Existential Psychotherapy

Daniel Sousa

Existential Psychotherapy

A Genetic-Phenomenological Approach

Daniel Sousa
Portuguese Society of Existential Psychotherapy
ISPA—University Institute
Lisbon, Portugal

ISBN 978-1-349-95216-8   ISBN 978-1-349-95217-5   (eBook)
DOI 10.1057/978-1-349-95217-5

Library of Congress Control Number: 2017936934

Cover illustration: Daniel Sousa

Printed on acid-free paper

This Palgrave Macmillan imprint is published by Springer Nature
The registered company is Nature America Inc.
The registered company address is: 1 New York Plaza, New York, NY 10004, U.S.A.

To my children
Margarida and Martim

ACKNOWLEDGEMENTS

It takes more than just the author to make a book.

I would like to start by thanking my partner, Sónia. For everything. For her real and special support which enabled me to see this project through. For her patience and friendship, for sharing with me the unfathomable paths of existence. This book is also the result of a personal and professional journey on which I have travelled with many people who mean a lot to me. I wish to thank my friends and colleagues Edgar Correia, José Carvalho Teixeira, Paula Ponce Leão and Victor Amorim Rodrigues, with whom I have had the please of developing the existential psychotherapy project in Portugal. Several other people have been very important. Ernesto Spinelli has without doubt been a mentor of existential psychotherapy whom I learned very early on to admire. Mick Cooper with whom it has been easy to maintain lively exchanges on research and perspectives on the existential approach. Simon Duplock and Lucia Moja who have played an important role in sharing their wisdom. Amedeo Giorgi is someone to whom I will always be grateful, for the human way in which he introduced me to the world of phenomenology. I would also like to thank Dan Zahavi for his work which has had a great influence on the way in which I have developed this theoretical model. This book is also the result of dialogues which I have conducted over the years with students of ISPA—University Institute and the Portuguese Society of Existential Psychotherapy. To all of them, thank you. Last but not least, as an existential psychotherapist I have had the privilege of encountering a great number of people who have trusted me enough to share their life experiences. Without doubt, to all of these I owe a large share of my development as a person and as a psychotherapist. Thank you.

CONTENTS

LIST OF FIGURES

LIST OF TABLES

INTRODUCTION

One of the expressions I most admire about existential psychotherapy was uttered by Rollo May, when he said that "existential psychotherapy may be understood not as a treatment as such, but rather as an encounter by the person with his own existence" (May 2000). This idea contains many of the elements that existential psychotherapy has defended over the decades. Over the time, in the writings and ideas of a various authors, this approach has defended a deep respect for human experience, a non-medical way of looking at human suffering, an intervention approach which is not centered on a technical stance, criticism of certain epistemological models for constructing scientific knowledge, and the overtechnologization of contemporary culture. Existential psychotherapy has its own history, community and internal debates. Like other theoretical models in psychotherapy, it also has a set of specific approaches which are distinct from each other (Cooper 2003). The existential approach is also recognized as being rooted in the influence of phenomenological-existential philosophy. This book does not propose to address the history of existential psychotherapy, nor does it propose to discuss the different sensibilities to be found in the approach. It is also not my intention to detail the points on which this approach differs from other theoretical models in psychotherapy, or to provide an introduction to the underlying concepts of existential phenomenology. These issues have all been sufficiently debated and the literature on them is plentiful, which is not to say that permanent discussion of these questions is not healthy. So without detaining the reader by describing the philosophical groundwork, the varying sensibilities in the approach, or their essential characteristics, I take the liberty of sharing a text which will defend a number of points I regard as important for the present and future of existential psychotherapy. In the first place, I believe that existential psychotherapy should not be characterized as a philosophical approach, despite benefiting from the epistemological wealth of existential phenomenology, as the central pillars of its theoretical foundations. Instead, existential psychotherapy is based on the concepts of phenomenological-existential psychology which, in turn, inform existential theory and clinical practice Secondly, I shall define and present a theoretical model for existential psychotherapy based on three essential concepts: the inner time-consciousness theory; the experiential self/narrative identity; and the theory of passive syntheses. These concepts are then placed in the framework of the static- and genetic-phenomenological methods. This will allow me the opportunity to present concepts based on existential phenomenology, which are conceptualized from a psychological point of view, and at the same time I shall seek to establish a basic framework for the practice of the existential approach. Just as any model of psychotherapy should do, this theoretical framework presents a rationale for human (psychological) development, an explanation for the experience of disturbance or human suffering, and a theory of change. Thirdly, as a result of this theoretical framework, I will argue that existential psychotherapy has a clinical practice which is based both on relational stances and on psychotherapeutic techniques (Sousa 2015), and that both are compatible with the theoretical underpinnings of the existential approach. Fourthly, I shall propose that existential psychotherapy should accommodate in its clinical practice what I call the principles of psychotherapeutical effectiveness, which are based on scientific research into psychotherapy and on empirical evidence. Fifthly, taking the preceding points into account, I consider that the genetic-phenomenological approach is closely linked to: a practice (also but not only) based on empirical evidence; the most effective therapeutic factors referred to in scientific research; the criteria of a *bona fide* psychotherapy. A *bona fide* psychotherapy is of course an intervention that sets out to be therapeutic, includes a rationale for the problems or issues that the client brings to the therapy, includes a number of therapeutic interventions consistent with the theoretical rationale, is based on psychological principles and is founded on a human and collaborative relationship between therapist and client.

Overview of the Book

In the first chapter we take a general view of the main debates today in the field of scientific research into psychotherapy. The chapter starts by defining a series of principles of effectiveness based on scientific evidence and clinical experience. These principles will serve as the basis for reading the main aspects to be addressed in the chapter. These are therapeutic principles which result from research and which I argue should be integrated into existential psychotherapy. Albeit without the pretension of dealing comprehensively with the subject of research into psychotherapy, the first chapter looks at many of the different issues debated today, from which existential psychotherapy has kept a distance. In addition to explaining which are the principles supported by scientific evidence and clinical experience, my aim, in this first chapter, is to help integrate and work towards collaboration between research and existential psychotherapy. The second chapter will present the theoretical groundwork for the genetic-phenomenological approach. One of the main objectives of this chapter is to raise the reader's awareness of the importance of familiarizing him or herself with some of the work of Edmund Husserl, who I believe is still largely unknown to the existential psychotherapy community. Husserl proposed not just one phenomenological method, but two. The first, which is best known to existential psychotherapists, involves essentially *epoché*, phenomenological reduction and description of phenomena. However, although this method is very important for clinical practice, Husserl said that phenomenology should be a new task when it centered on understanding the experience and the history of a particular person. And in this case, it should use the genetic method. Both methods, the static (descriptive) and the genetic (hermeneutic), function dialectically. The second chapter will present the foundations of static and genetic phenomenology and define the main concepts of this theoretical model: inner time-consciousness theory (a basis for understanding how pre-reflexive awareness functions); the experiential self (and its connection with narrative identity); and the theory of passive syntheses (an explanation of how the person constructs a network of intentional motivations, which may not all be consciously present). The aim of the third chapter is to present how the genetic-phenomenological approach in existential psychotherapy works in clinical practice. This chapter will therefore center on defining and explaining therapeutic interventions.

It starts with a summary of the theoretical foundations (addressed in Chap. 2) and principles of therapeutic effectiveness (referred to in Chap. 1) and integrates them; it then presents the aims of an existential intervention and goes on to define relational stances and intervention techniques in the genetic-phenomenological approach. It concludes with seven ways of conceptualizing a clinical case, in keeping with this model of existential psychotherapy. In the fourth and final, I will present some clinical vignettes and a clinical case study. The vignettes are primarily simple and designed to provide examples of issues I regard as important for incorporating into clinical existential practice, although they are not exclusive to this approach. The case study offers a deeper reading in order to show how the psychological concepts of existential psychotherapy can be used in reading a clinical case.

I would like to conclude with two brief notes. In this book, whenever I refer to existential psychotherapy, I consider it to be influenced by phenomenology and by philosophies of existence. I do not therefore hold that the existential approach is more phenomenological or more existential in its theoretical foundations; instead, both fields influence the existential approach. I use the words client and patient when I refer to people who have undergone psychotherapy. Neither word is satisfactory. Only the word person appears to do justice to the users of psychotherapy.

REFERENCES

Cooper, M. (2003). *Existencial therapies.* London: Sage Publications.

May, R. (2000). *A psicologia e o dilema humano.* Petropolis: Editora Vozes.

Sousa, D. (2015). Existential psychotherapy. The genetic-phenomenological approach: beyond a dichotomy between relating and skills. *Journal of Contemporary Psychotherapy, 45,* 69–77.

CHAPTER 1

Scientific Research into Psychotherapy

INTRODUCTION

To start a book on existential psychotherapy with a chapter devoted to scientific research might appear rather contradictory. Although there is today a huge body of knowledge based on research into psychotherapy, there is still an enormous gap between researchers and clinical practitioners (Lambert 2013b). Clinical practice and scientific research remain out of step with each other even though a series of proposals exist which seek to integrate them (Castonguay et al. 2013). Existential psychotherapy is no exception to this rule and is in fact very remote from mainstream research. Our approach sets out from two assumptions: (a) despite the controversies and debates, there are many benefits of integrating research into clinical practice; (b) existential psychotherapy, as proposed here, incorporates and interconnects its underlying theoretical and practical tenets with principles based on scientific effectiveness.

The main purpose of this chapter is to provide a brief description of some of the topics and issues currently considered in research into psychotherapy. No pretense is made of extensively covering the literature, as there are several sources that perform this task thoroughly (Wampold and Imel 2015; Lambert 2013b; Norcross 2011; Duncan et al. 2010; Cooper 2008). But we will start with a brief overview, in order to supply a context which will then allow us to focus on certain core aspects in the field of psychotherapy. So we will start by describing the medical and contextual models, and the differences between them. We will

© The Author(s) 2017
D. Sousa, *Existential Psychotherapy*,
DOI 10.1057/978-1-349-95217-5_1

find that, despite exponential growth in research, a clear dichotomy still exists in psychotherapy. In describing these two models, we will also gain a general perspective on the field, highlighting the main epistemological debates currently raging in psychotherapy. As a second step, we will enunciate some of the therapeutic factors which have attracted most attention over decades of research. These are regarded as core factors for therapeutic outcomes, and may be integrated into the clinical practice of any psychotherapist, irrespective of his theoretical orientation. We are referring to aspects such as the therapeutic relationship and maintaining it, above all in terms of what are called the human dimensions; establishing a relationship of active collaboration between client and therapist, leading to an agreement about aims and therapeutic tasks and increasing the client's expectations; acceptance of the client as an active person exerting particular influence over the therapeutic process; considering the therapist factors, in particular interpersonal skills, as aspects that exert a particular influence on psychotherapy; monitoring the therapeutic process and asking the client for feedback, in order for the therapist to be responsive and adapt the psychotherapy to the client; the therapist and the client being able to construct a rationale for the issues the client has brought to the psychotherapy. Research has systematically presented data on these aspects which, when combined, comprise a set of fundamentals for therapy. These can be regarded as *principles*, supported by a meta-theoretical vision; they present a degree of redundancy and exert mutual influence over the course of complex therapeutic processes. We like to regard these dimensions as *principles supported by scientific evidence and clinical experience*. Based on the literature, we will summarize a set of principles, which we will now enunciate and which will serve as guides to the reading of this chapter:

- to create and maintain a strong therapeutic alliance with clients. More than an alliance, establishing a real and human relationship with the client is an essential prerequisite (Gelso 2014). The therapeutic alliance is one of the most robust predictors of successful therapeutic outcomes (Zilcha-Mano et al. 2016; Horvath et al. 2011);
- the impact of the therapeutic alliance cuts across therapeutic models; however, it should not be regarded as solely responsible for therapeutic success. It should be cultivated in conjunction with an intervention plan, with the specifics of the client and the therapist's ability to design the most effective intervention (Norcross 2010);

- it is suggested that the psychotherapist should always regard the client as an active subject (Bohart and Tallman 2010), and that the success of the psychotherapy will depend significantly on how far the client believes in the rationale introduced by the therapist (or his model), and how far the client will engage with the goals and the therapeutic tasks (Wampold 2015; Laska and Wampold 2014). The client's contribution to the success of the psychotherapy is greater when compared to the specific type of intervention or even to the therapeutic relationship (Norcross and Wampold 2011);
- although it is essential to maintain a good therapeutic relationship, in which the client feels listened to, safe, empathically cared for, understood and not judged, these alone are not sufficient for success. It is also necessary for the psychotherapist to introduce a convincing rationale, which allows him, in conjunction with the client, to construct an explanation for the issues that the client has brought to the psychotherapy. More important than the scientific basis for the rationale introduced, is the client's acceptance that this makes sense, inducing him to take an active part in the therapeutic intervention, which in turn is provided by a therapist who believes in the same rationale and intervention (Wampold and Imel 2015);
- in addition to establishing and maintaining a strong therapeutic alliance, psychotherapists are encouraged to make use of the elements identified by research as most effective: empathic posture, consensus on aims, active collaboration between patient and therapist, obtaining feedback from the patient, and the therapist giving positive feedback to the patient (Norcross and Wampold 2011);
- in themselves, consensus about aims and therapeutic tasks, and also the level of collaboration between therapist and client, are the strongest predictors for successful therapeutic outcomes, and so therapists are encouraged to promote dialogue and ongoing adjustments concerning these dimensions (Lambert Cattani 2012; Tryon and Winograd 2011);
- psychotherapists are accordingly encouraged to keep monitoring their clients' expectations and perspectives regarding the relationship, concerning aims and the psychotherapeutic intervention. Monitoring leads to increased opportunities for furthering collaboration between the client and the therapist, for improving the relationship and tailoring the therapeutic interventions (Miller et al. 2015; Lambert and Cattani 2012). Positive and realistic expectations are associated with better therapeutic outcomes (Constantino et al. 2011);

- asking the patient for feedback about the therapeutic process is fundamental. The basic rationale for requesting feedback is to gather information on what is working and, above all, about what is not proving useful for the client, so as to make the psychotherapist more responsive and to tailor the intervention to the client. Monitoring the therapeutic process and receiving direct feedback from clients enhance therapeutic outcomes and reduce dropout rates (Lambert 2015; Lambert and Shimokawa 2011);
- the therapist's effects count for 5–9 times more than the theoretical models or specific techniques of the variance assigned to therapeutic change (Miller et al. 2015; Lutz et al. 2015). It appears crucial to consider the personal characteristics of the therapists and to further their interpersonal skills (Anderson et al. 2016). Research has shown that some therapists manage to maintain better therapeutic relationships and alliances, with highly diverse clients, and systematically achieve better therapeutic outcomes (Goldberg et al. 2016a; Imel et al. 2015; Owen et al. 2015; Baldwin and Imel 2013). The excellent performance achieved by these psychotherapists is not connected to their accumulated years of clinical experience, age, gender or theoretical model. (Owen et al. 2016; Goldberg et al. 2016b).
- psychotherapists who consistently achieve better therapeutic outcomes engage in deliberate practice with the aim of perfecting their clinical expertise. In particular, they are able to maintain excellent therapeutic relations, have exceptional personal skills and retain a sense of humility and professional self-criticism, combined with a convincing, credible and confidence-inspiring stance (Wampold et al., in press; Rønnestad 2016; Chow et al. 2015; Nissen-Lie et al. 2015b).
- the therapists' interpersonal and technical skills, applied to managing and repairing ruptures in the therapeutic alliance, appear crucial. When ruptures are repaired, the clients enjoy better therapeutic outcomes, drop out less and experience improvements in their quality of life and interpersonal functioning (Zilcha-Mano et al. 2016; Safran et al. 2014).
- a deep synergy exists between the therapeutic relationship, specific techniques and the characteristics of the client. They are in constant flux and influence each other (Castonguay 2013). Both scientific evidence and clinical experience point to this reciprocal and

complex interaction between the therapeutic relationship and psychotherapeutic interventions, between common factors and specific techniques, between the therapist's actions and the client's characteristics. In this sense, technical interventions are relational acts (Norcross and Lambert 2011; Safran and Muran 2006);

- different types of clients require different types of interventions and relationships. The psychotherapist must be able to establish and develop different relational stances, and adapt himself to the specific characteristics of each client and to the phase of change at which he finds himself (Owen and Hilsenroth 2014; Stiles 2013; Norcross et al. 2011). The capacity of the therapist to be responsive and adapt the intervention to the client is of particular importance (Stiles 2013). So it is essential not to be restricted to diagnostic categories, and to consider above all the client's potential and personal characteristics (Beutler et al. 2016);

- common factors are responsible for a good proportion of psychotherapeutic change, in conjunction with other factors, in particular, the type of intervention, the therapist's relational stance and the specific techniques applied. The therapist may consider the common factors as an essential basis of factors which enhance the therapeutic process (Wampold et al. 2016; Laska et al. 2014; Hubble et al. 2010);

- all psychotherapies structured with a convincing rationale for the client's problem, carried out by an empathic and careful therapist, which includes acceptance of the rationale by the client and his engagement in actions regarded as therapeutic, will have identical outcomes. The theoretical model and specific techniques are not, in themselves, critical to the outcome. Psychotherapy does not function on the same assumptions as medicine. Empirical evidence does not confirm that one particular model or specific techniques are crucial to the therapeutic outcome, on the contrary, that different psychotherapies lead to equivalent outcomes has been systematically corroborated by research (Wampold and Imel 2015; Bell et al. 2013; Stiles 2013);

- In general, therapists are therefore encouraged to develop psychotherapeutic interventions which combine the following factors: a theoretical rationale based on a psychological theory, the best scientific research to which they have access, clinical expertise, adapted to the client's characteristics, and a quality human relationship (Wampold 2015; Lambert and Norcross 2011).

The points highlighted here do not exhaust all the essential issues relating to psychological interventions, and fall far short of summarizing the complexity involved in psychotherapy. More detailed lists of therapeutic principles have been established (Beutler 2014; Castonguay 2013). Those mentioned above provide merely a summary of the main issues that this chapter sets out to address.

Lastly, the following should be noted in relation to the principles enumerated: they are based essentially on the contextual model with which the author identifies; it is understood that all these principles can be incorporated into existential clinical practice (as exemplified in Chap. 3); the theory and practice of existential psychotherapy set out here endorse and are in keeping with these principles of scientific effectiveness.

MEDICAL MODEL AND CONTEXTUAL MODEL: A DICHOTOMOUS WORLD

The history of psychotherapy has been marked by countless controversies, influenced by political, economic and social issues, which are connected to more specific questions of a scientific, academic and professional nature. The field is described as being divided into two great blocs: the medical model and the contextual model (Anderson et al. 2010). The medical model defends psychotherapies for specific diagnostic categories, known as empirically supported treatments (ESTs), where psychotherapy is scientifically validated on the sole basis of randomized clinical trials (RCT). It defends the manualization of psychotherapy based on specific techniques, regarded as engendering the processes of change that lead to cure. The contextual model believes that psychotherapies that include a given number of factors will have successful outcomes, and that there is no justification for restricting clinical decisions and the type of intervention on the sole basis of the diagnostic category. It also believes that RCTs are just one way of validating empirical knowledge in psychotherapy and that, rather than focusing on specific techniques, it is more important to implement psychological interventions based on common factors. The arguments on both sides have been debated in detail and are still open today (Beutler et al. 2016; Wampold 2015; Wampold and Imel 2015; Laska et al. 2014; Asnaani and Foa 2014; Laska and Wampold 2014; Baker and McFall 2014; Lambert and

Ogles 2014; Castonguay 2013; Norcross and Lambert 2011; Barlow 2004, 2010). However, detailed analysis of the literature looking at the complexity of the questions at stake shows that these questions cannot be easily separated from each other. Before we address some of the specific features of each model, we shall take a brief look at data concerning the absolute efficacy of psychotherapy, on which both models are in agreement.

The Efficacy of Psychotherapy

Historically, the division into opposing camps centered on discussion of the actual efficacy of psychotherapy. Hans Eysenck and Stanley Rachman were the precursors, from the 50s through to the 70s, in claiming that psychotherapy did not work, i.e. the outcomes failed to demonstrate the benefits of the psychotherapeutic interventions, which were less effective or equivalent to spontaneous remission, or could even be regarded as harmful to patients (Eysenck 1952). Ranged against them, Saul Rosenzweig and Allen Bergin countered that the evidence showed that psychotherapy was efficacious, pointing to a lack of rigor in the arguments employed by Eysenck and Rachman (Rosenzweig 1954; Bergin 1963). The late 70s and early 80s were crucial in creating a degree of order in the debate, with the introduction of the first meta-analysis (Smith and Glass 1977). The meta-analysis aggregated the findings of 375 studies comparing psychotherapeutic interventions with each other or with control groups. The findings confirmed that psychotherapy was beneficial, and there was no empirical evidence for the arguments of Eysenck and Rachman (Smith and Glass 1977). The second meta-analysis was statistically more sophisticated and considered a larger number of studies. It too confirmed that psychotherapy is efficacious, identifying a Cohen d of 0.85, greater than the first announced in 1977 (Smith et al. 1980). An effect size of 0.85 is regarded as a very high figure in social sciences and means that, at the end of therapy, individuals are, on average, 80% better compared to someone who has not undergone psychotherapy (Wampold and Imel 2015; Stiles 2013; Lambert 2013b). Meta-analyses are not immune to methodological criticism (Cooper 2008), but they are still regarded as essential for establishing the efficacy of psychotherapy (Lambert 2013b). They have grown exponentially in recent years, with 710 having been identified up to 2015 in PubMed, systematically confirming the efficacy of psychotherapy (Wampold and Imel 2015). There appears to be a consensus in support of efficacy which is both general and transversal to the medical and contextual models. Lambert (2013b) summarized data relating to efficacy and effectiveness:

- Psychotherapy is efficacious, on average a person will be 80% better in comparison to a person who has not received therapy or when compared to control or placebo groups;
- The research showed that psychotherapy produces positive results, both in experimental studies, where the conditions are controlled with an emphasis on internal validity (efficacy studies), and in natural settings where the stress is on external validity (effectiveness studies).
- The results of psychotherapy are statistically and clinically significant, causing remission of symptoms, helping to create new coping strategies and contributing to well-being. People have a tendency to maintain psychotherapeutic gains, producing positive effects over time and not merely at circumstantial level;
- Not only are the results of psychological interventions statistically superior to control conditions, but their effect is also superior to the effects of many medical treatments;
- Findings suggest that 50% of people who undergo psychotherapy achieve a clinically significant change after 20 sessions, whilst 50 sessions are needed for 75% of people to meet this criterion.

As we shall see further on in this chapter, despite the good news, the results of psychotherapy still face many challenges (Castonguay 2013). But we can point to one unquestionable finding: the successful results of psychological and psychotherapeutic interventions. However, the medical model and the contextual model appear to agree only on the absolute efficacy of psychotherapy. In all other dimensions, they set out from distinct assumptions (Wampold and Imel 2015, p. 75):

Relative Efficacy

| Medical Model | (a) there are differences between psychotherapeutic approaches, some will be more efficacious than others. A given treatment is more efficacious than another treatment, for a given disorder. |

Contextual Model   (a) Efficacy findings are generically equivalent for different psychotherapies, which are clearly intended to be therapeutic.

Therapeutic Effects

Medical Model   (a) The effects and impacts of the therapist on therapeutic outcomes are not significant, above all, when they follow treatments which are manualized and based on empirical evidence.

Contextual Model   (a) The effects of the therapist are relatively great, particularly when compared with the specific ingredients. Differences between therapists are above all due to relational factors.

General Effects

Medical Model   (a) Relational factors will not be critical to the outcomes of psychotherapy.

Contextual Model   (a) therapeutic alliance is correlated to outcomes.

(b) other relational factors, such as empathy, consensus concerning aims, collaboration and the real relationship, are associated with psychotherapeutic outcomes.

(c) expectations are important to outcomes.

(d) the therapist's allegiance to the theoretical model appears to be related to outcomes.

(e) cultural adaptations will enhance therapeutic effectiveness.

Specific Effects

Medical Model   (a) Removing a therapeutic element from a scientifically validated treatment will diminish its efficacy; and accordingly to introduce an element will increase its efficacy.

(b) A given treatment (A) may be more efficacious than another treatment (B) in treating certain symptoms (1) but not for treating other symptoms (2).

(c) Adherence to a given manual improves outcomes.

Contextual Model   (a) Removing a therapeutic element from a scientifically validated treatment will not diminish its efficacy; and accordingly to introduce an element will not increase its efficacy.

(b) Adherence to a given manual probably has no bearing on outcomes.

Medical Model

The rationale of the medical model is based on five assumptions: (1) the psychological problem is understood as an illness; (2) a biological explanations exists for the illness (in the case of psychotherapy, a psychological explanation); (3) identification of specific mechanisms which are the cause of change (cure); (4) therapeutic procedures consistent with the explanation of the illness and with the mechanisms of change; (5) the treatment is specific in the sense that it is more efficacious than a placebo treatment and because the treatment is supposed to operate specifically through the mechanism of change (Wampold and Imel 2015). One of the clearest ways in which the medical model was transposed to the world of psychotherapy was the adoption of what are called "empirically supported treatments" (ESTs). The first step was taken by Division 12 (Clinical Psychology Division) of the American Psychological Association (APA) (Chambless et al. 1998; Chambless and Hollon 1998). The key features of ESTs are: (a) they are empirically validated psychological treatments; (b) they presuppose that some therapies are more efficacious than others for specific disorders; (c) ESTs are scientifically validated solely by randomized clinical trials (RCTs) , regarded as the "gold standard" in research methodology; (d) psychotherapy manuals are designed which specify the therapeutic intervention, step by step; (e) they are intended for the diagnostic categories in the *Diagnostic and Statistical Manual of Mental Disorders* (DSM-5); (f) they argue that specific techniques account for therapeutic change; (g) emphasis on training and application of intervention model, to the detriment of relational factors (Crits-Christoph et al. 2014; Chambless and Hollon 1998). The impetus achieved by the ESTs led to calls for these interventions to be designated "psychological treatments", to distinguish them from other types of psychological interventions, which would be generically known as "psychotherapy". The former would be considered scientifically valid and they alone would be supported by health systems. The latter include all other psychotherapies regarded as not scientific, and should not be included in health systems (Barlow 2004).

ESTs brought a number of advantages to the world of psychotherapy: (a) they brought about an increase in scientific research; (b) they provided the political and social credibility essential in a world dominated by the medical view of human suffering and the use of medication for psychological disorders; (c) they helped to establish efficacy, contributing to recognition from the general public; (d) a means whereby psychotherapy can provide evidence of its efficacy in the face of growing economic pressure; (e) RCTs are one of the essential methodologies for investigating the efficacy of psychotherapy; (f) they helped to increase the inclusion of empirical data in clinical expertise (Castonguay 2013; Norcross and Lambert 2011).

Multiple limitations and criticisms have been laid at the door of ESTs. One of the prime concerns is for us not to fall into "empirical imperialism" or an "EST monopoly" (Castonguay et al. 2013; Slife et al. 2005), which would lead to the exclusion of other forms of scientific validation or other therapeutic approaches. In essence, lest we fall into a monotheistic vision of psychotherapy. Research findings have not shown that ESTs have better outcomes for specific disorders when compared with other psychotherapies (Beutler 2014). The assumption underlying ESTs to the effect that specific techniques or ingredients account for the therapeutic change has also not been borne out by empirical evidence. Research using a dismantling design seeks to test which specific ingredients are the causes of change. Studies conducted so far have concluded that even after removing the main techniques from a given psychotherapy, it maintains its efficacy (Stiles 2013; Laska et al. 2014;

Beutler 2014). The therapeutic manuals for ESTs appear to have three crucial restrictions. They limit the clinical decisions that the therapists have to take responsively from moment to moment, they ignore the client's characteristics, which are largely supplanted by the specifics of the diagnoses, and they disregard the impact of the therapist (Beutler et al. 2016; Norcross and Lambert 2011). The impact of the psychotherapists is greater than that of the theoretical model or the specific intervention (Miller et al. 2015; Wampold and Imel 2015). Adherence to psychotherapy manuals and specific techniques eventually results in rigidity and a lack of flexibility on the part of psychotherapists, and contributes to worse psychotherapeutic outcomes (Castonguay et al. 2010). This position is not undisputed by the defenders of ESTs, who suggest the application of particular, scientifically support treatments to specific diagnosis categories (Hofmann and Barlow 2014). The question is not whether psychotherapy works, but whether it is efficacious for a specific disorder (Chambless and Hollon 1998). In short, a huge contradiction appears to exist. The defenders of ESTs lay stress on the need for psychotherapy to be supported by scientific means, and these means fail to confirm the arguments of the ESTs. Despite the multiple limitations of RCTs, ESTs continue to be defended as the best solution for health systems (Crits-Christoph 1997). On the contrary, the elements associated with common factors have been repeatedly borne out by the empirical evidence (Duncan et al. 2010; Little 2010).

One of the questions highlighted in the literature as a fundamental error is the reduction of *evidence-based practice* (EBP) to *empirically supported treatments* (ESTs) (Lilienfeld 2013). For three essential reasons: (a) it greatly reduces the breadth of what evidence-based practice is; (b) ESTs do not even include the recommendations of the American Psychological Association (APA); (b) it contradicts a huge body of scientific research pointing to the importance of other factors which are neither explained nor supported by RCTs (Beutler 2016; Norcross and Lambert 2011; Duncan et al. 2010; Watchel 2010). The American Psychological Association's definition of EBPs should not therefore be confused with or reduced to ESTs, although evidence exists that managers, therapists, researchers, trainees and the general public have interpreted the two as synonymous (Laska et al. 2014). In the first place, the definition provided by the APA Task Force—"the integration of the best available research with clinical expertise in the context of patient characteristics, culture, and preferences"—does not single out RCTs as the only way of establishing the superiority of specific interventions. It considers that different types of research should be combined with the therapist's clinical expertise. So the APA's definition takes into account the impact of the therapist, of his interpersonal skills in the clinical intervention, and not exclusively the method of intervention. It also takes into account the fundamental role played by the individual client, with his or her expectations, preferences and culture, in determining the successful outcomes of psychotherapy. The APA Task Force also recommends introducing continuous forms of monitoring and adaptation of the client intervention (Hubble et al. 2010; APA Presidential Task Force on Evidence-Based Practice 2006). No explicit reference is made to the term "evidence-based treatments" or "psychotherapy treatments" which might point to a stronger connection with the medical model, just as the APA does not explicitly use the DSM as a preferred manual, as adopted by the proponents of ESTs (Wampold and Imel 2015).

In short, the ESTs movement, as we shall see in further detail below, appears to exclude dimensions that a vast body of research has corroborated over a period of decades: the therapeutic relationship and relational factors, the impact of the person of the therapist, his characteristics, technical and relational skills, the importance of the person of the client with his expectations, preferences and culture, the need to adapt the therapeutic intervention to the specific characteristics of the client which go beyond the diagnostic categories. This adaptation needs to be made in distinct ways at different stages in the therapeutic process, taking into consideration the management and maintenance of good therapeutic alliances (Beutler et al. 2016; Norcross and Lambert 2011). It therefore seems important to distinguish evidence-based practice from evidence-based treatments: the former emphasizes the need to combine empirical evidence with clinical expertise and with the clients' preferences, in order to reach informed decisions in individual cases; the latter is centered on identifying manualized treatments for specific conditions (Lilienfeld 2013; Little 2010). In addition, ways have been suggested of combining empirical evidence with clinical experience which largely supplant the reductionism of RCTs. The practice-oriented research paradigm—which includes patient-focused research, practice-based evidence and practice-research networks—encompasses a series of methodological and clinical procedures which make it possible to narrow the gap between science and clinical practice (Castonguay et al. 2013).

Contextual Model

There are several models based on common factors and the contextual model is one of the models derived from what are called common factors (Wampold and Imel 2015). It is based on 3 paths: (a) the real relationship; (b) expectations through explanation and agreement about tasks and goals; (c) facilitation of psychologically beneficial processes (Wampold 2015). However, before these factors go into action, an initial connection between client and therapist is established. Trust is a crucial factor. The client needs to feel safe and confident, and to feel sure that the therapist has the skills and understanding needed to help him. Several research projects have shown that creating and managing the alliance is vital from the first moments of psychotherapy (Horvath et al. 2011). One of the essential bases for therapy involves the client feeling committed to the therapist, feeling the setting as safe and potentially helpful, irrespective of the theoretical approach (Flückiger et al. 2012). It is known that most dropouts occur prematurely, at very early stages of the psychotherapy (Swift and Greenberg 2012).

After establishing an initial connection, the contextual model argues that a *real relationship* develops more deeply between client and therapist. A real relationship presupposes a personal relationship, which includes the ability of the client and the therapist to be sincere, authentic, open and honest, with the clear intention of benefiting from the therapeutic interaction (Gelso 2014). The real relationship is regarded, theoretically and methodologically, as a construct, distinct from the therapeutic alliance and the transferential and counter-transferential relationship (Gelso 2009). The real relationship refers to the personal dimensions between client and therapist, whilst the alliance focuses on the work that both put into collaborating, and derives from the real relationship. The transferential dimensions may eventually be present in the real relationship, but without defining it (Gelso 2014). The research suggests that the real relationship has greater impact on outcomes than the therapeutic alliance (Gelso et al. 2012). So research data appears to suggest what clinical experience has shown: the human relationship, relational factors, the person-to-person connection are crucial to and precede the establishment of a collaborative alliance. Of course, they both influence each other, but clients appear to value the human dimensions above all else. Indeed, empathy, one of the factors most closely associated with psychotherapy outcomes, is a fundamental characteristic of the real relationship. In addition, thanks to the therapeutic contract, in which confidentiality is an important aspect, the client knows she or he can feel safe to reveal emotionally difficult experiences, without running the risk of being criticized or abandoned (Wampold and Imel 2015).

The second path in the model has to do with *expectations through explanation and agreement about tasks and goals*. The creation of expectations has always been regarded as one of the crucial aspects of psychotherapy (Frank and Frank 1991; Goldfried 1980; Rosenzweig 1936). Expectations interconnect with the client's belief, with the internalization of the hope of resolving issues, which led him or her to seek help. In psychotherapy, expectations contribute around 15% to psychotherapeutic outcomes (Lambert and Norcross 2011). Research has demonstrated the importance of addressing, monitoring and working with the client's expectations, in order to reduce dropout rates and improve psychotherapy results (Constantino et al. 2012; Swift and Callahan 2011). There are two fundamental aspects for the contextual model. In the first place, the client's creation of the belief that participating in and completing the therapeutic tasks will help him to deal with his issues, in turn furthering the expectation that he has his own capabilities. Creating expectations is directly related to a convincing rationale for the issues that the client has brought to the psychotherapy, and also to therapeutic actions consistent with this rationale (Wampold 2015). This aspect stresses the need for the therapist and the client to establish a high level of collaboration, with regard to goals and therapeutic tasks. Lastly, it is important to stress that the most relevant issue concerning the rationale introduced for the client's problems is not its scientific validity, but rather that the explanation/rationale be accepted by the client and that the client should engage in therapeutic actions consistent with the rationale (Wampold and Imel 2015).

The third dimension has to do with *facilitation of psychologically beneficial processes*. The contextual model argues that all psychotherapy models include therapeutic factors consistent with the theoretical rationale. The specific ingredients are important to creating the expectations. They enhance client participation in actions regarded as therapeutic for the problems they have brought to the psychotherapy (Wampold 2015). Therapeutic interventions may have different goals (to alter maladaptive cognitive schemas, to express and deal better with emotions, to improve interpersonal relations), but what they have in common is that they diminish suffering and increase well-being (Wampold 2015). Therapeutic actions interrelate with the client's cognitive, emotional and behavioral factors.

SCIENTIFIC RESEARCH DATA IN PSYCHOTHERAPY

The consensus between the medical and contextual models ends at their agreement as to the absolute efficacy of psychotherapy. Their assumptions differ with regard to relative efficacy, general effects, specific effects and also the effects of the therapist. In the second part of this chapter we will look in more detail at the foundations for the principles of clinical and scientific effectiveness, mentioned at the start of the chapter. In this way we will clarify the points on which the medical and contextual models diverge.

The Dodo Bird Verdict—Different Psychotherapies Are Efficacious (Relative Efficacy)

The medical and contextual model have opposing assumptions on relative efficacy. For the medical model, it is presumable that certain psychotherapies (those containing "scientific" ingredients) are more effective. But for the contextual model, the type of psychotherapy is not at all crucial, meaning that different psychotherapies are equally effective, for the same type of problem. Since 1936, Rosenzweig has suggested that factors—at the time he called them *unrecognized factors*—common to all therapeutic models contributed more to psychotherapeutic change than specific models or techniques. Like the Dodo Bird in *Alice in Wonderland*, Rosenzweig declared: "Everybody has won, and all must have prizes." In other words, all psychotherapies are generically effective. One of the first analyses in the literature of the results of psychotherapy confirmed what Rosenzweig envisaged—there are no significant differences between the outcomes of different therapeutic approaches (Luborsky et al. 1975). Since then, the Dodo Bird verdict has been established in the literature as confirmation that different theoretical models are equivalent in terms of outcomes. However, this verdict set off a frantic race in the field. The proponents of different theoretical models all wanted to prove their own superiority. There are several methodological debates on how to determine the relative efficacy of psychotherapy. The first meta-analysis undertaken to overcome these methodological problems concludes that the differences between different psychotherapy models are non-existent, confirming the conjecture of the Dodo Bird verdict: "The results of our analysis demonstrated that the distribution of effect sizes produced by comparing two *bona fide* psychotherapeutic treatments was consistent with the hypothesis that the true difference is zero" (Wampold et al. 1997, p. 220). In other words, all psychotherapy that genuinely sets out to achieve therapeutic change will produce essentially the same results. A *bona fide* intervention means a psychotherapy which intends to be therapeutic. It is not an intervention which only features supportive, helping or relational elements. A *bona fide* psychotherapy includes the following elements: a convincing rationale for the client's problem; it is based on psychological principles; it has therapeutic actions consistent with the rationale; and it is based on a relationship of collaboration between the client and the therapist. As a rule, RCTs compare specific interventions, such as cognitive behavioral psychotherapy, with "supporting" therapies which do not include these factors (Wampold et al. 2010; Anderson et al. 2010).

Some of the criticisms leveled at the Dodo Bird verdict point out that it implies that therapists who work on the basis of common factors do not always use the same interventions, irrespective of the client's problem, or that, whatever the therapeutic procedure, the results will be positive (Barlow 2010). As we have seen, one of the assumptions of a *bona fide* therapy is that it sets out to be therapeutic, for a specific problem, so that the hypothesis of the contextual model is not that relational factors alone are enough. On the other hand, what the research shows is that a variety of psychotherapies are equally effective for specific disorders, not that a single psychotherapy is effective for different problems (Wampold and Imel 2015). The studies have confirmed three aspects: (a) the (positive) results of psychotherapies are not associated with theoretical models; (b) the results are not statistically associated with the duration of the psychotherapy; (c) the results are not statistically associated with specific techniques (Stiles 2013). Meta-analyses suggest the assumption of the contextual model, that psychotherapies are equivalent, even for certain specific disorders, such as anxiety or phobia, where insistent claims are made for the superiority of certain theoretical models, in particular, cognitive and behavioral models. One of the latest meta-analyses, which compares cognitive behavioral therapy (CBT) with other *bona fide* therapies concludes that: (a) CBT is defined in very different ways by different proponents, creating great difficulties in identifying which are the specific ingredients of the approach; (b) the findings have confirmed that there are no differences between CBT and other *bona fide* therapies, either for anxiety and depression, or for non-specific disorders (Baardseth et al. 2013). Despite the criticisms made of meta-analyses (Barlow 2010), and although certain studies suggest differences between therapies (Marcus et al. 2014), the *Dodo Bird verdict* has remained unassailable over decades of research (Wampold and Imel 2015). Research that compares efficacy between different types of intervention has not concluded that the diagnostic category or specific type of intervention are good predictors of outcome. In contrast, the common factors present in different types of intervention have presented systematically relevant results (Beutler 2016; Holt et al. 2015; Lambert and Ogles 2014; Lambert 2013b; Duncan et al. 2010). It is concluded that the type of intervention is not decisive, accounting for only 1% of the variance in results (Wampold and Imel 2015).

Lambert (2013b) proposed a model to explain the variance in psychotherapy outcomes:

- 40% are attributable to *extra-therapeutic factors*. These are above all aspects that the client takes to the psychotherapy: his motivation to change, cognitive and interpersonal skills, spontaneous remission, family and social support, and life events which may bring about an improvement in life quality.
- 30% are attributable to *common factors*. These are aspects which are above all present in the relationship, irrespective of the therapist's theoretical orientation. So the quality of the therapeutic relationship is the crucial aspect. Factors such as trust, acceptance, understanding, encouragement to explore new thoughts and behaviors and emotional relief are involved in good therapeutic relationships.
- 15% are related to the placebo effects. This has to do with the hope and expectation that the therapeutic process will have a positive effect. This is an effect similar to that of other treatment processes, i.e., the patient believes that he will in fact be helped to overcome his issues. Of course, it appears important for the client's and therapist's expectations to be aligned as to the restorative powers of the psychotherapy.
- 15% have to do with the *specific techniques*, such as transference interpretation in psychoanalysis, Rogerian unconditional positive regard, behavioral systematic exposure techniques, etc.

A recent meta-analysis aggregates several experimental studies which compared non-directive supportive therapy (NDST) with other *bona fide* therapies, for depression (Cuijeprs et al. 2012). NDST, normally called "supportive counseling", is regarded as an unstructured intervention, without specific interventions, involving basic relational skills, such as active listening. The meta-analysis concluded that: (a) NDST was efficacious for the treatment of depression in adults, although less efficacious when compared with other *bona fide* therapies; (b) most comparisons of NDST were with CBT and no significant differences were identified; (c) extra-therapeutic factors were estimated to account for around one-third of change (33.3%), around half was attributed to non-specific factors (49.6%) and specific factors contributed to around one sixth (17.1%) (Cuijeprs et al. 2012). These data have corroborated Lambert's model and emphasized that the efficacy of psychotherapy for depression in adults is mostly explained by non-specific factors, whilst specific factors account at best for a very small part.

More recently, Lambert (2015) adjusted the model to: 45% extra-therapeutic factors; 35% common factors; 20% factors relating to the therapist and 5% specific techniques (Lambert 2015). Less prominence is attached to specific factors and more to the effects of the therapist. The research has underlined that the relative efficacy of psychotherapy is inflated by the differences between psychotherapists (Miller et al. 2014). This means that the differences between specific models are even smaller. However, in the way in which it is presented, the data should be understood with caution. Not least because to divide the contribution of the different factors into "slices", might presuppose that they are not inter-related in a complex way, in the therapeutic process. The main factors that contribute to therapeutic change are mutually dependent (Norcross and Lambert 2011). In short, the research appears to support the *Dodo Bird verdict*, and also the limitations of ESTs, leading to what has been called the "decline of model mania," with a growth of interest in the common factors (Duncan et al. 2010).

Common Factors in Psychotherapy

As we have seen, Rosenzweig stressed the importance of common factors to the therapeutic process. Rather than the specific features of the model, he stressed that dimensions common to different theoretical models, as well as certain characteristics of the therapist, are more crucial to the psychotherapy (Rosenzweig 1936). Frank and Frank (1991) underlined the importance of certain essential components to the therapeutic processes: an emotionally charged relationship of trust with a person seeking to help (therapist); a context of support in which the client feels that something can be done to help him; and a rationale that promotes an explanation for the client's issues, and which "remoralises" the client (Frank and Frank 1991). This rationale, understood as a "myth", has to be accepted as plausible by the client and by the therapist, in order to be convincing and therapeutic. Lastly, a set of "rituals" consistent with the theoretical rationale represent the therapeutic tasks which should conduct the therapeutic goals and ensure mutual collaboration between client and therapist (Frank and Frank 1991). The common tasks also function as principles of change that cut across theoretical models: "(a) the facilitation of expectations that therapy will help; (b) the establishment of an optimal therapeutic alliance; (c) offering feedback that can help clients increase their awareness about what is contributing to their life problems; (d) the encouragement of corrective experiences; and (e) an emphasis on continued reality testing" (Goldfried 1980; Goldfried and Davila 2005). More recently, two task forces, one on *psychotherapy relationships that work* (Norcross 2011) and another on *principles of therapeutic change that work* (Castonguay and Beutler 2006), have masterfully brought together a body of evidence for common factors and principles of change, which can be regarded as meta-theoretical. Lambert (2013b) summarized the common factors (of support, learning and action) present, discernibly, in sequential form in therapeutic processes, irrespective of the theoretical model. Likewise, *Heart and Soul of Change* (Duncan et al. 2010), arguing that psychotherapy does not function like medicine, incorporates the main common factors that contribute to therapeutic change. Several authors have proposed a list of common factors. Any small list will necessarily have to include the following: "(a) an emotionally charged bond between the therapist and patient, (b) a confiding healing setting in which therapy takes place, (c) a therapist who provides a psychologically derived and culturally embedded explanation for emotional distress, (d) an explanation that is adaptive (i.e., provides viable and believable options for overcoming specific difficulties) and is accepted by the patient, and (e) a set of procedures or rituals engaged by the patient and therapist that leads the patient to enact something that is positive, helpful, or adaptive" (Laska et al. 2014, p. 469).

Several criticisms have been made of the common factors approach. The first is that it is not based on scientifically proven assumptions. It is based on aspects which are not confirmed by empirical evidence. The "common factors treatment" should therefore involve RCTs and empirical evidence. A second criticism argues that the common factors are really a mishmash of relational factors, without any theoretical framework, and that the therapeutic relationship would be sufficient for therapeutic change. For this reason, the common factors approach is often mistaken for a synonym of "supporting counseling". Another criticism is that common factors presuppose that a psychotherapy would be appropriate for all disorders (insofar as it is not specific). Consequently, therapists based on common factors can carry out any therapeutic action, which will be beneficial, even for any type of disorder. In other words, anything works with any clients—anything goes. In short, the common factors approach puts in jeopardy the recognition of psychotherapy as a psychological science. (Crits-Christoph et al. 2014; Asnaani and Foa 2014; Baker and McFall 2014; Hofmann and Barlow 2014; Barlow 2010). In essence, we already looked at these criticisms when we addressed the relative efficacy of psychotherapy, i.e., differences in outcome between different models. On the other hand, these criticisms originate in the assumptions of the medical model, which prioritizes the systematization of psychotherapy in a specific treatment, scientifically validated by RCTs, with specific techniques for particular diagnostic categories (Barlow 2004; Chambless and Hollon 1998).

The proponents of common factor models summarize their outlook in a number of fundamental points. In the first place, there is no such thing as "common factors treatment". No one argues that there is such a thing as common factors psychotherapy, but rather, as already explained at length, that different therapies have positive results, for specific disorders. A convincing theoretical rationale that provides an explanation for the client's problem is one of the common factors. There is accordingly a scientific framework, a theoretical rationale, not just the assumption that psychotherapy should function as a sum of relational dimensions. The therapeutic relationship, relational factors and an empathic therapist are all essential, but not exclusively responsible for the therapeutic change. However important these factors may be, it appears essential to add the specific therapeutic interventions, consistent with the theoretical rationale. And, of course, a client who actively engages with the psychotherapy. Common factors approaches should therefore not be regarded as "supportive counseling". Common factors do not mean that anything goes, for a good psychotherapeutic outcome. However, a common factors approach will envisage that some therapists will be more skillful and able in establishing therapeutic alliances, in adapting to different clients and making better use of their interpersonal skills. This stands in contrast to the rigidity of ESTs, which defend adherence to intervention manuals, to the exclusion of all else. The common factors present in different approaches do not preclude the need for the therapist to be trained in a therapeutic approach and to have skills to carry out therapeutic actions which are consistent with this theoretical model. In short, common factors models do not preclude common factors and specific ingredients being interrelated (Wampold and Imel 2015; Wampold 2015; Laska et al. 2014; Frank and Frank 1991)

As regards the criticism that they are unscientific, meta-analytical data confirms that the most efficacious elements for psychotherapeutic change are common factors, which have a far greater impact than specific factors. These are present in the different theoretical models, whilst the specific ingredients, the differences between therapies or the adherence to intervention manuals have very little impact(Wampold and Imel 2015):

Common Factors

(a) therapeutic alliance (effect size of 0.57)
(b) empathy (effect size of 0.63)
(c) consensus on goals/collaboration (effect size of 0.72)
(d) positive regard/affirmation (effect size of 0.56)
(e) congruence/genuineness (effect size of 0.49)
(f) expectations (effect size of 0.24)
(g) cultural adaptation of EBT (effect size of 0.32)
(h) therapists—RCTs (effect size of 0.35)
(i) therapists—Naturalistic (effect size of 0.55)

Specific Ingredients

(a) Differences between treatments (effect size of < 1.0)
(b) Specific ingredients (effect size of 0.0)
(c) Adherence to protocol (effect size of < 0.1)
(d) Skill assessed by ability to provide a specific therapy (effect size of 0.5)

These data confirm the factors which have the greatest impact on therapeutic change. As may be seen, the therapeutic alliance is a crucial factor, along with what are called relational factors, such as empathy, congruence, the genuineness of the therapist. It is crucial to the therapeutic process to create expectations and hope, and also to reach a consensus on goals and establish collaboration between the client and the therapist. As well as the data also pointing to the importance of interventions being adapted to the culture, another factor stands out: the therapist. Indeed, the effects of the therapist (a topic addressed in greater detail below) is one of the factors to which the literature most frequently draws attention. The therapist's effects count for 5–9 times more than the theoretical models or specific techniques (Miller et al. 2015; Lutz et al. 2015). When the therapist's effects are considered in meta-analyses, we find that the variance attributed to the theoretical model diminishes substantially (Owen et al. 2015). In other words, part of the credit we gave to the theoretical model is due to the specific contribution of the therapist and not to the therapeutic model. Today, the variance attributed to the psychotherapeutic model and to specific techniques is approximately 1% (Wampold and Imel 2015). In short, the systematization of research has lent further support for the summary list mentioned above for common factors: an empathic human relationship with a genuine and caring therapist, who creates expectations and fosters hope, provides an acceptable and convincing explanations for the client's issues, and a client who, in turn, believes that the therapeutic actions based on the alliance with the therapist will be beneficial and will help him to overcome his problems (Wampold et al. 2016).

Common factors have been grouped into: support factors, learning factors and action factors (Lambert 2013b). Common factors arise in a perceptibly sequential way over the course of therapeutic processes, and this is something that appears to occur irrespective of the theoretical model. All psychotherapies foster a collaborative endeavor that provides the person with: (1) increased confidence and security, along with a reduction in tension, fearfulness and anxiety, which (2) lead to changes in how the client conceptualizes his problems and anxieties which, in turn (3) makes it possible for clients to act differently because they deal with their fears, accept risks and work on their own problems.

Sequential list of common factors present in different psychotherapies (Lambert 2013b):

Support Factors—Catharsis/release of tension; Mitigation of isolation; Positive relationship; Reassurance; Safe environment; Identification with therapist; Therapeutic alliance; Therapist/client active participation; Recognition of therapist expertness; Therapist warmth, respect, empathy, acceptance, genuineness; Trust/open exploration;

Learning Factors—Advice; Affective re-experiencing; Assimilating problematic experiences; Cognitive learning; Corrective emotional experience; Feedback Insight, Rationale, Exploration of internal frame of reference; Changing expectations of personal effectiveness; Reframing of self-perceptions;

Action Factors—Facing fears; Cognitive mastery; Encouragement of experimenting with new behaviors; Taking risks; Mastery efforts; Modeling, Practice, Reality Testing; Success experiences; Working through; Behavioral/emotional regulation.

One final aspect which can in some way adjust and relate to the common factors has to do with stages of change. From a meta-theoretical perspective, the behavior of change is conceptualized as a process which is carried out over time, involving a progression through a series of five stages: pre-contemplation, contemplation, preparation, action and maintenance (Norcross et al. 2011). At the pre-contemplation stage, the patient is not yet ready to make changes in the near future and in many situations is unaware of his own issues. At the contemplation stage, patients have gained awareness of their problems, reflect seriously on the need to do something, but are not ready to make changes. It is at the preparation stage that they feel they are more willing to make changes and take the first steps in this direction. At the action stage, patients change behaviors, ways of dealing with their emotions and develop new perspectives on themselves and on others. The maintenance phase is characterized by consideration of the therapeutic gains. The recommendations for the stages of change are as follows (Norcross et al. 2011):

- Monitor and assess the stage of change at which the patient currently finds himself;
- Be careful not to intervene as if the patients were already at the action phase;
- Set realistic goals for moving from one stage of change to another;
- Be careful in approaching patients at the pre-contemplation phase;
- Adapt (responsiveness) the intervention to the stage which the patient has reached;
- Avoid disconnection between the stage of change and the therapeutic process;
- Bear in mind that the move from one stage to another is not necessarily linear;
- Adapt the relationship style to the stage of change.

Specific Ingredients (Relative Efficacy)

The prominence that research findings have attached to common factors does not preclude what has repeatedly been asserted in the literature: a permanent flow and interdependence between relational factors and specific techniques. Moreover, even common factors are not theoretically and empirically distinct from each other (Wampold and Imel 2015). What the research appears to suggest is that there is no empirical evidence to support the importance attached to the method of intervention in itself, or to the specific interventions as solely responsible for the therapeutic change. Testing relative efficacy—comparing the efficacy of two established psychotherapies which have been designated for a specific problem or disorder—is different from tests which seek to analyze the impact of specific techniques.

Component and dismantling studies set out to detect whether one specific ingredient is responsible for the therapeutic change. A study in the field of depression, which set out to test CBT based on Beck's theory, concludes that removing specific interventions from CBT had no impact on outcomes (Jacobson et al. 1996). In other words, even without the most important specific techniques in CBT, the psychological interventions were effective. The 150 patients were randomly divided into three types of intervention. One of the psychotherapies contained all the elements of CBT, another featured only some of the specific ingredients of CBT, but excluded elements regarded as essential, such as coping strategies to combat depressive thoughts. A third psychotherapy, behavioral activation (BA), was also tested. The authors concluded that there are no differences between the psychotherapies; the intervention which excluded essential elements of CBT did not have better outcomes; these data were maintained after follow-up (Jacobson et al. 1996). The psychotherapies were carried out by experienced psychotherapists, with a high level of adherence to CBT, like the program supervisor. This question is particularly importance, in view of the fact that the best therapeutic outcomes are attributed in part to the therapist's adherence to the theoretical model. In this study, greater adherence was not associated with better outcomes. In short, the authors concluded that the study confirmed "the failure to find evidence that the mechanisms addressed by the various treatments were associated with differential change in the targeted mechanisms" (Jacobson et al. 1996, p. 303).

A first meta-analysis was conducted to aggregate research and studies which sought to isolate specific elements of psychotherapeutic interventions, in order to test their efficacy (Ahn and Wampold 2001). It was found that the statistical difference, between psychotherapies with all their ingredients and psychotherapies without components regarded as critical, was not significantly different from zero (Ahn and Wampold 2001). All the studies included in this meta-analysis included therapeutic processes with positive outcomes. The specific elements removed and tested were ingredients regarded as essential by the proponents of the therapeutic interventions. This meta-analysis concluded that specific elements are inefficacious and that the manualization of psychotherapy is incongruous (Ahn and Wampold 2001). A more recent meta-analysis included three times as many studies as the first meta-analysis and also had the advantage of analyzing separately the results of dismantling and of the component studies (Bell et al. 2013). This meta-analysis identified no significant differences between psychotherapies with all their ingredients and psychotherapies without specific ingredients. However, it suggests there is a small effect size, when a given specific ingredient is added to an intervention. Even so, the effect of the added elements accounted for only 2% of the variance in outcomes (Wampold and Imel 2015; Bell et al. 2013). The various studies which have analyzed early responses offer another challenge to specific factors. Various research projects have shown that the response shown by clients in the early stages of psychotherapy occur before the main specific ingredients of the theoretical models are introduced (Lambert 2005). In short, contrary to the assumption made by the medical models and ESTs, removing or adding specific and essential ingredients did not alter the outcomes of the psychological interventions. Dismantling studies have repeatedly shown that empirical evidence confirms that the specific techniques of theoretical models have in themselves only a very small impact.

The Inter-relation Between Common Factors and Specific Factors

Whilst the impact of specific techniques is small, the literature contains various studies which point to the interdependence and mutual influence between common factors and specific factors. A meta-analysis has shown that different psychotherapies are equally effective for post-traumatic stress disorder (PTSD) (Benish et al. 2008). The authors concluded that there is no evidence to support an insistence that specific interventions be recommended for patients with PTSD. More important than the specific model is the consideration that clients come to the psychotherapy for highly varied reasons, with very different symptoms, and with very different worldviews and life experiences. We also know that the client derives the most from his psychotherapy when the psychotherapy rationale is in keeping with the client's worldview (Benish et al. 2008). Once again, the authors concluded that different psychotherapies are equally effective for PTSD. But more importantly, they showed that different psychotherapeutic interventions which were effective for PTSD combined several common factors and various specific factors (Wampold et al. 2010; Benish et al. 2008). Although all psychotherapies were equally efficacious, some contained an explicit focus on the trauma, others expressly excluded addressing the memories of the trauma, whilst some included exposure techniques and others excluded exposure to the trauma. So one of the central assumptions for specific PTSD interventions was not verified: centering the therapy on the trauma is *the* most importance mechanism of change (Wampold et al. 2010). The authors were able to identify to series of factors important to an intervention for PTSD. Some are used and others are excluded, making the task of distinguishing between common factors and specific factors extremely arduous: "(1) cogent psychological rationale that is acceptable to patient, (2) systematic set of treatment actions consistent with the rationale, (3) development and monitoring of a safe, respectful, and trusting therapeutic relationship, (4) collaborative agreement about tasks and goals of therapy, (5) nurturing hope and creating a sense of self-efficacy, (6) psychoeducation about PTSD, (7) opportunity to talk about trauma (i.e., tell stories), (8) ensuring the patient's safety, especially if the patient has been victimized as in the case of domestic violence, neighborhood violence, or abuse, (9) helping patients learn how to avoid revictimization, (10) identifying patient resources, strengths, survival skills and intra and interpersonal resources and building resilience, (11) teaching coping skills, (12) examination of behavioral chain of events, (13) exposure (covert in session and in vivo outside of session), (14) making sense of traumatic event and patient's reaction to event, (15) patient attribution of change to his or her own efforts, (16) encouragement to generate and use social supports, (17) relapse prevention" (Wampold et al. 2010, p. 931). In short, the different psychotherapies for PTSD are effective, use most of these interventions, but stress some to the detriment of others, making it very difficult to discern which is the most critical ingredient.

The empirical evidence does not therefore appear to support the argument that a set of specific mechanisms is responsible for therapeutic change (Wampold and Imel 2015; Wampold et al. 2010).

One study, with a different methodological approach, sought to identify the factors that most contribute to promoting insights in psychotherapy. The findings showed that the theoretical approach is not associated with more insights by clients (McAleavey and Castonguay 2013). Therapists who, in certain sessions, used more exploratory interventions than normal, for one client in particular, produced less insights than in other sessions with the same client. Likewise, in the case of therapists who used more exploratory interventions than other therapists, their clients reported less insights than with the latter. In contrast, therapists who introduced more directive interventions were able to achieve higher insight indices. However, a more detailed analysis of the findings shows the interrelation between common factors and specific techniques. Directive interventions were aggregated to a high insight index when they occurred in sessions which also featured high common factor indices (McAleavey and Castonguay 2013). A number of explanations may be offered for the negative association between exploratory interventions and insights. Overuse of the same type of intervention, in a single session or over sessions, may overburden the client and lead him to resist this type of intervention. It may also suggest a lack of flexibility on the part of the therapist. But the research suggests something more important: directive interventions were associated with a higher insight index only when the therapist also reported using, more than usual, interventions connoted with common factors. These data suggest the existence of a complex and bidirectional influence between common factors and specific interventions. On the one hand, technical interventions not always seem to be associated with specific therapeutic approaches, on the other, an either/or approach does not appear to offer the best explanation of the interdependence between common and specific factors (McAleavey and Castonguay 2013).

There are two other aspects which contribute greatly to the difficulty of distinguishing between common factors and specific ingredients. In the first place, psychotherapies, even more structured therapies such as CBT, differ considerably from each other. There are widely differing definitions of what a CBT is and what its most important mechanisms of change are. Secondly, psychotherapies are defined theoretically as distinct, using specific terminologies, but from a clinical practice perspective they actually present huge similarities (Wampold and Imel 2015; McAleavey and Castonguay 2013). A study which compared the interventions of experienced psychotherapists with cognitive and psychodynamic orientations, who conducted interventions for anxiety and depression, pointed to overlap between the interventions associated with the two theoretical models (Goldfried et al. 1998). What is more, the sessions considered by the therapists as clinically most significant included psychotherapeutic interventions from both theoretical models (Goldfried et al. 1998). Psychotherapists appear to have a tendency to use types of interventions from other theoretical orientations. The specific techniques applied are often extremely different from the central theoretical concepts in the theoretical model followed by the therapist (Cook et al. 2010; Thoma and Cecero 2009). In sum, research has produced evidence that: both the relationship and the techniques contribute to change; the therapeutic relationship contributes to the efficiency of the techniques; the relationship can be applied as a technique or a technique can be applied in the therapeutic relationship; both the relationship and the techniques are dependent on the client's engagement; the relationship, the techniques and the client's engagement vary during the therapeutic process (Goldfried and Davila 2005; Geller 2005; Hill 1995). The literature has emphasized the need to go beyond the narrow and simplistic view that divides the field into "techniques" and "relationship" (Castonguay and Beutler 2006), and that the common factors versus specific factors debate is not adequate to conceptualize the complexity inherent to the therapeutic process. Research has suggested a mutual dynamic and interdependence between common and specific factors (Hubble et al. 2009; Asay and Lambert 1999) and that there is an intersection between the therapeutic relationship and the therapeutic change techniques (Norcross and Lambert 2011).

It is argued that the field is not therefore restricted to what are regarded as false dichotomies. The influence of the participants (client and therapist), relational factors and the therapeutic interventions do not function in isolation. They are in constant flux and interaction, at a single session, and over the psychotherapeutic process (Beutler et al. 2016; Castonguay 2013). The Task Force that defined the principles of therapeutic change that work set out precisely to identify principles that would consider the effects of the relationship, the participants and the intervention, in order to achieve the best fit between a psychotherapy and a particular client. The principles of therapeutic intervention cut across theoretical models, and involve common factors and specific interventions. For the authors, the field of psychotherapy should move on from the division between the defenders of common factors and ESTs, and identify mediators and moderators who can adapt the psychotherapy to the client, and promote efficacious therapeutic changes (Beutler et al. 2016, 2014; Castonguay 2013). Classes of patterns, formulated in intervention principles, are also one of the ways of integrating research with clinical practice (Holt et al. 2015).

Therapeutic Alliance and Real Relationship

When questioned about the factors most closely associated with successful psychotherapeutic outcomes, therapists from the most varied theoretical models identified the therapeutic alliance as one of the most prominent. This was either as a pre-condition for change or as a change mechanism in itself (Norcross 2010). The therapeutic alliance has been a central concept in psychotherapeutic theories since the time of Freud (Horvath and Luborsky 1993). Since then the alliance has been conceptualized in very different ways and been the object of empirical studies using very different measurement instruments (Horvath et al. 2011). Bordin (1979) proposed a meta-theoretical definition—*working alliance,*—comprising three central aspects: (a) agreements on the therapeutic goals; (b) consensus on the tasks that make up therapy; (c) and a bond between the client and the therapist. In addition to including a relational dimension, this conceptualization places the tonic on active collaboration between client and therapist. Bordin referred to another aspect which subsequent literature has systematically regarded as crucial: monitoring and repair of ruptures in the therapeutic alliance (Bordin 1979, Safran and Muran 2000). The interest in common factors and the fact that psychotherapists acknowledge the usefulness of establishing a strong therapeutic alliance have led to this concept being increasingly adopted in clinical practice and in research. Meta-analyses have concluded that a positive and robust relationship exists between the therapeutic alliance and the success of psychotherapy (Falkenström et al. 2013). It also emerges that this positive relationship between the alliance and psychotherapy outcomes is independent of the theoretical approaches to the psychological disorders involved (Horvath et al. 2011; Horvath and Bedi 2002). The data confirm that the alliance in individual therapy, in therapy with children and adolescents and in couples and family therapy, and group cohesion in group therapy, are effective predictors (Norcross and Wampold 2011). Even so, a number of questions have been raised about the efficacy of the therapeutic alliance, in particular, methodological issues related to the research conducted (Crits-Christoph et al. 2011). This is the case of the "halo effect" which occurs when different variables (alliance and outcome) are measured by the same method or graded by the same person (client) (Ackerman and Hilsenroth 2003). A good alliance can be the result of the early therapeutic gains and not the cause of therapeutic change (Puschner et al. 2008; Tasca and Lampard 2013). In other words, the alliance may be graded positively by clients, because they feel they are experiencing rapid changes in the therapeutic process. In this case, the alliance would benefit from a positive client outlook, which is associated not with the alliance, but rather with the satisfaction at experiencing rapid improvements (Falkenström et al. 2013). Although the relationship between the therapeutic alliance and early therapeutic gains is acknowledged to be a two-way street, the data have pointed to the alliance having a robust impact, irrespective of the therapeutic gains experienced in the early stages of psychotherapy (Wampold and Imel 2015). These data reinforce the view of the alliance as a dynamic, in flux throughout the therapeutic process, as a change mechanism in psychotherapy (Falkenström et al. 2013).

Even in RCTs, where the therapists have to follow an intervention manual, and so the therapists have less interpersonal flexibility, the correlation between alliance and outcome is robust and particularly important in the early stages of the therapeutic process (Flückiger et al. 2012). The research also points to a statistically significant impact in the effect that the alliance has on changes which occur from session to session. For example, when the alliance is worse in a given session, the symptoms tend to worsen in the following sessions (Falkenström et al. 2013). So it is important to consider monitoring the level of the therapeutic alliance over the sessions, not least because in many circumstances the perception of the alliance may differ between client and therapists (Horvath et al. 2011). The therapeutic alliance arises from the interaction between client and therapist, between therapeutic interventions and the client's active engagement (Horvath et al. 2011). However, the empirical evidence suggests that the correlation between the alliance and the therapeutic outcome is due more to the therapist's contribution (Wampold and Imel 2015). Studies which have sought to dismantle the therapist's impacts, separating these from the client's contributions to the alliance, have concluded that therapist factors are a stronger predictor of psychotherapy outcomes (Baldwin et al. 2007; Dinger et al. 2008). The data indicated that therapist variability in the alliance predicted outcomes, whilst patient variability in the alliance was not related to therapeutic outcomes. Psychotherapists who were more effective were able to maintain better therapeutic alliances, over a variable set of clients (Baldwin et al. 2007; Dinger et al. 2008). Therapists who are empathic and genuine and have an open-minded and human attitude manages to have better therapeutic alliances and to bring about better therapeutic outcomes, including for specific areas, such as depression (Zuroff et al. 2010). The findings of a more recent meta-analysis, which looked at around 70 studies, have confirmed and expanded the findings of previous studies (Baldwin et al. 2007; Dinger et al. 2008; Zuroff et al. 2010), reasserting that therapist variability in the alliance is a statistically significant predictor of therapeutic outcomes, whilst this was not confirmed for patient variability (Del Re et al. 2012). The correlation between the alliance and therapeutic outcomes in the same therapist appears to be non-existent, whilst the correlation between different therapists appears to be relatively great. The data suggest that the therapist's contribution is more relevant to the therapeutic alliance and that some therapists manage to establish better alliances with different clients (Del Re et al. 2012).

Even the therapist's own experiences, both past and present, appear to have an impact on the quality of his therapeutic work (Rønnestad and Skovholt 2001). A recent study showed that the therapeutic alliance is influenced by the quality of the therapist's personal life, although the impact is scored in different ways by the client and the therapist (Nissen-Lie et al. 2013a). Clients were more sensitive to the distress levels in the therapist's private life, apparently communicated implicitly during sessions. At the same time, the therapists' scoring of the quality of the therapeutic alliance is influenced by their perception of personal well-being. This study underlines that some therapists have a better ability to establish good therapeutic alliances and that the quality of the therapist's private life therefore appears to influence their therapeutic work. Therapists appear to act, in part, under the influence of the quality of their personal life, which in turn influences the clients' perspective on the emotional connection with the therapists and the relational climate of the alliance (Nissen-Lie et al. 2013a). A literature review concluded that both personal attributes and technical attributes independent of theoretical models contributed positively to strong therapeutic alliances and to the management of ruptures in the alliance (Ackerman and Hilsenroth 2003). These data also reinforced the importance of self-reflection and self-awareness on the part of therapists, not only concerning their professional components, but also on their own personal lives and attributes (Nissen-Lie et al. 2013a; Rønnestad and Skovholt 2001). In short, empirical studies and meta-analyses have confirmed: (a) a positive and robust relationship between the quality of the alliance and psychotherapy outcomes (in different models); (b) some therapists have a better ability to establish strong therapeutic alliances with different types of clients; (c) the clients of therapists who form better therapeutic alliances have better therapeutic outcomes; (d) personal attributes and also certain interventions common to different theoretical approaches help to establish and manage good therapeutic alliances; (e) the alliance, together with the therapist's effects, are two of the strongest predictors in empirical research in psychotherapy (Nissen-Lie et al. 2013a; Del Re et al. 2012; Horvath et al. 2011; Zuroff et al. 2010).

The Real Relationship
As already mentioned, the contextual model refers to the importance of the concept of the real relationship, distinguishing it from the construct of the therapeutic alliance (Wampold 2015; Gelso 2014). The real relationship is conceptualized in a tripartite model, in which it is assumed that three dimensions are interrelated in psychotherapeutic relationships, irrespective of the theoretical model: a real relationship, a working alliance and a transferential and counter-transferential dimension. The three dimensions influence each other but have their own individual theoretical and empirical value (Gelso 2009, 2014). The real relationship is defined as "the personal relationship between therapist and patient marked by the extent to which each is genuine with the other and perceives/experiences the other in ways that befit the other" (Gelso 2014, p. 119). The real element encompasses two elements: realism and genuineness. The first refers to how client and therapist experience and perceive each other, how well they fit each other, rather than to projections based on relevant figures of the past. The second reflects the ability to be our true selves and to be authentic in the relationship. Two sub-elements are also considered: magnitude and valence. Magnitude has to do with how far the real relationship is present (realism and genuineness). Valence has to do with the positive and negative attitudes and feelings that client and therapist have for each other (Gelso 2009). This

conceptualization has been the subject of criticism, both epistemological and theoretical, from various spectra of the world of psychotherapy, psychoanalysts and humanists. However, its authors defend its theoretical, clinical and empirical value. In this last respect, a significant step forward has been taken: credible research instruments have been created (Gelso 2014). Empirical research has presented findings which require future confirmation but which even so are very promising: (a) from a client's perspective, the real relationship (in particular, the element of genuineness) was a predictor of outcome; (b) the real relationship was substantially more significant that the therapeutic alliance in predicting therapeutic outcomes (Gelso et al. 2012; Lo Coco et al. 2011). These findings were confirmed when a more recent study showed that clients who perceived that their therapists scored higher for the real relationship also gave higher scores to their therapeutic progress (Kivlighan et al. 2015). So for the clients, some therapists are able to establish better real and human relationships that other therapists. Clients who scored the therapists higher for the real relationship had better outcomes. However, the therapists' scoring of the real relationship was associated with worse therapeutic outcomes (Kivlighan et al. 2015). Research findings have shown how the construct of the real relationship is distinct from the working alliance. These findings have also underlined that therapists should pay special attention to creating and establishing an authentic personal relationship with clients (Gelso 2012).

These data are in keeping with a series of practical recommendations concerning the therapeutic relationship and alliance (Horvath et al. 2011; Norcross and Wampold 2011; Norcross 2010):

- The human relationship makes a significant and decisive contribution to therapeutic outcomes, in various psychotherapeutic models, and in different issues brought by clients to the therapy;
- Adapting the therapeutic relationship to the client, to his personal characteristics and expectations, helps to engage him and improves the therapeutic outcomes;
- Clients and therapists tend to have distinct perceptions of the therapeutic alliance, above all at the early stages of the therapeutic process. It is known that establishing the therapeutic relationship, from the very start of the therapy, is associated with therapeutic outcomes;
- It is therefore particularly important that the therapist should pay special attention to creating the alliance right from the outset.

Although it appears crucial to create a relationship which is human and one of trust, it is fundamental to achieve a high standard in working together and collaboration;

- Therapists are encouraged to monitor closely the therapeutic alliance, seeking client feedback on the relationship and the therapeutic process. The alliance is established and maintained through the actions of the clients and the therapist, in a relationship which should be one of mutual engagement and collaboration;
- Seeking patient feedback on the therapeutic relationship is fundamental. Some research data suggest that psychotherapists are less effective than clients in assessing the level of the alliance. The suggestion is to give the client a voice, to gather feedback systematically, and to take his views into account;
- The strength of the alliance may fluctuate and be subject to stresses in particular sessions over the therapeutic process. The therapist's interventions, his personal stance and interpersonal style, and the client's expectations overlap and influence each other. These are natural fluctuations which may help to strengthen the alliance when addressed in therapy by a flexible psychotherapist who is careful about these dimensions;
- Research has shown that specific actions by the therapist are critical to establishing strong alliances. Some therapists are systematically more able to establish better therapeutic alliances with highly varied clients. This suggests that therapists can improve this aspect over time and that their interpersonal skills and abilities are crucial;
- It is crucial for maintaining and managing a good therapeutic relationship that the therapists should not react defensively to negative reactions or even conflict.

Repair of Ruptures in the Therapeutic Alliance
Recent decades have seen a paradigm shift in most psychotherapy models: they have started to attach greater importance to the therapeutic relationship dimension and factors associated with the therapist's person, in particular interpersonal factors, to the detriment of a more exclusive focus on the model or therapeutic techniques (Nissen-Lie et al. 2013a). In particular, more attention is being paid to the truly human aspects of the therapeutic relationship (Safran and Muran 2006). But in addition to the human dimension, it has also been considered very important to understand the therapeutic alliance as something negotiated between

client and therapist. The concept of negotiation is designed to stress that (a) the therapeutic alliance is ongoing and continuously adjusted between client and therapist; (b) it therefore has a dimension which is not static, but instead constantly changing; (c) the alliance stems from the relationship itself; (d) the negotiation process, conscious and unconscious, ends up being in itself a change mechanism for the client, who develops an inter-subjective ability to cope and negotiate appropriately with himself and with others (Safran and Muran 2000). This paradigm shift has also led to interest in the concept and practice of repairing ruptures in the therapeutic alliance. Ruptures in the therapeutic alliance are defined as "problems in quality of relatedness" or "deteriorations in the communicative process" (or at least defined as *both* "breakdowns in collaboration" and "poor quality of relatedness") (Safran and Muran 2006, p. 289).

Meta-analyses have confirmed that managing and repairing cracks and ruptures in the alliance reduce dropout rates and help achieve better therapeutic outcomes (Safran et al. 2011). A study which compared therapist training in alliance-focused training (AFT) and CBT concluded that therapists trained in AFT were more able to have a more positive impact on the interpersonal process, from session to session. In addition, therapists trained in AFT were more able to foster deeper reflection on the therapeutic relationship and to address their own felt experience (Safran et al. 2014). A study which considered 241 dyads in therapeutic processes of 30 sessions, analyzed session by session, concluded that the strongest predictor of the outcome of a session were the changes occurring within the psychotherapy itself, reported by the client in his alliance assessment. This finding was in turn what contributed most to predicting what the client's predictions of the therapeutic outcome would be (Zilcha-Mano et al. 2016). The findings showed that specific changes made over the course of sessions in the management of the alliance and repairing of ruptures had an impact on the client and the therapist and change their perception, giving them a more positive outlook for the next session. Even so, merely the way in which the alliance was scored by the client had an impact not only on the client, but also an effect on the therapist's perception of the next session, called *significant partner effect*. However, whilst the study confirmed that the client's perception is a robust indicator, the same is not true of the therapist's perspective. The therapist's scoring of the alliance was not associated with how the client perceived it and or with the therapeutic outcome (Zilcha-Mano et al. 2016). The research demonstrates that therapists who were able to achieve micro-changes during sessions, to deal with fluctuations in the relationship, and to adapt the intervention to the client, managed to bring about better therapeutic outcomes.

This research confirmed a number of aspects described in the literature, stressing that therapists can be specifically trained to improve their skills to deal with ruptures in the alliance. When ruptures are repaired, the clients enjoy better therapeutic outcomes, dropout rates decrease, their quality of life gets better and they improve their interpersonal functioning (Zilcha-Mano et al. 2016; Safran et al. 2014; Crits-Christoph et al. 2006).

Clients are very reluctant to share negative feelings about the psychotherapy and the therapeutic relationship, partly out of fear of the therapist's reaction (Safran et al. 2011). It appears important that therapists pay particular attention to the slightest signs of discomfort from their clients, in view of their reluctance in expressing their emotions in relation to the therapeutic relationship. It is particularly important that clients should find the space and the confidence to be able to express their thoughts and emotions, whether negative or otherwise. It is also important that the therapist should not react defensively or even critically if the client verbalizes negative observations concerning the process or the relationship (Safran and Kraus 2014). Likewise, it is noted that it is critical that the therapist should take responsibility of what is happening in the relationship and of what may be felt by the client as a crack or rupture in the relationship. It is absolutely vital that the therapist should be able to empathize and validate the client's emotions. In some situations, changing the therapeutic goals and tasks may be enough to stabilize the relationship, in others, it is fundamental to look deeper into relational issues existing between client and therapist. Although it is sometimes recommended that connections be drawn between ruptures and the client's patterns of behavior or life experiences, this issue should be approached with particular care. Some data have suggested that, for many clients, connections between or interpretations linking what they experience in the therapeutic relationship and their past life experiences, may turn out badly for them, above all when they are frequent. The quality, rather than the quantity of transferential interpretations, appears to make a positive difference (Safran and Muran 2000; Safran et al. 2011)

Ruptures are inevitable events in therapeutic relationships. They are understood as opportunities for therapeutic change and not just as obstacles (Safran and Kraus 2014). Evolving concepts and promising empirical evidence, on management of ruptures in the therapeutic alliance, have yielded several theoretical and practical recommendations. When ruptures occur in the alliance, the interventions the therapist can consider include: (a) returning to the rationale of the therapeutic process, in addition to what is explained at the outset, can help to repair ruptures; (b) changing goals and tasks to make them more meaningful for the client and more in keeping with him; (c) clarify minor misunderstandings; explore relational issues associated with the rupture in the alliance; (d) sometimes link the rupture in the alliance to patterns in the client's life; (e) at certain times the therapist may try out a new relational stance without directly addressing this change on his own side with the client (Safran et al. 2011). More specifically, certain principles of meta-communication are suggested for negotiating ruptures in the therapeutic alliance: (1) skilful, careful and empathic exploration, so that the client feels free to express his subjectivity; (2) no immediate or premature drawing of parallels with other relationships, which may be experienced as blaming, instead of fostering intimacy between client and therapist; (3) the therapist takes responsibility for the relational dynamic without being defensive; (4) start in the here-and-now, accepting that meta-communication exists in the moment and in what the therapist thinks and feels in that situation; (5) in this sense, the client is helped when the therapist focuses on the concrete and the specific instead of using generalizations, through experiential focusing, rather than intellectualization; (6) monitoring and exploring the client's responses to the interventions, in order for the therapist to be able to intervene when he senses a relational breakdown; (7) clarify and reflect on the relational meaning of the therapist's interventions, both for the client and the therapist, insofar as the impacts of interventions are always mediated by his relational sense; (8) foster a collaborative spirit and a sense of "us" so as not to let the client feel isolated and alone; (9) the therapist explores his own experience and reveals issues in a prudent and cautious way; (10) bear in mind that resolving ruptures does not prevent fresh cracks from appearing in the therapeutic alliance (Safran and Kraus 2014). In short, the authors also refer to the importance of therapists not confusing meta-communication techniques with core skills for resolving ruptures in the alliance, in other words, being able to monitor and reflect, moment by moment, about what is happening in the therapeutic relationship (Safran and Kraus 2014).

Expectations, Agreement on Goals and Therapeutic Tasks

With the possible exception of the human connection, the alliance is not in itself therapeutic. It is essential for collaboration between client and therapist for goals and therapeutic tasks to be aligned. These factors combine to create expectations in the client, which will in turn be a *loko-motiv* for the therapeutic process (Wampold and Imel 2015). The meta-analyses suggest an important correlation between setting goals and therapeutic tasks on the one hand, and psychotherapy outcomes on the other (Tryon and Winograd 2011). The importance of clients' expectations for producing therapeutic change has been systematically referred to in the literature and is regarded as a common factor (Frank and Frank 1991; Goldfried 1980).

Literature reviews have pointed out that parties with high expectations of psychotherapy outcomes benefit more from it than clients who are not confident that the therapeutic intervention will help them get better (Delsignore and Schnyder 2007). Meta-analyses also confirm a positive correlation between clients' expectations and therapeutic outcomes (Constantino et al. 2011). The findings of meta-analyses indicate that, with a high level of consensus on goals, 67% of clients will have a positive outcome, whilst a psychotherapy with a low level of consensus about goals will have a success rate of around 33% (Lambert and Cattani 2012). Studies have shown that directly addressing client expectations of outcomes, the therapeutic process and the duration of psychotherapy all bring dropout rates down (Swift and Callahan 2011). On the other hand, clients' life goals, whether clear or ambiguous, can be adapted and re-established, as therapeutic goals and tasks, in order to boost the level of collaboration in the therapeutic alliance and therapeutic changes (Mackrill 2011). Studies have revealed strong associations between a consensus on goals and therapeutic tasks and a reduction in symptoms, with continued psychotherapy instead of dropping out, and developing more adaptive functioning. In the same way, a good level of collaboration is associated with positive therapeutic outcomes and better levels of well-being (Tryon and Winograd 2011). When therapists fail to adapt to their clients' goals, even when some therapeutic benefits exist, the general perception of clients is that the psychotherapy was not beneficial (Werbart et al. 2015). Many clients come to the psychotherapy with little advance knowledge of the procedures, or with biased expectations. For this reason, in view of the strong correlation between consensus on goals and a high level of collaboration between client and therapist, the practical suggestions include: (a) explain and clearly establish the therapeutic goals and tasks with clients; (b) therapists should not impose their own agenda, but instead pay heed to the clients' perspectives, motivations and goals; (c) regularly ask clients for feedback and their ideas, check their level of motivation and the phase of change; (d) provide the client with direct instructions and educate him about the importance of close and positive collaboration between them; (e) the therapist should check whether he and the client are on the same wavelength as the degree of collaboration towards the goals may fluctuate over the therapeutic process (Tryon and Winograd 2011). Clients' expectations have been conceptualized as expectations about outcomes and expectations about the process (Constantino et al. 2012). The former are more closely connected to beliefs about the effectiveness or otherwise of psychotherapy, and whether it can effectively be a source of help. The latter are related to the way in which the therapeutic process will take place, about the interaction between client and therapist, and about the duration of the therapy. Clients' expectations and beliefs about therapeutic outcomes exist even before the start of psychotherapy (Constantino et al. 2011). Assessing the level of expectations should serve in part to adjust goals and the intervention to the clients. Therapists can tell the clients about the psychotherapy, also explaining that fluctuations in expectations are only natural, as are fluctuations in the therapeutic process. This helps clients to cope with small frustrations and to reach a better understanding of what will happen between himself and the therapist. Fostering expectations empathically, adjusting them realistically, whilst at the same time managing to create in the client a belief that change for his issues is possible, contributes to an increase in the level of collaboration between client and therapist, and consequently helps the psychotherapy to advance successfully. Paying special attention to the level of the therapeutic alliance and possible ruptures may be particularly useful as both are related to the expectations that clients have of psychotherapy (Constantino et al. 2011, 2012). In conjunction, consensus on therapeutic goals and tasks, together with the clients' expectations are crucial elements for therapeutic change according to the contextual model (Wampold 2015). There is an interconnection and mutual influence between goals, expectations and the level of collaboration between client and therapist. Studies have shown that clients who are less self-critical and have higher expectations benefited more from the therapist's relational characteristics(empathy, congruence and positive regard). Even therapists who are relationally talented may be frustrated by more critical clients with lower expectations, and should therefore anticipate the level of their expectations and possible ruptures in the alliance (Zuroff et al. 2016). The client agreeing to and actively collaborating on therapeutic goals and tasks increases his expectations. These are in turn reinforced by acceptance by the client of a convincing rationale introduced by the therapist, which will be more adaptive to his issues. Studies have confirmed that the rationale for the therapeutic intervention is associated with the client's expectations of and commitment to the therapeutic process (Ahmed and Westra 2009). Lastly, collaboration between client and therapist is essential for them to work together on the therapeutic tasks and procedures, which should promote dimensions of relief and better well-being for the client (Laska et al. 2014).

Feedback Systems in Psychotherapy

As Carl Rogers famously said, "the facts are friendly". Psychotherapy is efficacious. Psychotherapy is an established practice and people who have had psychotherapy achieve better results than people who have not, both in terms of symptom reduction and in general well-being. What is more, psychotherapy is more efficacious than several scientifically established medical interventions, such as interventions in cardiology, geriatric medicine and asthma (Wampold 2007). No less important, research has shown that psychotherapy is at least as efficacious as pharmacological interventions for psychological disorders, with the advantage that its effects are longer lasting (Lambert 2013b; Wampold 2007).

Negative Therapeutic Outcomes and the Impacts of the Therapist

Despite the efficacy of psychotherapy, around 5–10% of adult clients are worse at the end of psychotherapy than when they started (Lambert and Shimokawa 2011). In children and adolescents, the percentages are higher, at between 14 and 24%(Lambert and Shimokawa 2011; Warren et al. 2010). It is estimated that between 40 and 60% drop out of psychotherapy (Boswell et al. 2015). Random clinical trials show that around two-thirds of adults have a positive outcome in approximately 14 sessions, but around one-third present no benefit or deteriorate

(Lambert 2013b). Data collected covering around 6000 clients in primary health care contexts show that only around one-third improved or showed any improvement, whilst approximately 8%, in a range between 3 and 14%, deteriorated during the therapeutic process or were worse when the process ended (Lambert 2013b). Around 30–50% of adult clients do not respond well to psychotherapy in health services (Boswell et al. 2015). There are clearly many reasons why people fail to obtain dividends from psychotherapy. It has been shown that life events and a lack of social support are in many circumstances the two dimensions which most contribute to the difficulty clients have in achieving therapeutic gains. The quality of life events and also the quality of social support appear to be significantly associated with both negative and positive changes, whilst the therapeutic alliance and motivation level are most closely associated with positive changes (Probst et al. 2015). But whilst there are factors that far transcend the actual context of psychotherapy, it is also important to continue looking deeper into the reasons, directly connected to therapeutic processes, which contribute to the fact that between 40 and 70% of people do not respond positively to psychological interventions (Imel et al. 2015).

Another aspect which has raised questions in the field has to do with what are called therapist factors, which have attracted increasing attention, as one of the variables that most contributes to change in clients (Goldberg et al. 2016a). We shall look at therapist factors in the next section, so for now it suffices to point to the great variability between the outcomes achieved by different therapists (Imel et al. 2015; Saxon and Barkham 2012) and to note that the therapist's impact on the variance attribute to therapeutic change is in the order of 5–7% (Baldwin and Imel 2013). This is a very high percentage and significantly higher than the factors associated with the theoretical models and the specific techniques. In short, some clients deteriorated over the course of therapy, other clients are worse when it ends, and there are sharp differences between the outcomes achieved by different therapists. Together, these are factors which contributed to the development of feedback systems in psychotherapy. In addition to these aspects, there are other factors which also contribute to the issue of feedback systems, in particular: (a) dropout rates remain relatively high, (b) therapists have difficulty in conducting a realistic assessment of their skills and the progress made by their clients.

Dropouts

In psychotherapy, dropping out is deemed to be when a client unilaterally interrupts the intervention prematurely, before recovering from the problems which led him to seek help and/or before completing the therapeutic intervention (Swift and Greenberg 2014). In a meta-analysis which took in 125 studies, the average dropout rate in psychotherapy was 46.86%. This is the median of the range of 30–60% of previous estimates of the dropout rate in psychotherapy (Wierzbicki and Pekarik 1993). The studies included in the meta-analysis considered different types of psychotherapeutic intervention, contexts and diagnoses. The dropout rate appears highest in the early stages of psychotherapy (Roos and Werbart 2013). Swift and Greenberg (2012) conducted a second meta-analysis which took in 669 studies, covering 83,834 clients and concluded that the dropout rate was around 19.7%, lower than that detected in the first meta-analysis two decades earlier. However, the early dropout rate in psychotherapy remains a concern, as the data from this meta-analysis shows that one in every five clients drops out (Swift and Greenberg 2012). Early dropouts were most associated with: younger clients, clients at university clinics, clients diagnosed with personality or eating disorders, and clients who had an intervention with no time limit, seen by trainee psychotherapists (Swift and Greenberg 2012). These data are in keeping with another meta-analysis which concluded that there was a relationship between weaker therapeutic alliances and higher dropout rates (Sharf et al. 2010). Moderator variables between the therapeutic alliance and dropouts were related to two factors: clients with lower educational attainment and a larger number of therapy sessions (Sharf et al. 2010). Dropouts were not associated with the theoretical orientation, with the type of intervention (individual or group, or with the therapist's age and gender. Although dropouts were not associated with the therapist's theoretical model, they were associated with his years of experience. More experienced therapists had lower dropout rates (17.2%) when compared with trainee psychotherapists (26.6%) (Swift and Greenberg 2012). A literature review identified dropout rates of around 35% and summarized the dimensions of the therapists and the therapeutic relationship which had an impact on dropouts (Roos and Werbart 2013). Therapists' experience, training and skills, together with concrete and emotional support for the clients, helped to diminish dropouts. At the same time, the quality of the therapeutic alliance, interpersonal factors between the client and the therapist, and preparation and information on the psychotherapy provided to clients at the outset were factors which reduced dropout rates (Roos and Werbart 2013). The more recent meta-analysis sought to study specifically the differences in dropout rates in specific disorders (Swift and Greenberg 2014). Of the 12 diagnostic categories considered, only depression and post-traumatic stress presented distinct dropout rates. These data suggested that the reasons for the dropout rate may be more associated with variables related to the characteristics of the clients, therapists and common factors associated with psychotherapies (Swift and Greenberg 2014). A set of practices were recommended for psychotherapists to deal with and seek to diminish dropouts: (a) give information on the duration of psychotherapy and change phases; (b) provide the clients with information on the roles expected of the client and therapist in the course of the psychotherapy; (c) incorporate the client's preferences; (d) increase the client's hope in the early stages of the psychotherapy; (e) foster good therapeutic alliances; (f) assess, monitor and talk about progress in the psychotherapy with the client (Swift et al. 2012).

Therapists' Self-assessments: Biased Over-Estimation

Several studies have shown that psychotherapists have an over-optimistic view of their own clinical abilities (Lambert 2015; Bowell et al. 2015). When psychotherapists are invited to assess their own skills and performance, and also to compare themselves with their peers, the findings indicates that 25% of mental health professions think they belong to the 90th percentile, when compared with their peers, and none acknowledge they are below average (Walfish et al. 2012). In addition, the findings indicate that psychotherapists have a biased view of the outcomes of their own clients: they overestimate the outcomes of clients who will improve and underestimate the number of their clients who get worse over the therapeutic process (Walfish et al. 2012). Therapists estimate that 85% of their clients have a positive outcome. However, the data shows that around 40% of processes in experimental trials have negative outcomes and around 60% in health services, which contrasts with the over-optimistic estimate made by therapists (Lambert 2015). Several studies have pointed out that therapists often lack the clinical judgment to assess properly the state of their clients (Hatfield et al. 2010). Positive self-assessments by psychotherapists of the levels of the real relationship were associated with worse therapeutic outcomes (Kivlighan et al. 2015). A comparison of psychotherapy outcomes measured using outcome instruments and the clinical notes of therapists shows that in 70% of cases therapists failed to identify deterioration by the client. Using their clinical assessment, therapists were only able to identify 21% of the situations in which clients got worse. It has also been found that an increase in symptoms was the therapists' preferred criterion for identifying a lack of therapeutic progress (Hatfield et al. 2010). Research which looked at 48 therapists (26 experienced and 22 trainees) set out to study how therapists were able to predict their clients' progress and outcomes (Hannan et al. 2005). The therapists were aware of the purpose of the study, 550 clients were included and statistical methods were used in order to predict client outcomes and levels of deterioration, based on data collected using Outcome Questionnaire-45 (OQ-45). During the therapeutic process and at the end of each session, therapists were asked whether they thought the client would get worse during the psychotherapy and end up in a worse state than at the start, and also whether, in this particular session, the client was worse than in the previous session. Although 40 of the total 550 clients ended in a worse overall state than when they started the therapy, the therapists were only able to predict that three would end the therapy in a worse state. However, only one of these three clients actually ended the therapy in a worse state, and this prediction was made by a trainee therapist and not an experienced therapist (Hannan et al. 2005). The data show that therapists have difficulty in anticipating situations where the clients will deteriorate during psychotherapy, or even end it in a more difficult situation. In contrast, the data collected using OQ-45, and then analyzed statistically, was able to predict that 36 clients would worsen, which means there was a success rate of 90% in prediction, insofar as 40 clients actually worsened (Hannan et al. 2005). In another study, with 48 clients, 10 of whom were in a worse state at the end of therapy, none of these were identified by the psychotherapists (Chapman et al. 2012). The therapists predicted that three clients would not respond well to the psychotherapy, but all of them experienced a significant improvement. This study also showed the psychotherapists to be poor predictors of the therapeutic alliance (Chapman et al. 2012). This aspect is also crucial as early identification of ruptures in the alliance may be decisive in positively turning around the process and avoiding dropouts. In short, the psychotherapists underestimated the clients who might not benefit or might even get worse with psychotherapy, and were inefficacious in assessing the level of the therapeutic alliance. (Chapman et al. 2012). Research looking at cognitive-behavioral therapists concludes that they significantly overestimate their abilities, as compared to the assessment by external evaluators regarded as experts in the approach (Brosan et al. 2008). The therapists regarded as less able were those who, proportionally, most overestimated their efficacy (Brosan et al. 2008). These data call into question a number of deeply rooted assumptions in the world of psychotherapy. In the first place, they question one of the most important tools of psychotherapists, which is their clinical assessment skills. They also question the assumption that, in order for a client to be able to improve, he must first get worse. Although it is known that, in many circumstances of the therapeutic process clients may go through difficult moments, several studies have shown that a positive start to psychotherapy is a good predictor of final outcomes (Lambert 2013b). Like many professions, psychotherapists appear to have a highly optimistic bias concerning their skills and performance (Lambert 2015). In general, people have a very optimistic view of their abilities in many social and professional domains (Kruger and Dunning 1999). Studies in social psychology have shown that when we are less skilled in certain tasks, we are also less able to recognize our limitations in performing the same tasks (Kruger and Dunning 1999). Although therapists consider that they improve their abilities over years of accumulating experience, some studies suggest that, on average, therapists not only do not evolve over time, but sometimes their efficacy diminishes (Goldberg et al. 2016b).

Monitoring and Feedback Systems

Despite the good news on the efficacy of psychotherapy, it is found that many clients do not benefit from psychotherapy, dropout rates remain high and therapists vary substantially amongst themselves in their success rates, are poor judges of clients' negative outcomes and overestimate their own efficacy (Duncan and Reese 2015). The introduction and development of routine outcome monitoring and feedback systems are designed, amongst other things, to help respond positively to these issues. One of the basic assumptions of feedback systems is that of providing therapists with information on their clients' progress (Lambert 2015). This information should provide the psychotherapist with something new. It is often not possible for the therapist to have enough time in the session to address the different areas of the client's psychological functioning. It is also very often the case that clients end up not addressing the issues which are affecting them most. With feedback systems, *the aim is to monitor the client's life, from his own perspective* (Lambert and Shimokawa 2011). Information is gathered from clients, in real time, and their progress is compared with an expected treatment response (ETR). The client's expected response is predicted using statistical methods, which compare the client's data with that of hundreds of thousands stored in data bases. Monitoring the process is intended to identify as early as possible any clients who are not benefiting from the intervention, in order to turn around their therapeutic process onto a positive course. The therapist is therefore able to review his relationship with the client and adapt the therapy to him (Lambert 2015). The rationale of feedback is that the therapist can be more responsive to the client's needs if he knows why the client is not benefiting from the psychotherapy (Lambert 2015). Feedback systems function as a warning sign for therapists. The feedback system picks up what they often fail to detect, in particular, clients who are on a downward curve in the therapeutic process (Lutz et al. 2015). As we have seen, many clients do not benefit from therapy. Process monitoring sets out to identify clients who are "not on track" (NOT), those who are not following the expected recovery trajectory and so at risk of dropping out or not deriving gains from the psychotherapy (Lambert 2015). The central aims of using feedback systems to monitor therapeutic processes are to adapt the intervention to the client's specific characteristics and thereby improve therapeutic outcomes and reduce dropout rates (Boswell et al. 2015).

A number of feedback systems have been developed over the years. Two of these, the Outcome Questionnaire System (OQ System) (Lambert 2015), and the Partners for Change Outcome Management System (PCOMS) (Miller et al. 2005), have been recognized in the Substance Abuse and Mental Health Administration's National Registry of Evidence-based Programs and Practices (Wampold 2015). PCOMS is based on two instruments: the Outcome Rating Scale (ORS) and the Session Rating Scale (SRS), where each of the measurements subdivides into four dimensions on which the client gives feedback after every session. The ORS sets out to assess how the client has been in the past week at different levels: individual (his personal well-being); interpersonal (family, more significant relationships) social (working and school relationships and friends) and in general (general well-being). The SRS looks at the sessions: the therapeutic relationship, aims and issues addressed, the method and approach, and how the session went in general. The ORS and SRS are given to clients at every session, the first at the start of the session and the second at the end. The aim of PCOMS is that the scales should be extremely quick to complete, and that client feedback is gathered at every session, whether or not the client is making a good recovery. Feedback is shared and discussed by client and therapist in their sessions (Miller et al. 2005). Michael Lambert pioneered the development of feedback systems in psychotherapy from the 90s onwards. He developed the OQ-System, based on the OQ-45, which includes 45 items designed to assess three fields of the client's functioning: symptoms of psychological disorder, interpersonal problems and social issues. OQ-45 provides an overall score for well-being, and partial scores from the sub-scales for symptoms, interpersonal relations and the social dimension. OQ-45 can be filled out by the client before starting the sessions and is expected to take around 5–7 min to complete. Both PCOMS and OQ-45 are supported by software which produces a recovery curve which can be statistically expected, in line with the distress level assessed at the start of the psychotherapy, in order to identify NOT clients. However, in addition to signaling, OQ-45 also sets out to identify which areas are preventing the client from making progress in the psychotherapy, and to help the therapist design strategies to deal with these obstacles (Lambert 2015). It includes the Assessment for Signal Clients (ASC), designed to assess problems which are blocking progress in the therapy, in particular, issues related to the therapeutic alliance, questions of motivations, lack of social supports and aspects related to life events. The ASC is related to the Clinical Support Tools (CST), developed with a decision clinical tree, allowing the therapist to identify the best therapeutic strategies to follow, on the basis of the survey conducted by ASC (Lambert 2015).

Several empirical studies and meta-analyses have shown that PCOMS and OQ-45 are empirically well supported (Wampold 2015; Reese et al. 2009). Miller and colleagues (2015) summarized the main impacts of using feedback systems: they are able to double therapeutic success rates and increase the proportion of clients with clinically significant change, they halved dropout rates, they reduced the number of clients at risk of deterioration by around one-third, and consequently primary health care costs are reduced (Miller et al. 2015). Meta-analyses show that clients who were at risk of deteriorating or at risk of not benefiting from psychotherapy were on average 70% better in cases where therapists received feedback. Of clients seen with feedback systems, only 9% deteriorated, and 38% had clinically significant changes. In contrast, for clients seen on a "treatment-as-usual" (TAU) basis, where therapists did not receive feedback, 20% deteriorated and 22% had a clinically significant improvement (Lambert and Shimokawa 2011; Shimokawa et al. 2010). The empirical evidence also confirms that the use of CST has positive impacts: clients were 76% better compared to clients seen on a "treatment-as-usual" basis. Deterioration rates fell to 6–53% of clients experienced clinically significant change (Lambert and Shimokawa 2011). In addition to feedback systems being able to identify clients at risk, the findings also point to the advantages of therapists benefiting from CST information: clients are less than one quarter as likely to deteriorate and 3.9 times more likely to experience clinically significant improvement (Lambert and Shimokawa 2011). A recent trial compared three variables in therapeutic processes: with or without a feedback system, short or long interventions, and feedback supplied to the client and the therapist or only to the therapist (De Jong et al. 2014). In situations where the clients were not making positive progress, it was found that the best results occurred in: short psychotherapy and when the client and therapist received feedback. It was also found that long-duration psychotherapies also benefited from receiving feedback. The study suggests that it may be more productive for both parties in the therapeutic process to receive feedback (De Jong et al. 2014). A study with psychosomatic patients concluded that the group which was at risk of deteriorating, with whom the therapists used OQ-45 and CST, had much better outcomes than the control group (Probst et al. 2013). All the patients who were at risk, and who recovered, belonged to the feedback group, in which the deterioration rate was 8.7%, as compared to a rate of 25% for the control group patients, in other words, patients deteriorated 65% less with the feedback system (Probst et al. 2013). Feedback systems have also proved useful in predicting the needs and developments of psychotherapeutic progress, with children and adolescents (Boswell et al. 2015; Kraus et al. 2015). A study with 299 young people that also includes the carers' perspective, found that the feedback group had much more positive impact in identifying problematic issues, as compared to the control group, which in turn led to more positive outcomes in psychotherapy (Douglas et al. 2015). An RCT involving 340 young people concluded that the group with a feedback system attained better therapeutic outcomes and that the therapeutic gains occurred earlier than in the control group (Bickman et al. 2011). ROM systems with feedback have achieved good results in community mental health services. Research shows that 36% of clients involved in psychotherapy with feedback in community services attained clinically significant improvements, in contrast to only 13% of clients without feedback (Gibbons et al. 2015). Feedback systems have been applied in group psychotherapies, with clinically more significant improvements and increased rates of retention in the therapeutic process for clients included in feedback groups (Slone et al. 2015). A review of the literature on interventions for substance abuse, with feedback systems, concludes that: clients have better final outcomes, a faster rate of recovery, a higher level of clinically significant change with remission of symptoms. The results were more significant for clients who were identified as at risk of being off-track. A crucial aspect that this highlighted was that off-track clients were identified much earlier (Goodman et al. 2013). This aspect is particularly important. Two of the best predictors of outcome have been found to be: the client's initial distress level and identification of clients at risk in the first few sessions (Lambert 2013b). Feedback systems have been shown to be able to identify between 80 and 100% of clients who will have poor therapeutic outcomes. In addition to their efficacy in detecting NOT clients, they are able to do this much earlier, sometimes in the first three sessions of psychotherapy, making it possible to reduce deterioration rates by 50% (Lambert 2013b; Reese et al. 2009). The findings have demonstrated this efficacy even in situations of clients with suicidal thoughts and at risk of suicide (Restifo et al. 2015). Indeed, several studies have shown how effective feedback systems are at identifying clients at risk, supplanting in some cases the clinical judgment of the therapists (Spielmans et al. 2006; Lutz et al. 2006; Ellsworth et al. 2006). Data have demonstrated that around 66.8% of clients believe that monitoring of therapeutic processes is completely right (Lutz et al. 2015).

However, some studies have presented more modest findings of the efficacy of feedback systems (Amble et al. 2015; Simon et al. 2012). The findings are not always consistent in demonstrating the advantage in long psychotherapies (Lutz et al. 2015). But above all, several research projects have shown that the efficacy of feedback systems depends on the therapist. Several factors relating to the therapist, including his motivation and his perception of the usefulness of incorporating feedback into clinical practice, contribute to whether feedback systems have more positive results (De Jong and De Goede 2015; Lutz et al. 2015; De Jong et al.2012; Simon et al. 2012). These studies are in keeping with the existing theories on feedback. Lambert and Shimokawa (2011) summarized a number of factors needed for feedback to result in more efficacious performance: the information provided must demonstrate that the therapist is not attaining standard levels; the therapist must actually be committed to improving his performance; he must be aware of the discrepancy between the actual results he achieves and new targets; the aim must be appealing and the therapist must believe that it can be achieved; the feedback source must be credible; whether feedback is immediate, frequent and systematic; whether it is simple and unambiguous; and whether it supplies concrete suggestions for improvement. In addition to therapist factors, other aspects stand in the way of acceptance of feedback systems. Firstly, the difficulties of implementing them (Wampold 2015). It is also necessary to assess the costs and benefits of implementation, and also the time that these systems demand from technical personnel (Lutz et al. 2015). Other barriers and obstacles to the implementation of feedback systems may include organizational culture issues, the difficulty of setting up feedback systems that respond to the different parties involved, and philosophical barriers (Boswell et al. 2015). Turnover in technical staff, data confidentiality and the way the data can be used to assess the skills of psychotherapists all add to the resistance to these systems (Miller et al. 2015). However, routine outcome monitoring (ROM) is one of the most promising areas for the future, for assessing the effectiveness of psychological interventions and of therapists (Emmelkamp et al. 2014), a position which has been defended by researchers and clinicians from around the world (Lutz et al. 2015). It may be particularly important to national health services, clinics, health centers, private institutions, hospitals and even for therapists in private practice. With ROM, closely linked to the practice-oriented research paradigm, integration between scientific research and clinical practice can be exponentially increased (Duncan and Reese 2015; Boswell et al. 2015). As we have seen, there are varied reasons for introducing feedback system and ROM, one of which is based on the evidence that the initial response to psychotherapy is a strong predictor of the evolution and final outcome of the psychotherapy (Lucock et al. 2015). In addition, in many circumstances therapists are poor predictors of the therapeutic evolution of their clients. The therapist's clinical assessment can be helped by prediction systems based on statistical algorithms (Lucock et al. 2015). Feedback systems can also be included as one of the ways of developing therapists' clinical expertise (Tracey et al. 2014). However, the existence of a feedback system in a service does not mean that the therapist includes these data in clinical practice. Studies have shown that half of therapists did not use the feedback (Miller et al. 2015; De Jong et al. 2012). The data also demonstrated that the more efficacious therapists were more sensitive to feedback systems than less efficacious therapists (Miller et al. 2015). Likewise, the findings suggest that therapists do not improve simply because they receive feedback or because they have a larger number of hours of clinical practice and have difficulties in identifying clients at risk of deteriorating or having negative outcomes in psychotherapy (Lambert 2015; Miller et al. 2015). Even in the application of ROM and feedback systems, these aspects point to one of the most relevant factors in research into psychotherapy: the therapist.

THE THERAPIST FACTORS

The literature suggests that therapist factors—defined as therapist factors with a direct impact on patient outcomes—contribute to approximately 5–9% of the variance attributed to therapeutic change. The literature has stressed two aspects: the variance attributed to therapist factors is significant, and there is a pronounced variability in effectiveness between different therapists (Goldberg et al. 2016a; Wampold and Imel 2015; Miller et al. 2015; Baldwin and Imel 2013; Miller et al. 2013). The variance in therapist factors is much greater than that for impact of the theoretical model and specific techniques, which are calculated at around 1% (Wampold and Imel 2015; Zuroff et al. 2010). Therapist impacts are more or less double the average effect identified in all studies of antidepressants, and are equivalent to a success rate of 65% in therapeutic interventions (Keenan and Shawn 2016). Even the therapeutic alliance, one of the strongest predictors of psychotherapeutic outcomes, contributes around 5% of these (Miller et al. 2013). The therapist himself is a crucial factor, whilst the theoretical model or the patient's diagnosis is not (Wampold 2011). A recent study which analyzed meta-analytical data reached two central conclusions: first, the specific effects of the therapists can contribute significantly to change, and second, when therapist effects are considered, between 65 and 80% of the effects attributed to the intervention (type of psychotherapy) ceased to be statistically significant (Owen et al. 2015). Both the variance of the therapist effect attributed to change, and the fact that some psychotherapists systematically achieved better outcomes and brought about improvements earlier in the therapeutic process have been verified irrespective of the theoretical model, the patient's disorder and the type of intervention (Lambert 2013b; Baldwin and Imel 2013).

Therapist factors have been identified as decisive in the psychotherapeutic literature since the 1930s (Lambert and Baldwin 2009), however, a huge gap continues to exist in our knowledge in this area of research (Castonguay 2013). Therapist factors have been considered the "neglected" variable in research (Garfield 1997). There was a resurgence in interest in this area in the 1980s. Empirical studies once again stressed that therapist factors were crucial and that there is a difference in efficacy between psychotherapists, unexplained by the theoretical model (Luborsky et al. 1986). In 1991, a meta-analysis concluded that therapist factors account for 9% of the variance attributed to therapeutic change (Crits-Christoph et al. 1991). More recent empirical research has borne out these findings. A study covering 6,146 patients and 581 therapists concluded that 5% of outcomes were attributed to the therapist (Wampold and Brown 2005). Some research in naturalistic settings has attributed a percentage of up to 17% to therapist factors (Lutz et al. 2007). These findings are also verified in studies with psychiatrists who sought to compare medication and placebos for depression (McKay et al. 2006). The psychiatrists accounted for respectively 6.7–9.1% of the variability in the outcomes in the Hamilton and Beck Measures of Depression, whilst medication contributed 5.9–3.4% (Mckay et al. 2006). The psychiatrists with the best personal skills had better outcomes administering the placebo than less effective psychiatrists supplying medication for depression. This shows that the factors associated with the psychiatrist were stronger than the factors associated with the treatment and that the former were more important to outcomes, even in situations where the supposed specific ingredient is a medicinal product (Mckay et al. 2006). In psychotherapy, recent studies which included evidence-based treatments for specific disorders, such as post-traumatic stress conclude that the variance attributed to therapists was 12% (Laska et al. 2013). This study revealed two equally important findings: differences in the person of the therapist are crucial even in more manualized interventions for specific situations; these therapists' supervisor was able to predict which therapists would be more efficacious on the basis of conversations during supervision and without having direct access to the interventions and the outcomes. Therapists who effectively addressed the patient's resistance to talking about the trauma, presented interpersonal flexibility and the ability to question themselves, and were not defensive in relation to feedback were those who succeeded in maintaining better therapeutic alliances (Laska et al. 2013). Studies with psychotherapists also present the variance of around 8% attributed to therapists, irrespective of the type of intervention (Kim et al. 2006). But this is even more significant with patients whose issues are severe. The more severe the patients' issues, the greater the impact of the therapist, in other words, the more skilful therapists were able to deal with more complex issues (Goldberg et al. 2016a; Saxon and Barkham 2012; Kim et al. 2006). This question points us towards variability among therapists.

Variability of Effectiveness Among Psychotherapists

The difference in effectiveness among psychotherapists is a controversial topic and raises many questions. However, the literature has systematically pointed to a huge degree of variability in efficacy between therapists (Baldwin and Imel 2013). Therapist effects are statistically significant in clinical trials, but also in naturalistic settings, and some therapists are consistently better than others; this difference is not attributable to chance or to patient characteristics (Kraus et al. 2016). As we have seen, studies which distinguished between therapist effects and patient effects, concluded that some therapists are more skilful in establishing robust therapeutic alliances. The patients of these therapists, who are felt to be empathic, genuine and human, achieve better therapeutic outcomes. The more skilful therapists establish better alliances with very varied patients (Zuroff et al. 2010; Dinger et al. 2008; Baldwin et al. 2007). Meta-analyses corroborate the findings: some therapists are consistently better at establishing therapeutic alliances; these therapists bring about better outcomes; the role of the therapist appears to be the most important thing in constructing the alliance and is a predictor of outcomes (Del Re et al. 2012). The variability identified between therapists is not explained by the therapist's age, gender, academic qualifications and years of experience, or by the patient's age, gender and diagnosis. Likewise, patients taking psycho-pharmacological medication benefited more from it when they underwent psychotherapy with more effective therapists (Wampold and Brown 2005). Research that took in 5,000 patients seen by 71 therapists concluded that there were enormous variabilities in outcomes between therapists. Some therapists succeeded systematically in bringing about better outcomes (Okiishi et al. 2006). The differences between therapists were not associated with gender, level of qualifications or the theoretical model. Therapists had approximately the same type of clinical cases but there were sometimes vast differences in the speed of the process of change. In addition, with less efficacious therapists the rate of deterioration was double than with the therapists regarded as more skilful (Okiishi et al. 2006). These findings have been borne out with different populations. In a sample of 10,812 patients (76% adults, 24% children and adolescents), seen by 281 therapists, it was found that certain more efficacious therapists brought about on average 53% more clinically significant change (Brown et al. 2005). Another study involving 3,222 therapists produced findings which were even more striking, identifying a larger number of inefficacious therapists, with whom patients ended their intervention on average 38% worse than at the outset (Kraus et al. 2011). More recent research suggests that the differences between therapists are even more significant in longer term interventions (Goldberg et al. 2016a). A study that included 5,828 patients and 158 therapists found that in interventions with a small number of sessions, the differences between therapists were not significant, but from the 16th session onwards, the patients of the more efficacious therapists had more positive outcomes (Goldberg et al. 2016a). The authors suggest that all therapists have basic skills for short interventions. But in longer interventions, with patients with a worse prognosis, more complex issues, less social support and less motivation, therapists more able to be empathic, who had a more sophisticated rationale and better interpersonal skills have better outcomes. In other words, parties who underwent longer therapies with more efficacious therapists were those who benefited most from the interventions (Goldberg et al. 2016a). The findings on variability of effectiveness between therapists are even more sobering when certain studies suggest that the best therapeutic outcomes are not associated with levels of training and years of clinical experience (Budge et al.2013; Nyman et al. 2010; Hersoug et al. 2009). The most recent study, which included 170 therapists working with 6,500 patients, over an average of 5 years, concluded that therapists did not improve their outcomes, either as a result of the number of cases or considering their years of experience. What is more, the findings suggest that therapists in general became less efficacious over time (Goldberg et al. 2016b). Although a percentage (39.41%) of therapists made progress, on average, there appears to be no evidence that the therapists improved over time

(Goldberg et al. 2016b). Studies using feedback systems show that the differences between therapists contributed 6.2% to therapeutic outcomes and 9% to differences between the lengths of intervention (Lutz et al. 2015). Therapists who were happier to accept and take on board the benefits of feedback, a higher level of intervention and identification with the organizational culture had better outcomes. In short, therapist factors influence the outcomes of interventions even in feedback situations (De Jong and De Goede 2015). These findings are extremely challenging for the profession at various levels. They should be approached with great caution. However, people who ask for psychological help want to know how they can best be served. Economic pressures on mental health services mean that the efficacy of psychological interventions has to be demonstrated, creating a need to clarify which professionals are most effective (Minami et al. 2012). A simulation has demonstrated that even a conservative estimate in which the therapist's influence on outcomes is 5% means that in 1 year, an effective therapist will have 94 positive outcomes in 120 clinical cases. A less effective therapist will have only 25 positive outcomes. These figures mean that the more effective therapist will have 700 more clinical cases with positive outcomes in 10 years, in comparison to the less effective therapist (Imel et al. 2015). These findings are in fact controversial and need to be handled with extreme care. However, one very positive consequence from a research point of view is that the research should focus much more on analyzing the therapist factors and much less, for example, on comparing specific interventions (Lambert and Baldwin 2009). Irrespective of organizational measures and decisions, it is the therapist's professional responsibility in the last instance to manage the therapeutic process appropriately (Krause and Lutz 2009). So it appears crucial to obtain information about the therapist's personal and professional qualities that contribute positively to therapeutic outcomes.

Personal and Professional Qualities of Psychotherapists

The person of the therapist is regarded as one of the most important factors in psychotherapy and one of the last frontiers for scientific exploration (Norcross and Lambert 2011; Duncan et al. 2010). Factors of a relational nature attributed to the therapist, such as empathy, being genuine and meaningful and giving positive feedback to the patient, are regarded by meta-analyses as demonstrably effective (Norcross and

Wampold 2011). Empathy is the relational factor most closely studied, accounting for approximately 9% of the variance in therapeutic outcomes (Elliot et al. 2011). The factors referred to, which consistently have the most impact on outcomes depending, at least in part, on the relational qualities of the therapists: the therapeutic alliance, empathy, consensus on aims and collaboration, positive affirmation of the patient, meaningfulness and genuineness (Wampold and Imel 2015). This data bears out a survey conducted of 2,000 psychotherapists working within the most varied therapeutic models (Cook et al. 2010). Although 79% of the therapists identified themselves as CBT psychotherapists, and only 31% as humanists, the five therapeutic practices most commonly used, which account for around 90%, are relational: warm and human welcome, care and respect; communicating that the patient is accepted and valued; communicating understanding of the patient's experience; empathizing with the patient's situation, having feelings, efforts; promoting clear and direct expression of the patient's feelings (Cook et al. 2010, p. 263). The following five types of intervention that complete the top ten were: making reflective or clarifying comments; focusing on cultivating the therapeutic relationship/alliance; encouraging the patient to develop healthy and recreational activities; encouraging emotional processing of experiences of distress; creating awareness of how patients relate to others (Cook et al. 2010, p. 263). These findings are also in keeping with the empirical studies that confirm that the therapist's interpersonal skills (e.g., expressing emotions, persuasiveness) are directly related to better therapeutic outcomes (Laska et al. 2013; Anderson et al. 2009). Experimental clinical studies which set out to consider the therapist's interpersonal skills as an independent variable confirmed that: patients seen by therapists with higher interpersonal skills ratings had better outcomes; patients seen by these therapists rated the therapeutic alliance more highly; the therapeutic alliance was also rated more highly over the course of therapeutic processes conducted by therapists with higher levels of interpersonal skills (Anderson et al. 2016). A final study concluded that the therapist's facilitative interpersonal skills, measured at the start of psychotherapy training, were able to predict the outcomes of the patients seen in the second, third and fourth years of these therapists' training (Anderson et al. 2016). The authors conclude that although interpersonal skills bring about better therapeutic outcomes, these are the result of an intricate interdependence between relational factors, patient factors and factors connected to specific interventions. This point is in agreement with studies that have shown that greater technical flexibility on the part of therapists, adapting themselves to patients' needs, produced better therapeutic outcomes (Owen and Hilsenroth 2014). Several studies have shown that the personal characteristics of therapists, such as being distant, disconnected or more indifferent, had a negative effect on outcomes (Hersoug et al. 2009). Research into dynamic psychotherapists with patients who failed to improve concluded that the therapeutic relationship was felt to be distant and artificial. Therapists were perceived by patients as being passive, bored, non-committal and reticent, and there was no change in these characteristics over the course of the psychotherapy (Werbart et al. 2015). Personal characteristics are directly related to levels of distress, felt by the therapists. Those who described themselves as submissive, standoffish and vindictive experienced higher levels of stressful involvement in the psychotherapy. These therapists may be less able to engage and maintain a positive therapeutic alliance, and may unconsciously provoke problematic reactions in their relationship with patients (Zeeck et al. 2012). These findings also point us to a factor regarded as crucial: the therapist's ability to be responsive (Stiles 2013). The therapist's ability to tailor the intervention to the patient, supplanting a reductive vision of the diagnosis, has been identified as one of the most important attributes for therapeutic interventions (Stiles 2013; Norcross and Wampold 2011; Stiles 2009). In the last instance, therapists are guided by a paradigmatic question in the literature: "*What* intervention, carried out by *whom*, is most effective for *this* individual with *this* specific problem, and in *what* set of circumstances?" (Paul 1967). Studies have shown that the characteristics of therapists, both interpersonal factors and intervention strategies that promote patient empowerment, are those which most directly influenced the engagement of patients (Holdsworth et al. 2014). Stress is laid on the interdependence between different aspects: the patient is an active subject in the therapeutic process; there is a mutual influence between patient and therapist factors, and also between relational and technical factors; the therapist's ability to be responsive is crucial to promoting the therapeutic process and the patient's idiosyncratic capacities (Norcross and Wampold 2011; Bohart and Tallman 2010; Stiles 2009).

A survey has been conducted of personal attributes and of techniques associated with good therapeutic alliances and successful therapeutic outcomes, irrespective of the theoretical models (Ackerman and Hilsenroth 2003). Personal attributes: being   flexible,   experienced,   honest, respectable, trustworthy, confiding, interested, attentive, friendly, welcoming and open. Techniques: exploration; depth; reflection; support; pointing out past therapeutic gains; accurate interpretations; facilitating expressions of affection; being pro-active; being affirmative; understanding; considering the patient's experience (Ackerman and Hilsenroth 2003, p. 28). Techniques and personal skills that had a negative influence on alliances and outcomes were also identified (Ackerman and Hilsenroth 2001). Personal attributes: rigidity; uncertainty; exploration; being critical; being distant; being tense; being distracted; being rash. Technique: over-structured therapeutic process; badly structured therapeutic process; inappropriate self-revelation; inadequate management of the therapeutic process; over-interpretation of transfer; inappropriate use of silence; disdain; superficial interventions (Ackerman and Hilsenroth 2001, p. 182). Although not yet properly recognized in mainstream research, qualitative studies have come a long way and offer a vast body of accumulated knowledge (Levitt 2015). The dimensions attributed above to therapists, regarded as the most important, have been borne out by qualitative meta-analyses, from the patient's perspective (Levitt et al. 2016; Ekroll and Rønnestad 2016). Patients felt that the therapists as being careful, empathic, caring, supportive, active, stimulating curiosity, engaging deeply, establishing human relations which offer security, not criticizing, even implicitly, highly understanding and listening attentively, and validating their patients' experiences (Levitt et al. 2016). In addition to being flexible and adapting to their patients' aims and expectations, therapists are perceived by patients as being competent and credible. Consequently, they are able to promote relational quality, accepting all the affects that arise, which in turn lead to changes in the patients' way of living and thinking, creating greater autonomy, a greater sense of self and self-awareness (Ekroll and Rønnestad 2016).

Recent data has confirmed the interdependence between the personal and professional factors of therapists. As already stated (in the section on the therapeutic alliance), the quality of the therapists' personal life has an impact on how the therapeutic alliance is rated by patients (Nissen-Lie et al. 2013a). A group of researchers assessed personal and professional characteristics in short and long therapies and concluded that therapists who are more active, more committed, more at ease in the interpersonal field and more extrovert, better able to engage patients in the process, had better outcomes in short therapies and achieved a faster reduction in symptoms (Heinonen et al. 2012). Less intrusive and more cautious therapists were more effective for patients who underwent longer therapies. Professional characteristics, in particular a lack of confidence in their abilities and in their satisfaction with their work as therapists, made for better therapeutic outcomes in longer interventions. The authors suggest that, in shorter interventions, it is necessary to introduce, earlier and appropriately, a therapeutic stance which transmits confidence, hope and interest, encouraging the patient to engage actively in resolving his issues (Heinonen et al. 2012). Good therapeutic outcomes were always influenced by an intense personal attitude, with an open style and an engaged and affirmative professional stance, stressing the interdependence between professional and personal dimensions (Heinonen et al. 2012). A similar study focused on the influence of therapist's professional and personal characteristics and the level of the therapeutic alliance, concluding that therapists with interpersonal skills enabling them to empathize with others, engage with human dimensions, who are open, able to communicate in a genuine way, concerned for their patients and optimistic, were rated better for the therapeutic alliance, in both short and long therapies (Heinonen et al. 2014). However, in long therapies, constructive techniques for dealing with deterioration in the alliance were more beneficial than interpersonal skills. Research findings show that "professional self-criticism" by the therapist had a positive correlation with interpersonal changes in patients and how they rated the alliance at the start of therapy. On the other hand, a "negative personal reaction" by therapists was associated with a negative impact on the therapeutic alliance and on higher levels of distress in patients (Nissen-Lie et al. 2010, 2013a). A healthy self-critical attitude on the part of therapists, combined with a sensitive and caring stance, being responsive and taking responsibility for cracks in the alliance with the patient, have positive impacts (Nissen-Lie et al. 2010, 2013a). These findings were confirmed by subsequent studies. The *interaction* between "professional self-criticism" and "self-affiliation" (how each sees himself as a person) was a predictor of more interpersonal changes in patients (Nissen-Lie et al. 2015a). The findings showed that these two dimensions had no impact when present unilaterally, but only when combined. On the other hand, active use by therapists of coping strategies, to deal with difficulties encountered in clinical practice, has been found to have positive impacts on the therapeutic process (Nissen-Lie et al. 2015a). These findings are corroborated by various researchers into "master therapists" who point to other dimensions which may be associated with an adequate level of self-criticism, in particular: humility, high ethical standards and a healthy sense of doubt as to their own abilities (Hook et al. 2013; Jennings et al. 2005, 2008). In general, research has revealed some highly important aspects. The person of the therapist and personal characteristics affect psychotherapy. The effectiveness of the therapist involves the interaction between professional factors and personal attributes (Heinonen et al. 2014; Nissen-Lie et al. 2013a; Nissen-Lie et al. 2010; Hersoug et al. 2009). What is more, the data suggest that a positive perception by therapists of their emotions has an effect on their reading of the alliance but has no effective impact on the patient, as he does not perceive them in the same way. However, negative reactions by therapists have an effective and negative effect on patients' perception of the therapeutic alliance. Similarly, feelings of distress, grief and pressure on the part of therapists have been seen to have an unfavorable effect on the alliance from the patient's perspective, although it had no effect on the therapist's perception (Nissen-Lie et al. 2015b). The findings have borne out the literature: the therapists' vision does not coincide with that of the patients, also creating a greater need for self-monitoring by therapists (Zuroff et al. 2016). In addition to the practical repercussions of these data, it is no less important to consider also the relevance they may have for the training of psychotherapists (Hersoug et al. 2009; Castonguay et al. 2010). The title of one of the articles says it all: "Love yourself as person, doubt yourself as therapist" (Nissen-Lie et al. 2015a).

Wampold (2011) has defined 14 qualities and actions of efficacious therapists:

(1) "good interpersonal skills (including empathy, verbal fluency, emotional modulation, acceptance and warmth, interpersonal perception and focus on the other);

(2) the patients of the most efficacious therapists feel that their therapists are trustworthy, understand them and believe that the therapists can help them. These factors of acceptance, understanding and expertise are critical at the early stages of the process;

(3) the therapists are able to establish good therapeutic alliances with very different patients. In addition to relational ties, it is important that therapists should be very clear about aims and therapeutic tasks;

(4) therapists held to create an acceptable and adaptive explanation for the patient's problems. The explanation should be consistent with the therapeutic practice, in this case, psychological; the explanation

should be acceptable to the patient and fit in with his worldview, values and culture, meaning that the intervention is adapted to the patient;

(5) the effective therapist develops an intervention plan consistent with the explanation provided and is adaptive insofar as the intervention will help the patient to overcome his obstacles;

(6) the therapist manages to be influential, persuasive and convincing, leading the patient to raise his hopes and expectations and so to engage with the therapeutic actions;

(7) conducts genuine and ongoing monitoring of the therapeutic process, either formally using instruments, or else informally and directly with the patient. The therapist is particularly sensitive if the patients are deteriorating;

(8) the efficacious therapist is flexible and will adapt the intervention if the patients is not experiencing positive progress;

(9) does not avoid difficult material and uses it therapeutically;

(10) communicate hope and optimism in a consistent, secure and realistic way;

(11) is aware of the patient's characteristics and his social and cultural context;

(12) is aware of his own psychological processes and how they can influence the therapeutic processes;

(13) is *au fait* with scientific research on the patient's issues;

(14) seeks to develop his therapeutic skills on an ongoing basis".

Clinical Expertise and Deliberate Practice

The fact that research has identified therapists who have better outcomes than others raises questions on clinical expertise. How can we define expertise in psychotherapy? What makes psychotherapists develop greater expertise? What therapist characteristics cause their patients to have 50% more improvement than those seen by other therapists? (Tracey et al. 2014; Miller et al. 2008). The debate is contentious. The first thorny issue is defining the concept. A distinction has been drawn between expertise and competence (Sperry and Carlson 2014). Expertise is regarded as a high level of proficiency, a superior level of performance, in knowledge, skills, ability to make professional judgments about situations, and in personal and technical qualities. Competence presupposes merely adequate performance in this areas and domains (Sperry and Carlson 2014). The definition of expertise implies three assumptions:

(1) it is specific to a given domain or profession; (2) it is perfected over time; (3) it is a designation attributed to an individual, rather than a particular grade or level of performance (Wampold et al., in press). The expertise of psychotherapists has been defined by reputation, by performance or by patient outcomes (Rønnestad 2016; Tracey et al. 2014). Although all have their limitations, it has been suggested that the best criterion is patient outcomes (Wampold et al., in press; Tracey et al. 2014). However, this criterion should be filled out by what therapists do (performance) in order to compile clear indications on the substance of their superior performance (Rønnestad 2016). But there is one point on which the authors appear to agree: experience is not synonymous with expertise (Wampold et al. in press; Miller et al. 2015; Tracey et al. 2014). Years of experience do not necessarily translate into increased clinical expertise (Goldberg et al. 2016b). Studies have also shown that trainees in psychotherapy courses achieve outcomes identical to experienced psychotherapists (Owen et al. 2016). Even so, clinical experience may play an important role and some studies have stressed that more experienced therapists tend to be more flexible, deal better with more complex situations and more severe problems, and produce case conceptualizations which are more succinct and more complex (Tschuschke et al. 2015; Oddli et al. 2014a). More experienced therapists tend to organize information systematically in a way that reflects deeper knowledge, focus on what is more relevant, have a more incisive and less descriptive intervention and are better able to adjust to new situations (Oddli et al. 2014a). But several studies have in fact concluded that the fact that a psychotherapist has worked for longer, or seen more patients, is no guarantee of increased clinical expertise or better outcomes (Goldberg et al. 2016b; Miller et al. 2008, 2015). Most psychotherapists do not improve over time, therapists progress over their training but the improvements are not statistically significant, and inexperienced therapists are in many circumstances just as efficacious as their more experienced colleagues (Wampold et al., in press). Questions relating to the lack of adequate and concrete feedback on therapists' performance, the absence of participation in deliberate practice, involving specific procedures, as well as the failure to assess outcomes using objective methods, and the inadequacy of therapist self-assessment are all factors identified as standing in the way of improving clinical expertise (Tracey et al. 2014). The literature has dubbed as "master therapists" those who achieve outcomes substantially superior to their peers (Rønnestad and Skovholt 2013; Jennings

and Skovholt 1999). Research has pointed to some of their characteristics: (a) they have charisma and are skilled in immediately establishing a strong connection with the patient, and they manage to be persuasive, implicitly or explicitly, in promoting trust and expectations of change; (b) personal style and skills that allow them to engage in a collaborative relationship, in which the patient quickly feels validated and accepted as a person; (c) they are extremely variable and flexible in strategies, and are actively engaged so as to address the patient's issues creatively but securely; (d) flexibility, considering a nonlinear logic, is maintained over the course of psychotherapy, the therapists follow implicit and intuitive processes, helping to steer patients, although taking decisions which are sensitive to the context and the moment; (e) ability to focus the patient on his capabilities and inner resources; (f) ability to deal with a huge variety of patients, even those who present severer issues and distress; (g) are able not to get involved in dysfunctional processes and promote optimism, focus on the patients' resources, fostering in them a deep feeling of meaning and the ability to understand themselves and the world (Ekroll and Rønnestad 2016; Rønnestad 2016; Hansen et al. 2015; Oddli et al. 2014a, b). Clinical expertise can be divided into three domains: cognitive, emotional and relational (Rønnestad and Skovholt 2013; Jennings and Skovholt 1999). In the cognitive domain, therapists value ambiguity and complexity; they draw on a store of wisdom; they are ceaselessly curious and voracious learners; they have a deep understanding of the human condition; they have cultural knowledge and competence. In the emotional domain they have maturity and a healthy awareness of their emotional well-being; they are genuinely humble and emotionally receptive; they have great self-awareness and an enormous willingness to grow, and they are passionately involved with their life; they are aware of the emotional impacts on their work. In relational terms, they have excellent interpersonal skills, they believe in the therapeutic alliance and trust in their patients' resources, they genuinely accept feedback from others, they are ethically discriminating and have great relational insight and are generously accepting (Rønnestad and Skovholt 2013; Jennings and Skovholt 1999).

Although there are descriptions of the personal and professional characteristics of therapists, which are believed to have direct impacts on outcomes, there is still a shortage of empirical studies which undertake an objective assessment of these dimensions (Chow et al. 2015). On the other hand, there is promising evidence that outcome monitoring routines and feedback systems improve therapeutic outcomes and reduce dropout rates, above all for clinical cases at risk of deterioration (Lambert 2015). However, neither is it clear, nor has it been confirmed that these systems result in an improvement in therapists' skills (Goldberg et al. 2016c). Deliberate practice has been suggested as a way of improving therapists' skills (Miller et al. 2015; Chow et al. 2015). Miller et al. have conducted research into deliberate practice in psychotherapy (Miller et al. 2015, 2008), based on the work of the psychologist K. Anders Ericsson, on the performance of experts in various fields and professions (Ericsson 2009; Ericsson et al. 1993). Deliberate practice is a training activity structured around specific tasks, that performs a fundamental role in the understanding of skills acquisition and explaining individual differences, in the performance of specialists in different professional areas (Platz et al. 2014). Meta-analyses and studies of deliberate practice in the most varied professions—musicians, sportsmen, doctors, air traffic controllers, etc.—have shown that the best practice more, acquire deeper knowledge of their area, systematically gather feedback on their performance, invest double the time in training and study activities and, above all, go about learning in a structured way, to surpass their habitual results and performance (Platz et al. 2014; Coughlan et al. 2014; Miller et al. 2008; Ericsson 2009; Lehmann and Ericsson 1997; Ericsson et al. 1993). Experts work harder (Miller et al. 2008). But it's not enough just to do more. It is necessary to do it in a structured way, that allows the individual exceed his own skills (Ericsson et al. 1993). Data gathered on deliberate practice in various fields bears out studies which show that more hours of psychotherapy or years of experience are not necessarily synonymous with better results (Goldberg et al. 2016a). Experience is not enough: "To be efficacious, deliberate practice must be focused on achieving specific aims, beyond the habitual skill level of the person achieving the performance, guided by conscious monitoring of results, and carried out over long periods of time" (Chow et al. 2015). What is the starting point for deliberate practice? Awareness of the individual's present level of performance (Ericsson 2009; Miller et al. 2008). Major barriers in the field of psychotherapy to starting deliberate practice have to do with: the difficulties that therapists have in recognizing deterioration in their patients; therapists overestimate their own skills; and make erroneous estimates of their patients' outcomes (Bowell et al. 2015; Walfish et al. 2012; Hatfield et al. 2010). In short, they lack a realistic awareness of their own skills (Kruger and Dunning 1999). In contrast, therapists regarded as experts have a "situational awareness" that allows them to be good observers, both realistic and attentive, and to assess and compare their performance critically with their peers (Ericsson 2009; Miller et al. 2008). Studies show that therapists reputed to be experts are open in a way that makes them more receptive to patients and available to receive their negative feedback. It is not uncommon for these therapists to have lower scores for the therapeutic at the start of therapy, which allows them to address problems in the relationship with the patient in a genuine way. In contrast, therapists regarded as average sometimes receive negative feedback at an advanced stage in the therapy, when the patients already feel disconnected from the therapy and the relationship (Miller et al. 2008). In short, three components are regarded as crucial for superior performance and to enhance therapists' skills: (a) setting a basic level of efficacy; (b) obtaining, systematic, continuous and formal feedback; (c) deliberate practice (Miller et al. 2013). Introducing objective measures which complement the clinical evaluation of therapists makes it possible to establish the level of effectiveness, and a starting point for real awareness of the outcomes of interventions. The advantages of feedback systems are many and have already been described. But the use of feedback depends on the therapists who, in many circumstances end up not taking advantage of patient feedback, and/or not actively engaging in the use of feedback measures (De Jong and De Goede 2015; Lutz et al. 2015). So it is particularly important for the therapist to be motivated and to acknowledge the advantages of feedback. The metaphor used concerning feedback systems is that of satnav. Feedback functions like a satnav device that provides information on the terrain and on routes and warns us to avoid a given route, but without teaching us to improve our driving skills (Miller et al. 2013). Deliberate practice is viewed as the third critical factors for improving therapists' skills (Miller et al. 2015). With deliberate practice, psychotherapists devote time exclusively to reflecting on their performance, carry out tasks, analyze feedback sources, pinpoint errors, seek to improve specific aspects of their therapeutic practices, try out, rehearse and follow plans with tasks to achieve improvements (Miller et al. 2015; Ericsson 2009). Deliberate practice involves setting challenges at above the current level of attainment, which should be done within a learning space felt to be safe and secure, where feedback on the intervention is provided immediately, allowing the therapist to gradually hone his skills (Chow et al. 2015; Ericsson 2009). In a study carried out with 69 therapists who saw 4,580 patients, the therapist effects accounted for around 5.1% of the variance attributed to the therapeutic change (Chow et al. 2015). This finding is consistent with others in the literature (Baldwin and Imel 2013). In a sub-sample of this universe, of 17 therapists who followed 1,632 patients, therapist characteristics (age, gender, years of clinical experience, academic qualification, degree of theoretical integration) were poor predictors of outcomes (Chow et al. 2015). However, the time that therapists spent with the specific aim of improving their skills was a significant predictor of patient outcomes. The group of therapists with the best outcomes invested on average 2.81 times more time in deliberate practice in a typical working week (Chow et al. 2015). A research project designed to assess the efficacy of psychotherapists over 7 years, considering 153 psychotherapists and 5,128 patients, concluded that the intentional use of outcome monitoring routines, planning and use of feedback systems, combined with deliberate practice, resulted in a gradual improvement in the skills of psychotherapists (Goldberg et al. 2016c). The findings indicate a small but significant statistical increase in the effectiveness of psychotherapy over time. Although the effect is small, it is important to remember that small effects are magnified when considered on a large scale (Imel et al. 2015). It was also found that therapists were able to improve their performance and outcomes, year after years, whenever they combined monitoring, feedback and deliberate practice (Goldberg et al. 2016c). Even so, the authors suggest that care has to be taken in interpreting the findings, pointing to the need to replicate them in future studies. It is important to recall that a large part of the variability of outcomes is due to the patient (Baldwin and Imel 2013; Bohart and Wade 2013). Indeed, some patients will have good outcomes irrespective of their therapist, because they are motivated, have a lower comorbidity index, enjoy greater social and family support, are willing to change and have sufficient financial resources to cover ongoing care (Wampold et al., in press). Care is required not to put too much pressure on psychotherapists for them to demonstrate their efficacy. Monitoring, feedback and deliberate practice should be understood as aids for improving the skills of psychotherapists, and not merely as instruments for evaluating outcomes. Lastly, caution is suggested in interpreting these outcomes, for the purposes of organizational decision-making. The data should be used for constructive procedures that contribute to ongoing improvements in the professional development of psychotherapists, and not for appraisals used to penalize under-performers (Goldberg et al. 2016c). In short, the empirical evidence, as it exists today, suggests that the most efficacious therapists combine the following characteristics: they form good therapeutic alliances with different types of patient; they have excellent interpersonal skills which prove particularly useful in more challenging situations; they are professionally self-critical; they engage in deliberate practice and training over the course of their professional development (Wampold et al., in press).

REFERENCES

Ackerman, S. J., & Hilsenroth, M. J. (2001). A review of therapist characteristics and techniques negatively impacting the therapeutic alliance. *Psychotherapy, 38,* 2.

Ackerman, S. J., & Hilsenroth, M. J. (2003). A review of therapist characteristics and techniques positively impacting the therapeutic alliance. *Clinical Psychology Review, 23,* 1–33.

Ahmed, M., & Westra, H. A. (2009). Impact of a treatment rationale on expectancy and engagement in cognitive behavioral therapy for social anxiety. *Cognitive Therapy and Research, 33,* 314–322.

Ahn, H., & Wampold, B. E. (2001). Where oh where are the specific ingredients? A meta-analysis of component studies in counseling and psychotherapy. *Journal of Counseling Psychology, 48*(3), 251–257.

Amble, I., Gude, T., Stubdal, S., Andersen, B. J., & Wampold, B. E. (2015). The effect of implementing the Outcome Questionnaire-45.2 feedback system in Norway: A multisite randomized clinical trial in a naturalistic setting. *Psychotherapy Research, 25*(6), 669–677.

Anderson, T., Olges, B. M., Patterson, C. L., Lambert, M. J., & Vermeersch, D. A. (2009). Therapist effects: Facilitative interpersonal skills as a predictor of therapist success. *Journal of Clinical Psychology, 65*(7), 755–768.

Anderson, T., Lunnen, K. M., & Ogles, B. M. (2010). Putting models and techniques in context. In S. D. Miller, B. L. Duncan, M. A. Hubble, & B. E. Wampold (Eds.), *The heart and soul of change* (2nd ed., pp. 143–166). Washington, DC: American Psychological Association.

Anderson, T., Crowley, M. E. J., Himawan, L., Holmberg, J. K., & Uhlin, B. D. (2016). Therapist facilitative interpersonal skills and training status: A randomized clinical trial on alliance and outcome. *Psychotherapy Research, 26*(5), 511–529.

APA Presidential Task Force on Evidence-Based Practice. (2006). Evidence-based practice in psychology. *American Psychologist, 61,* 271–285.

Asay, T. P., & Lambert, M. J. (1999). The empirical case for the common factors in therapy: Quantitative findings. In M. A. Hubble, B. L. Duncan, &

S. D. Miller (Eds.), *The heart and soul of change—what works in therapy* (pp. 33–55). Washington, DC: American Psychological Association.

Asnaani, A., & Foa, E. B. (2014). Expanding the lens of evidence-based practice in psychotherapy to include a common factors perspective: Comment on Laska, Gurman, and Wampold. *Psychotherapy, 51*(4), 487–490.

Baardseth, T. P., Goldberg, S. B., Pace, B. T. Wislocki, A. P., Frost, N.D., Siddiqui, J.R., ... Wampold, B. E. (2013). Cognitive-behavioral therapy versus other therapies: Redux. *Clinical Psychology Review, 33*, 395–405.

Baker, T. B., & McFall, R. (2014). The promise of science-based training and application in psychological clinical science. *Psychotherapy, 51*(4), 482–486.

Baldwin, S. A., & Imel, Z. E. (2013). Therapists effects. Findings and methods. In M. Lambert (Ed.), *Bergin and Garfield's handbook of psychotherapy and behavior change* (pp. 258–297). New Jersey: Wiley.

Baldwin, S. A., Wampold, B. E., & Imel, Z. E. (2007). Untangling the alliance–outcome correlation: Exploring the relative importance of therapist and patient variability in the alliance. *Journal of Consulting and Clinical Psychology, 75*(6), 842–852.

Barlow, D. H. (2004). Psychological treatments. *American Psychologist, 59*(9), 869–878.

Barlow, D. H. (2010). The Dodo Bird-again-and again. *The Behavior Therapist, 33*(1), 15–16.

Bell, E. C., Marcus, D. K., & Godlad, J. K. (2013). Are the parts as good as the whole? A meta-analysis of component treatment studies. *Journal of Consulting and Clinical Psychology, 81*(4), 722–736.

Benish, S. G., Imel, Z. E., & Wampold, B. E. (2008). The relative efficacy of bona fide psychotherapies for treating post-traumatic stress disorder: A meta-analysis of direct comparisons. *Clinical Psychology Review, 28*, 746–758.

Bergin, A. E. (1963). The effects of psychotherapy: Negative results revisited. *Journal of Counseling Psychology, 10*, 244–250.

Beutler, L. E. (2014). Welcome to the party but.... *Psychotherapy, 51*(4), 496–499.

Beutler, L. E., Someah, K., Kimpara, S., & Miller, K. (2016). Selecting the most appropriate treatment for each patient. *International Journal of Clinical and Health Psychology, 16*, 99–108.

Bickman, L., Kelley, S. D., Breda, C., Andrade, A. R., & Riemer, M. (2011). Effects of routine feedback to clinicians on mental health outcomes of youths: Results of a randomized trial. *Psychiatric Services, 62*(12), 1423–1429.

Bohart, A. C., & Tallman, K. (2010). Clients: The neglected common factor in psychotherapy. In B. L. Duncan, S. D. Miller, B. E. Wampold, & M. A. Hubble (Eds.), *The heart and soul of change: Delivering what works in therapy* (2nd ed., pp. 83–111). Washington, DC: American Psychological Association.

Bohart, A. C., & Wade, A. G. (2013). The client in psychotherapy. In M. J. Lambert (Ed.), *Bergin and Garfield's handbook of psychotherapy and behavior change* (6th ed., pp. 219–257). Hoboken, NJ: Wiley.

Bordin, E. S. (1979). The generalizability of the psychoanalytic concept of the working alliance. *Psychotherapy: Theory, Research & Practice, 16*(3), 252–260.

Boswell, J. F., Kraus, D. R., Castonguay, L. G., & Youn, S. J. (2015). Treatment outcome package: Measuring and facilitating multidimensional change. *Psychotherapy, 52*(4), 422–431.

Brosan, L., Reynolds, S., & Moore, R. G. (2008). Self-evaluation of cognitive therapy performance: Do therapists know how competent they are? *Behavioural and Cognitive Psychotherapy, 36*(5), 581–587.

Brown, G. S., Lambert, M., Jones, E. R., & Minami, T. (2005). Identifying highly effective psychotherapists in a managed care environment. *The American Journal of Managed Care, 11*(8), 513–520.

Budge, S. L., Owen, J. J., Kopta, S. M., Minami, T., Hanson, M. R., & Hirsch, G. (2013). Differences among trainees in client outcomes associated with the phase model of change. *Psychotherapy, 50*(2), 150–157.

Castonguay, L. G. (2013). Psychotherapy outcome: A problem worth re-revisiting 50 years later. *Psychotherapy, 50,* 52–67.

Castonguay, L. G., & Beutler, L. E. (2006). *Principles of therapeutic change that work.* New York: Oxford University Press.

Castonguay, L. G., Boswell, J. F., Zack, S. E., Baker, A., Boutselis, M. A., Chiswick, N. R., ... Holtforth, M.G. (2010). Helpful and hindering events in psychotherapy: A practice research network study. *Psychotherapy Theory, Research, Practice, 47*(3), 327–344.

Castonguay, L. G., Barkham, M., Lutz, W., & McAleavey, A. (2013). Practice-oriented research. Approaches and applications. In M. Lambert (Ed.), Bergin and Garfield's handbook of psychotherapy and Behavior Change, 85–133. New Jersey: Wiley.

Chambless, D. L., & Hollon, S. D. (1998). Defining empirically supported therapies. *Journal of Consulting and Clinical Psychology, 66,* 7–18.

Chambless, D. L., Baker, M. J. Baucom, D. H., Beutler, L. E., Calhoun, K. S., Crits-Christoph, P., ... Woody, S. R. (1998). Update on empirically validated therapies, II. *The Clinical Psychologist, 51*(1), 3–16.

Chapman, C., Burlingame, G. M., Gleave, R., Rees, F., Beecher, M., & Porter, G. S. (2012). Clinical prediction in group psychotherapy. *Psychotherapy Research, 22*(6), 673–681.

Chow, D., Miller, S. D., Seidel, J. A., Kane, R. T., Thornton, J. A., & Andrews, W. (2015). The role of deliberate practice in the development of highly effective psychotherapists. *Psychotherapy, 52*(3), 337–345.

Constantino, M. J., Arnkoff, D. B., Glass, C. R., Ametrano, R. M., & Smith, J. Z. (2011). Expectations. *Journal of Clinical Psychology: In session, 67*(2), 184–192.

Constantino, M. J., Ametrano, R. M., & Greenberg, R. P. (2012). Clinician interventions and participant characteristics that foster adaptive patient expectations for psychotherapy and psychotherapeutic Change. *Psychotherapy, 49*(4), 557–569.

Cook, J. M., Elhai, J., Biyanova, T., & Schnurr, P. (2010). What do psychotherapists really do in practice? An internet study of over 2,000 practitioners. *Psychotherapy Theory, Research, Practice, Training, 47*(2), 260–267.

Cooper, M. (2008). *Essential research findings in counselling and psychotherapy. The facts are friendly.* London: Sage.

Coughlan, E. K., Williams, A. M., McRobert, A. P., & Ford, P. R. (2014). How experts practice: A novel test of deliberate practice theory. *Journal of Experimental Psychology. Learning, Memory, and Cognition, 40*(2), 449–458.

Crits-Christoph, P. (1997). Limitations of the Dodo Bird verdict and the role of clinical trials in psychotherapy research: Comment on Wampold et al. *Psychological Bulletin, 122*(3), 216–220.

Crits-Christoph, P., Baranackie, K., Kurcias, J. S., Beck, A. T., Carrol, K., Perry, K., … Zitrin, C. (1991). Meta-analysis of therapist effects in psychotherapy outcome studies. *Psychotherapy Research, 1*(2), 81–91.

Crits-Christoph, P., Connolly Gibbons, M. B., Crits-Christoph, K., Narducci, J., Schamberger, M., & Gallop, R.(2006). Can therapists be trained to improve their alliances? A preliminary study of alliance-fosteringpsychotherapy. *Psychotherapy Research, 16*(3), 268–281.

Crits-Christoph, P., Connolly Gibbons, M. B., Hamilton, J., Ring-Kurtz, S., & Gallop, R. (2011). The dependability of alliance assessments: The alliance–outcome correlation is larger than you might think. *Journal of Consulting and Clinical Psychology, 79*, 267–278.

Crits-Christoph, P., Chambless, D. L., & Markell, H. M. (2014). Moving evidence-based practice forward successfully: Commentary on Laska, Gurman, and Wampold. *Psychotherapy, 51*(4), 491–495.

Cuijeprs, P., Driessen, E., Hollon, S. D., Van Oppen, P., Barth, J., & Andresson, G. (2012). The efficacy of non-directive supportive therapy for adult depression: A meta-analysis. *Clinical Psychology Review, 32*, 280–291.

De Jong, K., & De Goede, M. (2015). Why do some therapists not deal with outcome monitoring feedback? A feasibility study on the effect of regulatory focus and person—organization fit on attitude and outcome. *Psychotherapy Research, 25*(6), 661–668.

De Jong, K., Van Sluis, P., Nugter, M. A., Heiseder, W. J., & Spinhoven, P. (2012). Understanding the differential impact of outcome monitoring:

Therapist variables that moderate feedback effects in a randomized clinical trial. *Psychotherapy Research, 22*(4), 464–474.

De Jong, K., Timman, R., Hakkaart-Van Roijen, L., Vermeulen, P., Kooiman, K., Passchier, J., et al. (2014). The effect of outcome monitoring feedback to clinicians and patients in short and long-term psychotherapy: A randomized controlled trial. *Psychotherapy Research, 24*(6), 629–639.

Del Re, A. C., Flückiger, C., Horvath, A. O., Symonds, D., & Wampold, B. E. (2012). Therapist effects in the therapeutic alliance–outcome relationship: A restricted-maximum likelihood meta-analysis. *Clinical Psychology Review, 32*(7), 642–649.

Delsignore, A., & Schnyder, U. (2007). Control expectancies as predictors of psychotherapy outcome: A systematic review. *British Journal of Clinical Psychology, 46*, 467–483.

Dinger, U., Strack, M., Leichsenring, F., Wilmers, F., & Schauenburg, H. (2008). Therapist effects on outcome and alliance in inpatient psychotherapy. *Journal of Clinical Psychology, 64*, 344–354.

Douglas, S. R., Jonghyuk, B., Andrade, A. R. V., Tomlinson, M. M., Hargraves, R. P., & Bickman, L. (2015). Feedback mechanisms of change: How problem alerts reported by youth clients and their caregivers impact clinician-reported session content. *Psychotherapy Research, 25*(6), 678–693.

Duncan, B. L., & Reese, R. J. (2015). The Partners for Change Outcome Management System (PCOMS). Revisiting the client's frame of reference. *Psychotherapy, 52*(4), 391–401.

Duncan, B. L., Miller, S. D., Wampold, B. E., & Hubble, M. A. (2010). *The heart and soul of change: Delivering what works in therapy* (2nd ed.). Washington, DC: American Psychological Association.

Ekroll, V. B. S., & Rønnestad, M. H. (2016). Processes and changes experienced by clients during and after naturalistic good-outcome therapies conducted by experienced psychotherapists. *Psychotherapy Research*, 1–19.

Elliott, R., Bohart, A. C., Watson, J. C., & Greenberg, L. S. (2011). Empathy. *Psychotherapy, 48*, 43–49.

Ellsworth, J. R., Lambert, M. J., & Johnson, J. (2006). A comparison of the Outcome Questionnaire-45 and Outcome Questionnaire-30 in classification and prediction of treatment outcome. *Clinical Psychology and Psychotherapy, 13*, 380–391.

Emmelkamp, P. M. G., David, D., Beckers, T., Muris, P., Cuijpers, P., Lutz, W., … Vervliet, B. (2014). Advancing psychotherapy and evidence-based psychological interventions. *International Journal of Methods in Psychiatric Research, 23*(S1), 58–91.

Ericsson, K. A. (Ed.). (2009). *Development of professional expertise: Toward measurement of expert performance and design of optimal learning environments.* New York: Cambridge University Press.

Ericsson, K. A., Krampe, R. T., & Tesch-Romer, C. (1993). The role of deliberate practice in the acquisition of expert performance. *Psychological Review, 100*(3), 363–406.

Eysenck, H. J. (1952). The effects of psychotherapy: An evaluation. *Journal of Consulting Psychology, 16,* 319–324.

Falkenström, F., Granström, F., & Holmqvist, R. (2013). Therapeutic alliance predicts symptomatic improvement session by session. *Journal of Counseling Psychology, 60*(3), 317–328.

Flückiger, C., Del Re, A. C., Wampold, B. E., Symonds, D., & Horvath, A. O. (2012). How central is the alliance in psychotherapy? A multilevel longitudinal meta-analysis. *Journal of Counseling Psychology, 59*(1), 10–17.

Frank, J. D., & Frank, J. B. (1991). *Persuasion and healing. A comparative study of psychotherapy* (3rd ed.). Baltimore: John Hopkins University Press.

Garfield, S. (1997). The therapist as a neglected variable in psychotherapy research. *Clinical Psychology: Science and Practice, 4*(1), 40–43.

Geller, J. D. (2005). Style and its contribution to a patient-specific model of therapeutic technique. *Psychotherapy: Theory, Research, Practice. Training, 42,* 469–482.

Gelso, C. J. (2009). The real relationship in a postmodern world: Theoretical and empirical explorations. *Psychotherapy Research, 19*(3), 253–264.

Gelso, C. J. (2014). A tripartite model of the therapeutic relationship: Theory, research, and practice. *Psychotherapy Research, 24*(2), 117–131.

Gelso, C. J., Kivlighan, D. M., Busa-Knepp, J., Spiegel, E. B., Ain, S., Hummel, A. M., ... Markin, R. D. (2012). The unfolding of the real relationship and the outcome of brief psychotherapy. *Journal of Counseling Psychology, 59*(4), 495–506.

Gibbons, M. B. C., Thompson, D. L., Eisen, S. V., Kurtz, J. E., Mack, R. A., Lee, J. K., ... Crits-Christoph, P. (2015). The effectiveness of clinician feedback in the treatment of depression in the community mental health system. *Journal of Consulting and Clinical Psychology, 83*(4), 748–759.

Goldberg, S. B., Hoyt, W. T., Nissen-lie, H. A., Nielsen, S. L., & Wampold, B. E. (2016a). Unpacking the therapist effect: Impact of treatment length differs for high- and low-performing therapists. *Psychotherapy Research.*

Goldberg, S. B., Miller, S. D., Nielsen, S. L., Rousmaniere, T., Whipple, J., Hoyt, W. T., & Wampold, B. E. (2016b). Do psychotherapists improve with time and experience? A longitudinal analysis of outcomes in a clinical setting. *Journal of Counseling Psychology, 63*(1), 1–11.

Goldberg, S. B., Babins-Wagner, R., Rousmaniere, T., Berzins, S., Hoyt, W. T., Whipple, J., ... Wampold, B. E. (2016c). Creating a climate for therapist improvement: A case study of an agency focused on outcome and deliberate practice. *Psychotherapy, 53*(3), 367–375.

Goldfried, M. (1980). Toward the delineation of therapeutic change principles. *American Psychologist, 35*(11), 991–999.

Goldfried, M. R., & Davila, J. (2005). The role of the relationship and technique in therapeutic change. *Psychotherapy: Theory, Research, Practice, Training, 42,* 421–430.

Goldfried, M. R., Patrick, J., Raue, P. J., & Castonguay, L. G. (1998). The therapeutic focus in significant sessions of master therapists: A comparison of cognitive-behavioral and psychodynamic-interpersonal interventions. *Journal of Consulting and Clinical Psychology, 66*(5), 803–810.

Goodman, J. D., McKay, J. R., & DePhilippis, D. (2013). Progress monitoring in mental health and addiction treatment: A means of improving care. *Professional Psychology: Research and Practice, 44*(4), 231–246.

Hannan, C., Lambert, M. J., Harmon, C., Nielsen, S. L., Smart, D. W., Shimokawa, K., & Sutton, S. W. (2005). A lab test and algorithms for identifying clients at risk for treatment failure. *Journal of Clinical Psychology, 61,* 155–163.

Hansen, B. P., Lambert, M. J., & Vlass, E. N. (2015). Sudden gains and sudden losses in the clients of a "Supershrink": 10 case studies. *Pragmatic Case Studies in Psychotherapy, 11*(3), 154–201.

Hatfield, D., McCullough, L., Frantz, S. H. B., & Krieger, K. (2010). Do we know when our clients get worse? An investigation of therapists' ability to detect negative client change. *Clinical Psychology and Psychotherapy, 17,* 25–32.

Heinonen, E., Lindfors, O., Laaksonen, M. A., & Knekt, P. (2012). Therapists' professional and personal characteristics as predictors of outcome in short- and long-term psychotherapy. *Journal of Affective Disorders, 138,* 301–312.

Heinonen, E., Lindfors, O., Härkänen, T., Virtala, E., Jääskeläinen, T., & Knekt, P. (2014). Therapists' professional and personal characteristics as predictors of working alliance in short-term and long-term psychotherapies. *Clinical Psychology and Psychotherapy, 21,* 475–494.

Hersoug, A. G., Høglend, P., Havik, O., Lippe, A. V. D., & Monsen, J. (2009). Therapist characteristics influencing the quality of alliance in long-term psychotherapy. *Clinical Psychology and Psychotherapy, 16,* 100–110.

Hill, C. (1995). Therapist techniques, client involvement, and the therapeutic relationship: Inextricably intertwined in the therapy process. *Psychotherapy: Theory, Research, Practice, Training, 42,* 431–442.

Hofmann, S. G., & Barlow, D. H. (2014). Evidence-based psychological interventions and the common factors approach: The beginnings of a rapprochement? *Psychotherapy, 51*(4), 510–513.

Holdsworth, E., Bowen, E., Brown, S., & Howat, D. (2014). Client engagement in psychotherapeutic treatment and associations with client characteristics, and treatment factors. *Clinical Psychology Review, 34,* 428–450.

Holt, H., Beutler, L. E., Kimpara, S., Macias, S., Haug, N. A., Shiloff, N., ... Stein, M. (2015). Evidence-based supervision: Tracking outcome and teaching principles of change in clinical supervision to bring science to integrative practice. *Psychotherapy, 52*(2), 185–189.

Hook, J. N., Davis, D. E., Owen, J., Worthington, E. J., & Utsey, S. O. (2013). Cultural humility: Measuring openness to culturally diverse clients. *Journal of Counseling Psychology, 60*(3), 353–366.

Horvath, A. O., & Bedi, R. P. (2002). The alliance. In J. C. Norcross (Ed.), *Psychotherapy relationships that work* (pp.37–69). New York: Oxford University Press.

Horvath, A. O., & Luborsky, L. (1993). The role of the therapeutic alliance in psychotherapy. *Journal of Consulting and Clinical Psychology, 61*(4), 561–573.

Horvath, A. O., Del Re, A. C., Fluckiger, C., & Symonds, D. (2011). Alliance in individual psychotherapy. In Norcross, J. (Ed.), *Psychotherapy relationships that work* (2nd ed., pp. 76–89). New York: Oxford University Press.

Hubble, M. A., Duncan, B. L., Miller, S. C., & Wampold, B. E. (2010). Introduction. In B. L. Duncan, S. C. Miller, B. E. Wampold, & M. A. Hubble (Eds.), *The heart and soul of change: Delivering what works in therapy* (pp. 23–46). Washington, DC: American Psychological Association.

Imel, Z. A., Sheng, E., Baldwin, S. A., & Atkins, D. C. (2015). Removing very low-performing therapists: A simulation of performance-based retention in psychotherapy. *Psychotherapy, 52*(3), 329–336.

Jacobson, N. S., Dobson, K. S., Truax, P., Addis, M. E., Koerner, K., Gollan, J. K., ... Prince, S. E. (1996). Component analysis of cognitive-behavioral treatment for depression. *Journal of Consulting and Clinical Psychology, 64*(2), 295–304.

Jennings, L., & Skovholt, T. M. (1999). The cognitive, emotional, and relational characteristics of master therapists. *Journal of Counseling Psychology, 46*(1), 3–11.

Jennings, L., Sovereign, A., Bottorff, N., Mussell, M. P., & Vye, C. (2005). Nine ethical values of master therapists. *Journal of Mental Health Counseling, 27*(1), 32–47.

Jennings, L., D'Rozario, V., Goh, M., Sovereign, A., Brogger, M., & Skovholt, T. (2008). Psychotherapy expertise in Singapore: A qualitative investigation. *Psychotherapy Research, 18*(5), 508–522.

Keenan, K., & Shawn, R. (2016). The good therapist: Evidence regarding the therapist's contribution to psychotherapy. In Cain, D. J., Keenan, K., & Shawn, R. (Eds.), *Humanistic psychotherapies: Handbook of research and practice* (2nd ed., pp. 421–454). Washington, DC: American Psychological Association.

Kim, D., Wampold, B. E., & Bolt, D. M. (2006). Therapist effects in psychotherapy: A random-effects modeling of the National Institute of Mental

Health Treatment of Depression Collaborative Research Program data. *Psychotherapy Research, 16*(2), 161–172.

Kivlighan, D. M., Jr., Gelso, C. J., Hummel, A. M., Ain, S., & Markin, R. D. (2015). The therapist, the client, and the real relationship: An actor–partner interdependence analysis of treatment outcome. *Journal of Counseling Psychology, 62*(2), 314–320.

Kraus, D. R., Castonguay, L., Boswell, J. F., Nordberg, S. S., & Hayes, J. A. (2011). Therapists effectiveness: Implications for accountability and patient care. *Psychotherapy Research, 21*(3), 267–276.

Kraus, D. R., Baxter, E. E., Alexander, P. C., & Bentley, J. H. (2015). The Treatment Outcome Package (TOP): A multi-dimensional level of care matrix for child welfare. *Children and Youth Services Review, 57,* 171–178.

Kraus, D. R., Bentley, J. H., Alexander, P. C., Boswell, J. F., Constantino, M. J., Baxter, E. E., et al. (2016). Predicting therapist effectiveness from their own practice-based evidence. *Journal of Consulting and Clinical Psychology, 84*(6), 473–483.

Krause, M. S., & Lutz, W. (2009). Process transforms inputs to determine outcomes: Therapists are responsible for managing process. *Clinical Psychology: Science and Practice, 16*(1), 73–81.

Kruger, J., & Dunning, D. (1999). Unskilled and unaware of it: How difficulties in recognizing one's own incompetence lead to inflated self-assessments. *Journal of Personality and Social Psychology, 77*(6), 1121–1134.

Lambert, M. J. (2005). Early response in psychotherapy: Further evidence for the importance of common factors rather "placebo effects". *Journal of Clinical Psychology, 61*(7), 855–869.

Lambert, M. J. (2013a). *Bergin and Garfield's handbook of psychotherapy and behavior change*. Hoboken, NJ: Wiley.

Lambert, M. J. (2013b). Outcome in psychotherapy: The past and important advances. *Psychotherapy, 50*(1), 42–51.

Lambert, M. J. (2015). Progress feedback and the OQ-System: The past and the future. *Psychotherapy, 52*(4), 381–390.

Lambert, M. J., & Baldwin, S. A. (2009). Some observations on studying therapists instead of treatment packages. *Clinical Psychology Science Practice, 16,* 82–85.

Lambert, M. J., & Cattani, K. (2012). Practice-friendly research review: Collaboration in routine care. *Journal of Clinical Psychology. In Session, 68*(2), 209–220.

Lambert, M. J., & Ogles, B. M. (2014). Common factors: Post hoc explanation or empirically based therapy approach? *Psychotherapy, 51*(4), 500–504.

Lambert, M. J., & Shimokawa, K. (2011). Collecting client feedback. *Psychotherapy, 48*(1), 72–79.

Laska, K. M., & Wampold, B. E. (2014). Ten things to remember about common factor theory. *Psychotherapy, 51*(4), 519–524.

Laska, K. M., Smith, T. L., Wislocki, A. P., Minami, T., & Wampold, B. E. (2013). Uniformity of evidence-based treatments in practice? Therapist effects in the delivery of cognitive processing therapy for PTSD. *Journal of Counseling Psychology, 60*(1), 31–41.

Laska, K. M., Gurman, A. S., & Wampold, B. E. (2014). Expanding the lens of evidence-based practice in psychotherapy: A common factors perspective. *Psychotherapy, 51*(4), 467–481.

Lehmann, A. C., & Ericsson, K. A. (1997). Research on expert performance and deliberate practice: Implications for the education of amateur musicians and music students. *Psychomusicology, 16*, 40–58.

Levitt, H. M. (2015). Qualitative psychotherapy research: The journey so far and future directions. *Psychotherapy, 52*(1), 31–37.

Levitt, H. M., Pomerville, A., & Surace, F. I. (2016). A qualitative meta-analysis examining clients' experiences of psychotherapy: A new agenda. *Psychological Bulletin, 142*(8), 801–830.

Lilienfeld, S. O., Ritschel, L. A., Lynn, S. J., Cautin, R. L., & Latzman, R. D. (2013). Why many clinical psychologists are resistant to evidence-based practice: Root causes and constructive remedies. *Clinical Psychology Review, 33*, 883–900.

Little, J. H. (2010). In B. L. Duncan, S. D. Miller, B. E. Wampold & Hubble, M. A. (Eds.), *The heart and soul of change: Delivering what works in therapy* (2nd ed., pp. 167–198). Washington, DC: American Psychological Association.

Lo Coco, G., Gullo, S., Prestano, C., & Gelso, C. J. (2011). Relation of the real relationship and the working alliance to the outcome of brief psychotherapy. *Psychotherapy, 48*(4), 359–367.

Luborsky, L., Singer, B., & Luborsky, L. (1975). Comparative studies of psychotherapies: Is it true that "everyone has won and all must have prizes"? *Archives of General Psychiatry, 32*, 995–1008.

Luborsky, L., Crits-Christoph, P., McLellan, A. T., Woody, G. Piper, W., Liberman, B., … Pilkonis, P. (1986). Do therapists vary much in their success? Findings from four outcome studies. *American Journal of Orthopsychiatry, 56*(4), 501–512.

Lucock, M., Halstead, J., Leach, C., Barkham, M., Tucker, S., Randal, C., … Saxon, D. (2015). A mixed-method investigation of patient monitoring and enhanced feedback in routine practice: Barriers and facilitators. *Psychotherapy Research, 25*(6), 633–646.

Lutz, W., Lambert, M. J., Harmon, S. C., Tschitsaz, A., Schürch, E., & Stulz, N. (2006). The probability of treatment success, failure and duration— what can be learned from empirical data to support decision making in clinical practice? *Clinical Psychology and Psychotherapy, 13*, 223–232.

Lutz, W., Leon, S. C., Martinovich, Z., Lyons, J. S., & Stiles, W. B. (2007). Therapist effects in outpatient psychotherapy: A three-level growth curve approach. *Journal of Counselling Psychology, 54*(1), 32–39.

Lutz, W., Rubel, J., Schiefele, A. K., Zimmemann, D., Bohnke, J. R., & Wittmann, W. W. (2015). Feedback and therapist effects in the context of treatment outcome and treatment length. *Psychotherapy Research, 25*(6), 647–660.

Mackrill, T. (2011). Differentiating life goals and therapeutic goals: Expanding our understanding of the working alliance. *British Journal of Guidance and Counselling, 39*(1), 25–39.

Marcus, D. K., O'Connel, D., Norris, A. L., & Sawaqdeh, A. (2014). Is the Dodo bird endangered in the 21st century? A meta-analysis of treatment comparison studies. *Clinical Psychology Review, 34*, 519–530.

McKay, K. M., Imel, Z. E., & Wampold, B. E. (2006). Psychiatrist effects in the psychopharmacological treatment of depression. *Journal of Affective Disorders, 92*, 287–290.

Miller, S. D., Duncan, B. L., Sorrell, R., & Brown, G. S. (2005). The partners for change outcome system. *Journal of Clinical Psychology. In Session, 61*, 199–208.

Miller, S.D., Hubble, M., & Duncan, B. (2008). Supershrinks: What is the secret of their success? *Psychotherapy in Australia, 14*(4), 14.

Miller, S. D., Hubble, M. A., Chow, D. L., & Seidel, J. A. (2013). The outcome of psychotherapy: Yesterday, today, and tomorrow. *Psychotherapy, 50*(1), 88–97.

Miller, S. D., Hubble, M. A., Chow, D. L., & Seidel, J. A. (2015). Beyond measures and monitoring: Realizing the potential of feedback-informed treatment. *Psychotherapy, 52*(4), 449–457.

Minami, T., Brown, G. S., McCulloch, J. M., & Bolstrom, B. J. (2012). Benchmarking therapists: Furthering the benchmarking method in its application to clinical pratice. *Quality and Quantity: International Journal of Methodology, 46*, 1699–1708.

Nissen-Lie, H. A., Monsen, J. T., Ulleberg, P., & Rønnestad, M. H. (2010). Therapist predictors of early patient-rated working alliance: A multilevel approach. *Psychotherapy Research, 20*(6), 627–646.

Nissen-Lie, H. A., Havik, O. E., Høglend, P. A., Monsen, J. T., & Rønnestad, M. H. (2013a). The contribution of the quality of therapists' personal lives to the development of the working alliance. *Journal of Counseling Psychology, 60*(4), 483–495.

Nissen-Lie, H. A., Monsen, J. T., Ulleberg, P., & Rønnestad, M. H. (2013b). Psychotherapists' self-reports of their interpersonal functioning and difficulties in practice as predictors of patient outcome. *Psychotherapy Research, 23*(1), 86–104.

Nissen-Lie, H. A., Havik, O. E., Høglend, P. A., Rønnestad, M. H., & Monsen, J. T. (2015a). Patient and therapist perspectives on alliance development: Therapists' practice experiences as predictors. *Clinical Psychology and Psychotherapy, 22*(4), 317–327.

Nissen-Lie, H. A., Rønnestad, M. H., Høglend, P. A., Havik, O. E., Solbakken, O. A., Stiles, T. C., & Monsen, J. T. (2015b). Love yourself as a person, doubt yourself as a therapist? *Clinical Psychology & Psychotherapy.*

Norcross, J. (2010). The therapeutic relationship. In B. L. Duncan, S. D. Miller, B. E. Wampold, & M. A. Hubble (Eds.), *The heart and soul of change: Delivering what works in therapy* (2nd ed., pp. 113–141). Washington, DC: American Psychological Association.

Norcross, J. (2011). *Psychotherapy relationships that work* (2nd ed.). New York: Oxford University Press.

Norcross, J. & Lambert, M. (2011). Psychotherapy relationships that work II. *Psyhcotherapy, 48*(1), 4–8.

Norcross, J. C., & Wampold, B. E. (2011). What works for whom: Tailoring psychotherapy to the person. *Journal of Clinical Psychology. In Session, 67*(2), 127–132.

Norcross, J. C., Krebs, P. M., & Prochaska, J. O. (2011). Stages of Change. *Journal of Clinical Psychology. In Session, 67*(2), 143–154.

Nyman, S. J., Nafziger, M. A., & Smith, T. B. (2010). Client outcomes across counselor training level within a multitiered supervision model. *Journal of Counseling & Development, 88*, 204–209.

Oddli, H. W., Halvorsen, M. S., & Rønnestad, M. H. (2014a). Expertise demonstrated: What does it mean to be an expert psychotherapist? Retrieved from http://societyforpsychotherapy.org/expertise-demonstrated.

Oddli, H. W., McLeod, J., Reichelt, S., & Rønnestad, M. H. (2014b). Strategies used by experienced therapists to explore client goals in early sessions of psychotherapy. *European Journal of Psychotherapy & Counselling, 16*(3), 245–266.

Okiishi, J. C., Lambert, M. J., Eggett, D., Nielsen, L., Dayton, D. D., & Vermeersch, D. A. (2006). An analysis of therapist treatment effects: Toward providing feedback to individual therapists on their clients' psychotherapy outcome. *Journal of Clinical Psychology, 62*(9), 1157–1172.

Owen, J., & Hilsenroth, M. J. (2014). Treatment adherence: The importance of therapist flexibility in relation to therapy outcomes. *Journal of Counseling Psychology, 61*(2), 280–288.

Owen, J., Drinane, J. M., Idigo, K. C., & Valentine, J. C. (2015). Psychotherapist effects in meta-analyses: How accurate are treatment effects? *Psychotherapy, 52*(3), 321–328.

Owen, J., Wampold, B. E., Kopta, M., Rousmaniere, T., & Miller, S. D. (2016). As good as it gets? Therapy outcomes of trainees over time. *Journal Of Counseling Psychology, 63*(1), 12–19.

Paul, G. (1967). Strategy in outcome research in psychotherapy. *Journal of Consulting Psychology, 31,* 109–118.

Platz, F., Kopiez, R., Lehmann, A. C., & Wolf, A. (2014). The influence of deliberate practice on musical achievement: A meta-analysis. *Frontiers in Psychology, 5,* 1–13.

Probst, T., Lambert, M. J., Loew, T. H., Dahlbender, R. W., Göllner, R., & Tritt, K. (2013). Feedback on patient progress and clinical support tools for therapists: Improved outcome for patients at risk of treatment failure in psychosomatic in- patient therapy under the conditions of routine practice. *Journal of Psychosomatic Research, 75*(3), 255–261.

Probst, T., Lambert, M. J., Loew, T. H., Dahlbender, R. W., & Tritt, K. (2015). Extreme deviations from expected recovery curves and their associations with therapeutic alliance, social support, motivation, and life events in psychosomatic in-patient therapy. *Psychotherapy Research, 25*(6), 714–723.

Puschner, B., Wolf, M., & Kraft, S. (2008). Helping alliance and outcome in psychotherapy: What predicts what in routine outpatient treatment? *Psychotherapy Research, 18*(2), 167–178.

Reese, R. J., Norsworthy, L. A., & Rowlands, S. R. (2009). Does a continuous feedback system improve psychotherapy outcome? *Psychotherapy Theory, Research, Practice, Training, 46*(4), 418–431.

Restifo, E., Kashyap, S., Hooke, G. R., & Page, A. C. (2015). Daily monitoring of temporal trajectories of suicidal ideation predict self-injury: A novel application of patient progress monitoring. *Psychotherapy Research, 25*(6), 705–713.

Rønnestad, M. H. (2016). Is expertise in psychotherapy a useful construct? *Psychotherapy Bulletin, 51*(1), 11–13.

Rønnestad, M. H., & Skovholt, T. M. (2001). Learning arenas for professional development: Retrospective accounts of senior psychotherapists. *Professional Psychology: Research and Practice, 32*(2), 181–187.

Rønnestad, M. H., & Skovholt, T. M. (2013). *The developing practitioner: Growth and stagnation of therapists and counselors.* New York: Routledge.

Roos, J., & Werbart, A. (2013). Therapist and relationship factors influencing dropout from individual psychotherapy: A literature review. *Psychotherapy Research, 23*(4), 394–418.

Rosenzweig, S. (1936). Some implicit common factors in diverse methods of psychotherapy. *American Journal of Orthopsychiatry, 6,* 412–415.

Rosenzweig, S. (1954). A transvaluation of psychotherapy; a reply to Hans Eysenck. *The Journal of Abnormal and Social Psychology, 49,* 298–304.

Safran, J. D., & Kraus, J. (2014). Alliance ruptures, impasses, and enactments: A relational perspective. *Psychotherapy, 51*(3), 381–387.

Safran, J. D., & Muran, J. C. (2000). *Negotiating the therapeutic alliance.* New York: Guildford.

Safran, J. D., & Muran, J. C. (2006). Has the concept of the therapeutic alliance outlived its usefulness? *Psychotherapy: Theory, Research, Practice, Training, 43*(3), 286–291.

Safran, J. D., Muran, J. C., & Eubanks-Carter, F. (2011). Repairing alliance ruptures. *Psychotherapy, 48*(1), 80–87.

Safran, J. D., Muran, J. C., Demaria, A., Boutwell, C., Eubanks-Carter, C., & Winston, A. (2014). Investigating the impact of alliance-focused training on interpersonal process and therapists' capacity for experiential reflection. *Psychotherapy Research, 24*(3), 269–285.

Saxon, D., & Barkham, M. (2012). Patterns of therapist variability: Therapist effects and the contribution of patient severity and risk. *Journal of Consulting and Clinical Psychology, 80*(4), 535–546.

Sharf, J., Primavera, L. H., & Diener, M. J. (2010). Dropout and therapeutic alliance: A meta-analysis of adult individual psychotherapy. *Psychotherapy Theory, Research, Practice, Training, 47*(4), 637–645.

Shimokawa, K., Lambert, M. J., & Smart, D. W. (2010). Enhancing treatment outcome of patients at risk of treatment failure: Meta-analytic and mega-analytic review of a psychotherapy quality assurance system. *Journal of Consulting and Clinical Psychology, 78*, 298–311.

Simon, W., Lambert, M. J., Harris, M. W., Busath, G., & Vazquez, A. (2012). Providing patient progress information and clinical support tools to therapists: Effects on patients at risk of treatment failure. *Psychotherapy Research, 22*(6), 638–647.

Slife, B. D., Wiggins, B. J., & Graham, J. T. (2005). Avoiding an EST monopoly: Toward a pluralism of philosophies and methods. *Journal of Contemporary Psychotherapy, 35*(1), 83–97.

Slone, N. C., Mathews-Duvall, S., Reese, R. J., & Kodet, J. (2015). Evaluating the efficacy of client feedback in group psychotherapy. *Group Dynamics: Theory, Research, and Practice, 19*(2), 122–136.

Smith, M. L., & Glass, G. V. (1977). Meta-analysis of psychotherapy outcome studies. *American Psychologist, 32*(9), 752–760.

Smith, M. L., Glass, G. V., & Miller, T. I. (1980). *The benefits of psychotherapy.* Baltimore: The John Hopkins University Press.

Sperry, L., & Carlson, J. (2014). *How master therapists work: Effecting change from the first through the last session and beyond.* New York: Routledge.

Spielmans, G. I., Masters, K. S., & Lambert, M. J. (2006). A comparison of rational versus empirical methods in the prediction of psychotherapy outcome. *Clinical Psychology and Psychotherapy, 13*, 202–214.

Stiles, W. B. (2009). Responsiveness as an obstacle for psychotherapy outcome research: It's worse than you think. *Clinical Psychology: Science and Practice, 16*, 86–91.

Stiles, W. B. (2013). The variables problem and progress in psychotherapy research. *Psychotherapy, 50*(1), 33–41.

Swift, J. K., & Callahan, J. L. (2011). Decreasing treatment dropout by addressing expectations for treatment length. *Psychotherapy Research, 21*(2), 193–200.

Swift, J. K., & Greenberg, R. P. (2012). Premature discontinuation in adult psychotherapy: A meta-analysis. *Journal of Consulting and Clinical Psychology, 80*(4), 547–559.

Swift, J. K., & Greenberg, R. P. (2014). A treatment by disorder meta-analysis of dropout from psychotherapy. *Journal of Psychotherapy Integration, 24*(3), 193–207.

Tasca, G. A., & Lampard, A. M. (2013). Reciprocal influence of alliance to the group and outcome in day treatment for eating disorders. *Journal of Counseling Psychology, 59*(4), 507–517.

Thoma, N. C., & Cecero, J. J. (2009). Is integrative use of techniques in psychotherapy the exception or the rule? Results of a national survey of doctoral-level practitioners. *Psychotherapy Theory, Research, Practice, 46*(4), 405–417.

Tracey, T. J. G., Wampold, B. E., Lichtenberg, J. W., & Goodyear, R. K. (2014). Expertise in psychotherapy. An elusive goal? *American Psychologist, 69*(3), 218–229.

Tryon, G. S., & Winograd, G. (2011). Goal consensus and collaboration. *Psychotherapy, 48*(1), 50–57.

Tschuschke, V., Crameri, A., Koehler, M., Berglar, J., Muth, K., Staczan, P., ... Koemeda-Lutz, M. (2015). The role of therapists' treatment adherence, professional experience, therapeutic alliance, and clients' severity of psychological problems: Prediction of treatment outcome in eight different psychotherapy approaches. Preliminary results of a naturalistic study. *Psychotherapy Research, 25*(4), 420–434.

Wachtel, P. (2010). Beyond "Tratamentos empriricamente suportados". Problematic assumptions in the pursuit of evidence-based practice. *Psychoanalytic Psychology, 27*(3), 251–272.

Walfish, S., McAlister, B., O'Donnell, P., & Lambert, M. J. (2012). An investigation of self-assessment bias in mental health providers. *Psychological Reports, 110*(2), 639–644.

Wampold, B. E. (2007). Psychotherapy: The humanistic (and effective) treatment. *American Psychologist, 62*(8), 857–873.

Wampold, B. E. (2011). *Qualities and actions of effective therapists.* American Psychological Association. Retrieved from https://www.apa.org/education/ce/effective-therapists.pdf.

Wampold, B. (2015). Humanism as a common factor in psychotherapy.In *The handbook of humanistic psychology: Theory, research, and practice* (2nd ed., pp. 400–408) (e-book). Thousand Oaks, CA: Sage.

Wampold, B. E., & Brown, G. S. (2005). Estimating variability in outcomes attributable to therapists: A naturalistic study of outcomes in managed care. *Journal of Consulting and Clinical Psychology, 73*(5), 914–923.

Wampold, B. E., & Imel, Z. E. (2015). *The great psychotherapy debate: The evidence for what makes psychotherapy work* (2nd ed.). New York: Routledge.

Wampold, B. E., Mondin, G. W., Moody, M., Stich, F., Benson, K., & Ahn, H. (1997). A meta-analysis of outcomes studies comparing bona fide psychotherapies: Empirically: "All must have prizes". *Psychological Bulletin, 122*, 203–215.

Wampold, B. E., Imel, Z. E., Laska, K. M., Benish, S. Miller, S. D., Flückiger, C., ... Budge, S. (2010). Determining what works in the treatment of PTSD. *Clinical Psychology Review 30*, 923–933.

Wampold, B. E., Frost, N. D., & Yulish, N. E. (2016). Placebo effects in psychotherapy: A flawed concept and a contorted history. *Psychology of Consciousness: Theory, Research, and Practice, 3*(2), 108–120.

Wampold, B. E., Lichtenberg, J. W., Goodyear, R. K., & Tracey, T. J. G. (in press). Clinical expertise: A critical issue in the age of evidence-based practice. In S. Dimidjian (Ed.), *Evidence-based practice in action*. New York: Guilford.

Warren, J. S., Nelson, P. L., Mondragon, S. A., Baldwin, S. A., & Burlingame, G. M. (2010). Youth psychotherapy change trajectories and outcomes in usual care: Community mental health versus managed care settings. *Journal of Consulting and Clinical Psychology, 78*(2), 144–155.

Werbart, A., Von Below, C., Brun, J., & Gunnarsdottir, H. (2015). 'Spinning one's wheels': Nonimproved patients view their psychotherapy. *Psychotherapy Research, 25*(5), 546–564.

Wierzbicki, M., & Pekarik, G. (1993). A meta-analysis of psychotherapy dropout. *Professional Psychology: Research and Practice, 24*(2), 190–195.

Zeeck, A., Orlinsky, D. E., Hermann, S., Joos, A., Wirsching, M., Weidmann, W., et al. (2012). Stressful involvement in psychotherapeutic work: Therapist, client and process correlates. *Psychotherapy Research, 22*(5), 543–555.

Zilcha-Mano, S., Eubanks-Carter, F., Muran, J. C., Hungr, C., Safran, J. D., & Winston, A. (2016). The relationship between alliance and outcome: Analysis of a two-person perspective on alliance and session outcome. *Journal of Consulting and Clinical Psychology, 84*(6), 484–496.

Zuroff, D. C., Kelly, A. C., Leybman, M. J., Blatt, S. J., & Wampold, B. E. (2010). Between-therapist and within-therapist differences in the quality of the therapeutic relationship: Effects on maladjustment and self-critical perfectionism. *Journal of Clinical Psychology, 66*(7), 681–697.

Zuroff, D. C., Shahar, G., Blatt, S. J., Kelly, A. C., & Leybman, M. J. (2016). Predictors and moderators of between-therapists and within-therapist. Differences in depressed outpatients' experiences of the rogerian conditions. *Journal of Counseling Psychology, 63*(2), 162–172.

CHAPTER 2

Static and Genetic Phenomenology

The aim of this chapter is to present arguments to support the central claim that phenomenology covers two broad interconnected areas, namely *static phenomenology* and *genetic phenomenology*. Both constructs will be used in the sense originally intended by Edmund Husserl. There are three interconnected points that need to be made about the subject in general:

1. Static phenomenology is a base for an eidetic psychology with its own object of study (i.e., intentional consciousness) and a clearly defined research method. It's object of study is the intentional experience. The static method has several methodological steps and its final goal is the definition of the invariant structures of human experience. However, for existential psychotherapy, besides de focus on the intentional experiences, the main aspects of the static method are: the epoché, the psychological-phenomenological reduction and the description of the human experiences.

2. Genetic phenomenology, on the other hand, underpins a form of psychology that goes beyond the mere description of the intentional structures of consciousness. This deals with subjects such as pre-reflective and reflective consciousness; the phenomenological

---

This chapter has some parts based on a original paper: Phenomenological Psychology: Husserl's Static and Genetic Methods. *Journal Phenomenological Psychology,* 45, pp. 27–60.

© The Author(s) 2017   85
D. Sousa, *Existential Psychotherapy,*
DOI 10.1057/978-1-349-95217-5_2

notion of self; the creation of identity (the *persona*), constituted in an intersubjective space; and the analysis of passive geneses and the layers of meaning in the stream of temporal awareness. The genetic method enables us to plunge into layers of human existence that are pre-reflective, passive and anonymous, though nonetheless active. Genetic-phenomenological analysis is research into facticity, as proposed by Husserl. It is the basis of *one* form of existential phenomenological psychotherapy.

Between the static and genetic methods, there is constant dialectic. Constitutive phenomenology based on eidetic dimensions (static phenomenology) enables theoretical bases to be established, which are then explored in more depth and applied using the genetic method. The results yielded by this process are then subjected to regressive movements, and offset the results of descriptive research into a particular object of study. Husserl maintained a constant interrelationship between the two methods: "these are fundamental questions concerning the distinction, but also the ordering of necessary phenomenological investigations. Where they are concerned, I will always speak of *static* and *genetic* phenomenology" (Husserl 2001a, p. 643) (Fig. 2.1).

"Static" phenomenology investigates the processes of noetic-noematic constitution and elaborates typologies and general notions about human beings in connection with the world (Husserl 2001a). It focuses on the intentional structures of experience that form part of the human being. Static research is more general and abstract in nature and is not concerned with the existential specificity of the self and its individual history: "...I can doubtlessly designate phenomenological

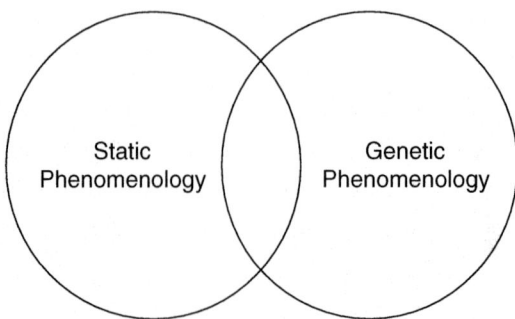

Fig. 2.1 Static and genetic phenomenology

investigations as static, investigations that attend to the correlations between constituting consciousness and the constituted objectlike formations, and exclude genetic problems altogether" (Husserl 2001a, pp. 639, 640). However, according to Husserl, we can have "a new task", when this is applied to personal individuality (Husserl 2001a, p. 639). Thus, another function of the phenomenological project is to consider the specificity of the personal history, which is constantly in the process of becoming. Phenomenology is transported to a more concrete dimension, to the level of facticity, where the object of study becomes the self and its personal characteristics, motivations and intentions, always limited by horizons that have been previously constituted, actively and passively. "Of particular importance, but noticed very late, is the fact that reflective, so-called "internal, experience has very many levels and depth-dimensions and is exceedingly difficult to put into practice whenever one strives to go beyond the most superficial level" (Husserl 1977, p. 21). Genetic investigation aims to explore the rational and affective, conscious and pre-reflective dimensions of a historical temporal awareness, influenced by past sedimented meanings and by future expectations and desires. When Husserl comes up against the depth of personal existence, he inflects the ambit of phenomenology. "Finally, we have the phenomenology of monadic individuality, and included in it, the phenomenology of a genesis integral to it, a genesis in which the unity of the monad arises, in which the monad is by becoming. …By the phenomenology of genesis attending to original becoming in the temporal stream, which itself is an originally constituting becoming, and by attending to the so-called 'motivations' that functions genetically, a phenomenology of consciousness shows how consciousness arises out of consciousness" (Husserl 2001a, p. 639).

The dual dimension of phenomenology is nevertheless unified by a common project. Husserl mentions the notion of the "leading clue" (Husserl 2001a, p. 633) to describe the constant dynamic and connection between the static and genetic methods. The two methods are mutually integrative and do not function exclusively in separation. That is to say, descriptive research throws up clues that lead to genetic phenomenology when this is located at the individual level of self. Certain eidetic knowledges, elaborated and typified, about the general structures of experience, may be applied to particular cases. Genetic research, for its part, can also produce clues leading to static phenomenology; by articulating eidetic knowledge at the individual level, it stimulates further questions and new research possibilities. Our purpose is to adapt Husserl's static and genetic methods to the context of existential psychotherapy. However, the static and the genetic dimensions of phenomenology don't entail only a methodological scope, rather it presupposes theoretical underpinnings. Therefore, we will start to present some issues regarding the static method. Secondly, we will proceed by presenting several theoretical aspects linked to the genetic phenomenology.

STATIC PHENOMENOLOGY

Phenomenology sprang from a double project: to present a method suitable for the study of mental processes and, in parallel, to deepen some philosophical principles that would establish a renewed scientific paradigm. Phenomenology, bases its project, in part, as *phenomenological psychology*. It is this particular aspect that most interests us. The fundamental principle required for any understanding of the object of study of phenomenological psychology is the concept of intentionality. Its *object of study* is *intentional experience*, or the *meaning of human experience*. In adopting the concept of intentionality, psychologists are not limited to understanding the psychic phenomenon, as something exclusively mental, although the objective is to study human consciousness. Husserl stressed that all consciousness is consciousness *of* something. Acts of consciousness such as perception, imagination, memory and hallucination, are intentional as they direct themselves, or *aim toward*, an object—the intentional object. If consciousness has *real* elements that are in an empirical domain, it also has *ideal* elements that with their dimension of meaning exceeding the spatial-temporal dimension, the empirical contingency. It is the intentional component of consciousness that places its object of study, the intentional experience, at the level of sense and meaning. "Whatever becomes accessible to us through reflection has a noteworthy general character: that of being consciousness *of* something, of having something as an object of consciousness, or to be aware of it correlatively—we are speaking here of intentionality. This is the essential character of mental life in the full sense of the word, and is thus inseparable of it" (Husserl 1997, p. 217). Husserl highlighted that one does not love, hate, hallucinate, perceive, imagine or simply recall, but one loves someone, one hates something, one hallucinates on something, one perceives an object, one imagines a wish or recalls a past achievement.

So, it is of crucial importance to understand that phenomenological analysis seeks to study in parallel the object and the subject implied within an act of consciousness. The concept of Husserlian intentionality implies that the intentional object cannot be analyzed correctly, without its subjective correlate, the act of intentional consciousness. One cannot be studied or analyzed, without the other. Phenomenological considers, for example, in a perception, the act of intentional subjectivity—that of perceiving—and the object to which the act of consciousness of perceiving is directed (in this case, this text that I am now reading, the object *while* perceived). Neither the intentional object, nor the intentional act, may be separately understood. This is valid even when the object does not, or no longer exists. Intentional consciousness may involve non-existent objects. Obviously, this does not suggest that one accepts the existence of non-real objects; however, the intentional acts have the capacity of targeting objects even when the referent no longer exists (Gallagher and Zahavi 2008). Husserl also added that intentional relations are always lived in a perspectival context. We are not only aware of a determined object, we are aware of an object in a particular manner. The intentional object is presented to consciousness from a determined way and involved in a specific context. Consider, for example, the computer on which this text is being written. The computer is never given in its totality, always in or from a perspective, and one may be changed substantially in each intentional act. The mode of the object's appearing to me and to consciousness may be distinct. Not only may I not perceive the computer as a whole but always from a perspective (in front, behind, from above, etc.), such that it may be given different meanings according to each new or different perspective. I may, for example, be annoyed, since the computer represents a space of work for me, when I would prefer to be engaging in a more leisurely activity, or on the contrary, be glad that a particular piece of work is about to be completed. I may be in a state of anticipation or expectation in waiting for an urgent reply by e-mail, or experiencing pleasure due to the fact that the computer has an aesthetically modern design. It may evoke a particular concern, given that the computer will bear subsequent financial running costs, as this been a common experience with other computers. There is an intrinsic relationship, namely that between the subjective act and the intentional act that allows a constituting of the meaning of an experience; in Husserl, the *intentional experience.*

The Static Method

The static method includes five steps: the *époché*, the phenomenological reduction, the description, the eidetic analysis, and inter-subjective results. To the therapeutic process, the first four dimensions are the ones important. The last one is out of the scope of this text, since is specifically important to the validation of qualitative research (Sousa 2014).

Epoché

Essentially *epoché* means to put in brackets, suspend the belief of natural attitude. In order to analyze human experience, we must abstain ourselves from considering the factual and empirical dimension of natural reality, so as to concentrate ourselves exclusively on what is given to consciousness, *such as it is presented* to consciousness. It does not deal with denying the world, natural reality, to doubt or enter in some mystical process of negation of objects and situations, but rather develops systematically, an attitude that makes explicitly the intentional mental processes. "The purpose of the epoché is not to doubt, neglect, abandon, or exclude reality from consideration; rather the aim is to suspend or neutralize a certain dogmatic *attitude* towards reality, thereby allowing us to focus more narrowly and directly on reality as it is given—how it makes its appearance to us in experience. In short, the epoché entails a change of attitude towards reality, and not an exclusion of reality" (Gallagher and Zahavi 2008, p. 23). It is important to stress that the *epoché* is not a methodological step achieved in one moment. Many authors have speculated on the possibility of practicing the *epoché*, and of applying it. It is a methodological instrument that helps the therapist to centre himself on his object of study, seeking to avoid the bias of the naturalist vision. The crucial aspect of it is in excluding empirical dogmatism and the belief in a natural attitude. In the same way, any previously acquired knowledge about the kind of experience being described by the other is initially suspended. Obviously, it is not strictly true to say that the therapist is set free forever from his preconceived opinions. However, he may throughout the process of learning promote a critical exercise that permits him to recognize the bias of the descriptions that he is analyzing being influenced by previous theoretical constructs. Likewise, it does not imply a turn "inwards" of the subject, nor an exclusive concentration on the subjectivity of personal vision. Contrarily, the intentional experience cannot be understood in merely mental terms, the *epoché* is a tool that makes possible a more lucid and clarifying approach, in the form of how experiences are perceived by the person.

Psychological-Phenomenological Reduction

The second step of the method is the *psychological-phenomenological reduction*. The *epoché* and phenomenological reduction may be understood as two methodological instruments, used in parallel. "Whereas the purpose of the epoché is to suspend or bracket a certain natural attitude towards the world thereby allowing us to focus on the modes or ways in which things appear to us, the aim of the phenomenological reduction is to analyze the correlation interdependence between specific structures of subjectivity and specific modes of appearance or givenness" (Gallagher and Zahavi 2008, p. 25). How can we understand this for the practice of psychotherapy? The main aspect is that the use of both the epoché and the phenomenological reduction allows the therapist to truly focus on the lived experience of the other. It is very hard to listen to other person and try to really capture the experience of the person that is describing his experiences. The static method is of great value for the therapist develops a kind of awareness focused on the other. Husserl considered the phenomenological reduction a central tool for the psychologist (Husserl 1998). The reduction used by the therapist, shall be in accordance with the reduction that Husserl designated as *psychological-phenomenological reduction*, not making use of a subsequent methodological step, the transcendental reduction: "Thus in order to attain the pure and actual subject matter of the required 'descriptive psychology', a fully consciously practiced method is required which I call the *phenomenological-psychological reduction*—taken in this context as a method for psychology" (Husserl 1970, p. 236). The *epoché* and phenomenological reduction do not imply an emptying of the *self* or of our past knowledge. The phenomenological reduction is a task for a critical consciousness, a methodological instrument, that seeks to reveal human experiences such as it are presented in a given situation.

Descriptions

The *phenomenological description* intends to avoid the explanation of a determined phenomenon by means of external factors to this, limiting itself to the phenomenon such as it is *given*. The description already contains in itself, intrinsically, an understanding of the phenomenon. However, a good description is that one that describes the events with the greatest detail as is possible; including the cognitive emotion lived by the subject. The objective is to return with the greatest fidelity possible on the experience as lived, and such as it is lived at the moment in which it occurs. This descriptive methodological indication sometimes is neglected by therapists. The capacity of analyzing evidence in a descriptive way is something that calls for specific training, a considerable degree of aptitude, of self-critical capacity, such that it deepens the competencies of descriptive analysis (Spiegelberg 1994). The phenomenological description does not presuppose the simple acceptance of evidence uncritically rather they need to be carefully vetted by the trained eyes of the therapist. It is essential to highlight that, one of the fundamental reasons for Husserl stressing the need to describe intentional acts is linked to the fact that not all have the same cognitive value.

Eidetic Analysis

The fourth element of the phenomenological method is the *eidetic analysis—imaginative free variation*. Husserl stressed that is also possible to accede, through a conceptual analysis, to essential dimensions of the experiences. The eidetic reduction allows acceding dimensions, characteristics and properties that make a determined experience, which it is, leaving aside merely contingent factual variations. It is the aim to determine the essence of the experience, such as it appears to consciousness, be it a physical object, a perception, a sensation, or a lived situation. The objective is to identify the fundamental characteristics of the phenomenon, establishing, by way of a variative reflection, the particularities from which the phenomenon does not depend, to be such as it is. If, by removing the characteristics, the experience is no longer recognized, then that characteristic is considered essential. Should it not be prevalent, the characteristic is regarded as accidental, particular, and not fundamental for the *eidos*, for the essence of the phenomenon. The eidetic analysis in the scope of phenomenological psychology and psychotherapy is aimed at achieving synthesis of psychological meanings.

To sum up, the use of the static method applied to existential psychotherapy takes into account the following steps (Husserl 1970, 1997, 2001c):

1. *Epoché*, suspension of the natural attitude and previous knowledge;
2. *Phenomenological Reduction*, to centre upon the object such as it appears to consciousness and, on its subjectivity such that it experiences the intentional object such as it is lived;
3. *Descriptive*, phenomenological analysis implies a description of phenomena such as targeted by intentional consciousness;
4. *Eidetic Analysis*, permits through imaginative free variation, the elucidation of invariant structures, the essences, of the experiences.

GENETIC PHENOMENOLOGY

Between 1917 and 1921 Edmund Husserl developed what he called the *genetic-phenomenological method*, which would complement the *static-phenomenological method* and added an explanatory dimension to the descriptive static method: "In a certain way, we can therefore distinguish 'explanatory' phenomenology as a phenomenology of regulated genesis, and 'descriptive' phenomenology as a phenomenology of possible essential shapes (no matter how they have come to pass) in pure consciousness and their teleological ordering in the realm of possible reason under the headings, 'object' and 'sense'. In my lectures, I did not say 'descriptive', but rather 'static' phenomenology " (Husserl 2001a, p. 629).

The static method is characterized by its attempt to describe the way in which objects are manifested to consciousness, elaborating essential structures of experience which are expressed in eidetic dimensions, general and typified. The self is understood as defined and developed, without consideration of the cultural and historical context, or the meanings that have been temporally elaborated during the course of a unique personal development. Hence, the static method remains formal and abstract, seeking to investigate the type of procedures and acts of consciousness that are involved in the formation of meaning, but it is limitative as regards the origin of meaning and the genesis of the sense attributed to experience. As for the genetic method, this is directly connected to time consciousness theory, which Husserl began working on in 1893 and first demonstrated in his 1905 lectures. The crucial question is as follows: when the temporal dimension of consciousness is considered, the phenomenological method becomes "static", as it excludes the factitious dimension of self, its personal and individual history, sedimented in layers of meaning, which are in part pre-reflective, non-thematic and anonymous to the self, but which nevertheless continue to influence its experience of itself with the other and with the world. For Husserl, the self is never static, absolute and defined, but is rather situated in a *living present*. This means that the self extends uninterruptedly beyond the present moment, influenced by its past history and conditioned by its expectations (explicit or implicit) of the future. Intentional consciousness never *exists* only in the present moment; it inhabits the paradox of the here-and-now, which experiences its existence through a temporal flux which is simultaneously a being-here, a being-no-longer-here and a being-not-yet-there (Montavont 1999). Husserl uses the term "person" in relation to this facticity, a process of becoming, which constitutes time and is constituted in time, the centre of a surrounding world (Husserl 1989). Person and world are inseparably interrelated. As we shall see, the genetic method plumbs the depths of facticity of existence, assuming that the self has a cluster of abilities and characteristics, habits sedimented throughout its experiential process, which are not immediately accessible but which passively influence the person's action. Each experience has a deep temporally constituted dimension which only the genetic method can explore (Donohoe 2004). The process of genetic-phenomenological analysis will in part be a distillation of the sedimented layers of meaning that intersubjectively constitutes the subject's personality and his experiential horizons. From that interrelational context from which human existence derives, there may emerge conflicts, existential tensions and traumatic processes, for their part sedimented in dissociative processes that operate at the pre-reflective level (Spinelli 1997; Stolorow 2007). Existential psychotherapy's work of clarification focuses upon the anguish and dissociative processes that form part of the being-in-the-world (Spinelli 1997). There are three main aspects to the rationale underlying the genetic-phenomenological applied to existential psychotherapy: inner time-consciousness theory, the experiential self and the theory of passive geneses. This theoretical structure will be framed by the method of genetic-phenomenological analysis, which will in term be complemented by other concepts. In short, the aim is to present a theory based upon existential phenomenological psychology which has repercussions for existential psychotherapy (i.e., upon the phenomenological conception of self; the constitution of passive geneses which form the existential ground of the person; the way in which the person's interaction with the surrounding world not only contributes to development of personal identity but may also open up the possibility of psychological disturbances resulting from traumatic processes between the sedimentations of self and the experiences gleaned in the surrounding world).

Inner Time-Consciousness Theory

Husserl considered inner time-consciousness theory to be the corner-stone of the theoretical edifice of phenomenology (Husserl 1977). It reflects and expresses the fundamental aim of the phenomenological project: to understand how subjectivity can manifest itself, how it is a *constituent* of beings in the world and how it *is constituted* to itself. Husserl wondered how consciousness perceives an object with temporal extension, such as a melody, but also asked how consciousness has manifested itself (Husserl 1994, p. 56). According to him, it would be impossible to perceive objects with temporal extension if consciousness could only apprehend the "now" moment of the object and if the stream of consciousness were no more than the sum of a series of unconnected "nows" (Zahavi 1999). To explain the apprehension of temporal objects, and situations involving changes and successions, three technical terms are used: *primordial impression, retention* and *protention*. Let us consider a sequence of three sounds making up a melody. When the first sound is heard (the now moment of the object), the *primordial impression* is activated. This never occurs in isolation, as that would not enable the object's temporality to be perceived; thus, it is always accompanied by a *retention* (i.e., of the moment-just-passed), which allows access to the moment it dives into the past. Simultaneously, *protention* is a more-or-less undefined form that intuits the moment that is about to happen. Consciousness perceives temporal objects "in blocs", in a three-part dynamic temporal structure in which the temporal phases (past, present and future) of the object are presentified "together" in a concentrated form. Thus, in inner time consciousness, retention and protention are not past or future in relation to the primordial impression but presented together with it. Retention and protention should, however, be distinguished from thematic recollection and expectation. The former are passive activities that occur without any intentional action on the part of the subject; that is to say, there is no active contribution from the consciousness. Thematic recollection and expectation, on the other hand, are independent intentional acts that depend at least in part upon the subject's actions, i.e., they are voluntary (Merleau-Ponty 2002).

The primordial impression—retention—protention structure is constantly being updated and altered in the stream of consciousness. Each new retention is always retention of the previous primordial impression and of the primordial impression that preceded that. As time passes, objects and the experience of them lose qualities and definition.

Retentions gradually weaken until they eventually become impercepti-ble (Husserl 1994; Zahavi 1999, 2005; Bernet et al. 1993). The crucial question from the psychological point of view is that *the example of sound may be extended to any kind of experience lived in the first-person perspec-tive.* What is given in the self in "living flesh" (Husserl 2001a, p. 217) undergoes a transformation during the continuous retentional process in the stream of consciousness. It is successively relegated to the past, so that the continuous emergence of new primordial impressions occurs inseparably from a retentional transformation.

Manifestation of Subjectivity and Temporality

For Husserl, inner time-consciousness theory had a much more impor-tant aim than merely explaining the perception of temporal objects. It had to do with the very manifestation of subjectivity (Zahavi 1999). Therefore it is important to mention the concept of *double intentional-ity: transversal intentionality (Querintentionalität) and longitudinal intentionality (Längsintentionalität)* (Husserl 1994). Let us go back to the example of the melody. When we hear a sound, an intentional act occurs, enabling an intentional object, different from consciousness, to manifest itself. The act is intentional because it allows the manifes-tation of something different from itself, but at the same time the act is also manifested to itself. This is therefore a double intentionality, in which the object is given by means of the act which, as well as manifest-ing the intentional object, also manifests itself: "from the last explana-tions, we can give the following response: there is a single unique flow of consciousness which constitutes the temporal unity immanent in the sound, and at the same time, the very unity of the flow of consciousness" (Husserl 1994, p. 107). There are two intentionalities that are insepara-bly united and intertwined, effectively two sides of the same coin. The intentional act and the stream of consciousness are integral inseparable parts (Mohanty 2008). Each retention implies a double intentionality. The intentional act is called the transversal intentionality of retention. The intentionality of retentions (that is, the flow of consciousness itself) is called longitudinal intentionality. This is not a supplementary reten-tion that is added to the retention of sounds. If it were, this would imply infinite regression. As well as being intentional and making possible the manifestation of something different from itself (the intentional object), the act is characterized by an "inner consciousness", in the sense that it is manifested to itself (Husserl 1994). For Zahavi, one of the crucial questions arising from a correct interpretation of double intentionality is that *inner time-consciousness is the pre-reflective consciousness of acts of consciousness and lived experiences* (Zahavi 1999, p. 71). As Sartre also mentioned, inner time-consciousness theory is the most appropriate place for understanding Husserl's explanation of the pre-reflective structure of consciousness (Sartre 1994b). The stream of temporal awareness is the name given to a pre-reflective consciousness, which is not an intentional act, an internal object or temporal unity, but rather a basic permanent dimension of human consciousness (Husserl 1989). Experiences become the object for consciousness only when reflexivity is introduced; for Husserl, the object is at this point transcendental in relation to consciousness, i.e., there exists a *difference* between the object and intentional consciousness. The flux of consciousness and intentional acts are not two distinct flows but two different ways of manifesting a single stream.

Pre-reflective Consciousness and Temporal Identity

It is important to remember that retentional pre-reflective consciousness is a modification, in the sense that, when the primordial impression becomes retention, we are not only before the object as it was given (for example, the melody), but as it was *experienced* (Zahavi 2003). Effectively, the *stream of consciousness of retentions and protentions form a chain of experiences* that transcend natural givens; they are not experienced neutrally in their crude form (Rodemeyer 2003). Therefore, Husserl's theory demonstrates how all experience is constituted in temporal awareness, a consciousness that is not thematic and which is the province of a non-objectified self. Every experience is retained in the stream of consciousness, even when it is not constituted as a reflective object or instituted in objective time, forming a backdrop that constitutes the experiential horizon. Longitudinal intentionality anchors subjectivity, as Merleau-Ponty pointed out; retentions and protentions are intentionalities that fasten subjectivity to its surroundings (Merleau-Ponty 2002). Through time awareness, the pre-objectified self is continuously and uninterruptedly lived in a multiplicity of experiences that are constantly being updated in the retentional chain, while it nevertheless recognizes itself pre-reflectively as the same over time, despite the changes. Consciousness is a stream of lived experiences, in other words, a flowing manifold. But these many different types of lived experiences are all known to me as "my experiences". Through their all belonging to "me", these experiences all belong together, and thus they form a unity. This synthetic unity of the diversity of the *stream of lived experiences* is, according to Husserl, temporality (Held 2003). In this sense, *inner-time consciousness is the primordial space for the constitution of identity.* There is unity, a flow of consciousness, a self, a personality (Husserl 1989).

Husserl's concept of inner time-consciousness is a theory about the notion of a basic identity established in time, where the lived present is an opening, a present in depth, *ek-static*, which enables the experiences of subjectivity and the constitution of selfhood to be scrutinized. Time consciousness is the basis of selfhood, meaning and reason (Merleau-Ponty 2002). *The temporality of consciousness enables the experiential world of subjectivity to be analyzed.* If time is the thread with which the personal narrative is woven, it is understandable that the dynamic structure of temporal awareness is affected by the presence of existential tensions and psychological disturbances. Stolorow and his colleagues imported phenomenology to psychoanalysis and, over the course of several decades, developed the notion of "dynamic intersubjective fields", which presupposes a focus on affectivity in human experience and considers it to be both regulated and compromised by relational systems (Stolorow 2007). This idea was always central in existential psychotherapy, which "assumes that all reflections upon our lived experience reveal that existence is relationally-derived" (Spinelli 1997, p. 96). What Stolorow means is that the presence of emotional trauma in the human experience seriously compromises the *ek-static* unity of temporal existence (Stolorow 2007). Traumatic experience causes the temporal awareness of the past to congeal in the present, so that one remains captive there or returns constantly to it, while the future loses significance. The line of flux of temporal awareness collapses, which means that clinical dissociation may be understood in terms of a disorganization of personal meaning sustained by temporality (Stolorow 2007). The dynamic structure of temporal awareness will necessarily have to be considered from the therapeutic perspective when there are dissociative processes arising out of existential tensions and conflicts.

Experiential Selfhood

While recognizing that it is reductive to work with only one notion of self (the term is multi-faceted), Zahavi, basing himself on classical names from phenomenology such as Husserl, Heidegger, Sartre and Merleau-Ponty, suggests that there is an *"experiential dimension of self-hood"* (Zahavi 2007, 2005). This is a basic form of selfhood, a core self (the 'experiential self') which precedes and underpins the narrative self (or, if we prefer, the constitution of personal identity). *The fundamental question of the phenomenological theory of pre-reflective consciousness is that, in an experiential dimension, all and any experience in a first-person perspective immediately implies a basic awareness of self* (Husserl 1994; Heidegger 1988; Sartre 1994b; Merleau-Ponty 2002). In order to gain access to a *core self*, it is necessary to investigate experiences lived in the first person. For example, when I perceive an object, experience an emotion, recall a past event or bring forth a thought, I simultaneously have a basic pre-reflective awareness of myself. To be self-aware is to have first-person experiences that are characterized by the quality of being *mine*. The basic dimension of human existence and the constitution of self does not take place in opposition to the stream of consciousness or separately from it; on the contrary, the core self is submerged in the experiential world, i.e., in the experiential flow of temporal awareness. Thus, self-understanding implies an investigation into the experiential interaction between the self and the world, which is clearly the main aim of existential psychotherapy. The experiential self is the conceptual articulation of the being-in-the-world: "It is possible to identify this pre-reflective sense of mineness with a minimal, or core, sense of self .... In other words, the idea is to link an experiential sense of self to the particular first-person givenness that characterizes our experiential life; it is the first-personal givenness that constitutes the *mineness* or *ipseity* of experience. (…) To be self-aware is not to interrupt the experiential interactions with the world in order to turn the gaze inward; on the contrary, self awareness is always the self-awareness of a world—immersed self" (Zahavi 2005, pp. 125, 126).

As Sartre points out, if I feel pleasure, I am aware of feeling pleasure; the experience of pleasure does not exist first, to which the awareness of feeling pleasure is later added. Pleasure is awareness of feeling pleasure. The way of being of subjectivity is to be aware (Sartre 1994b). "For the law of being in the knowing subject is *to-be-conscious*" (Sartre 1943,

p. 17). Perceiving a table is not a matter of affirming that the table exists in itself, but that it exists for *me* (Sartre 1943). The awareness of an object is simultaneously a pre-reflective consciousness, a non-positional consciousness (Sartre 1943). For Sartre, this basic selfhood does not yet mean self-awareness. It is necessary to distinguish between pre-reflective consciousness, and reflective consciousness, which is now self-knowledge (Sartre 1943). We will see below that, for Husserl, inter-subjectivity is constitutional; but here what matters is the fact that any experience lived in the first person is totally exclusive and unique. "But this unique distinctive character is clear, consisting in this, that an all-inclusive synthesis pervades the streaming of lived experiences and all existence synthetically constituted in them as persisting, an all inclusive synthesis by means of which even unreflectedly I am constantly a pole of identity in relation to which everything else is 'objective'" (Husserl 1977, p. 208). Merleau-Ponty also indicated that through temporality there arises *selfhood*; that is to say, consciousness always maintains a relationship of itself for itself (Merleau-Ponty 2002). If there are qualitative differences in the way experiences are lived, there is a quality that remains unaltered—the fact that the experiences are *mine* (Heidegger 1962). Along similar lines, Heidegger understands that the essence of *Dasein* lies in the existence that is characterized by a *being of mine*. The *Dasein* is unveiled in and through facticity, a being thrown into the world, with a pre-comprehension and an intrinsic connection to himself, prior to any interpretative movement: "We are ourselves the entities to be analyzed. The Being of any such entity *is in each case mine*. Because Dasein has *in each case mineness* (Jemeinigkeit), one must always use a personal pronoun when one address it: 'I am', 'you are'. Furthermore, in each case Dasein is mine to be in one way or another" (Heidegger 1962, p. 67).

Experiential Self—"Streaming" and "Standing"

Experiences lived in the first-person perspective *are* in inner time consciousness in a non-thematic position, submerged in a horizon of potential and possibilities (Held 2003). The self of inner time consciousness is primordial and originary, as it slips through the retentional time chain of consciousness, although remaining constantly self-aware. At a deep dimension of self, *streaming* and *standing* are one and the same inner time-consciousness (Held 2003). This gives rise to the paradox of the person that knows himself and recognizes himself as the same subjectivity over time, but who simultaneously identifies with a multiplicity of different experiences, and who is in constant change (Husserl 1989). This is what Husserl called the "living present" (Husserl 1970). Although the self lives constantly in a chain of experiences that go on throughout life, and cannot be identified outside that flow, the self given in the first-person perspective is at the same time an *invariant* dimension that is maintained throughout the multiplicity of experiences (Zahavi 2005). As stated: "through this pre-objective self-identification, my primordial ego, on the one hand is something unchanging, that is, it is standing and remaining; on the other hand, through this pre-objective self-distancing, it is some-thing living and streaming, that is, something that can become something different in comparison to what it was before. Thus my ego, in its deepest dimension, is a living being, wherein 'standing' and 'streaming' are one" (Held 2003, p. 47). At this level, it is not a matter of the subject's transparency to himself, or of a reflective process of construction of self-knowledge (Zahavi 2003). The crucial aspect is the direct connection between the phenomena experienced and the first-person perspective, in which there already exists a primordial non-thematic pre-objective dimension of self. Nothing can be present to the self if it is not self-aware. The experiential self may constitute itself as a person, construct its personal identity through language and narrative processes—above all, as we shall see, through the intersubjective space and relational networks—but the experiential self is a base structure of consciousness that precedes any narrative dimension (Zahavi 2007). From the psychological point of view, what is important is that the experiential self cannot be understood or considered independently of its connection with the world. The self is, in first place, present in the experiential life, intrinsically connected to the other and to the world. The experiential self, as it is defined by phenomenologists, is similarly conceptualized in existential—phenomenological psychotherapy, which considers an irreducible *grounding of relatedness* (Spinelli 2007, p. 12) as the first principle of self: "phenomenologically influenced perspectives on the self begin by asserting its indissoluble and indivisible *interrelational grounding*. Nothing meaningful can be stated or experienced about 'self' without an implicit reliance upon the self's interrelational placement *in the world*" (Spinelli 2001, p. 41).

Phenomenology of Passivity: The Depths of Facticity

Following Husserl, it is possible to go one step deeper to understand the meaning that is present in the background of lived experiences, which always contain a dimension that is veiled and obscure. Later, it will be important to distinguish the notion of self from the concept of person, a distinction that leads to an explanation of the intersubjective constitution of personal identity, thus enabling closer connections to be made with psychology and with psychotherapy. However, for Husserl, there are also intrinsic motivations belonging to each subject, which are veiled, hidden, and are not immediately accessible. These are what Husserl considered to be a backdrop of experiences that the self does not immediately understand, but which nevertheless continue to "knock on the door of consciousness" (Husserl 1989, p. 105). These are geneses of meaning that have been established passively, without the participation of the active self, and which have gradually formed *sedimentations and habits* that become part of the subject's history and influence his experience. Research using the genetic method acquires pertinence when the aim is to understand not only the active self but to deal with the depth of passive experience that involves the development of the person, and his present and future expectations. The genetic method thus makes vertical connections between the basic self and a personal identity, and between progressive and regressive movements of *intentional motivations.* It also deals with multiple associations that occur in passive geneses in the dynamic structure of temporal consciousness, where the active self is not the main actor but nevertheless has an influence. Our starting point was inner time-consciousness theory; however, this on its own may be formal and abstract, as Husserl himself pointed out, if it is not directly related to the contents of facticity and the existential dimension of subjectivity that is always imbued with personal characteristics, memory and affectivity. It is in that connection, it is argued, that inner time-consciousness theory and passive geneses allow phenomenology to go beyond the descriptive mode to elaborate a theory of change and personal development, a theory which is concerned above all with the constitution of a personality or personal identity that can be applied to psychology and psychotherapy. See, for example, the lectures on phenomenological psychology that he gave in Freiburg in 1925, in which he refers to passive geneses as an integral part of the constitutions of personality, to the necessary connection between time consciousness and facticity, and how the collapse of certain personal assumptions may bring about radical changes in the subject: "As regards the psychic life of the lower passive levels, it is everywhere the presupposition for personality" (Husserl 1977, p. 100). "However, the psyche is not just streaming life, but a life in which, inevitably, distinctive new unities, habitualities are constituted, that is, the passive and active abilities, abilities of perception, abilities of feeling, abilities of memory, intellectual abilities etc. (…) personal characteristics which are variable and in fact never resting, and which eventually, in a collapse, can change totally; among them are the strictly so-called character traits; the unity of mental individuality which persists even through character changes, permeates all that" (Husserl 1977, p. 107).

Active and Passive Self

Already in *Ideas II*, Husserl refers to the free self that decides and acts, but mentions that this active self is only one dimension of existence; a great deal of personal experience involves a passive self. Even when the self is active, part of it is only passively active. Husserl clearly states at various points in his oeuvre that, even in a hidden dimension, the self *is not* a nothing (Husserl 1977, 1989). Investigating the geneses of meaning throughout the process of personal development implies considering the way the self is in constant contact with what Husserl calls *hyle* (Depraz 2001) (i.e., all the sensorial givens of experience, such as "instincts", sensations like pleasure or pain, various types of feelings, well-being and illness, all of which form part of the passive dimension of the experience of self and influences it, even before being thematized) (Husserl 1989). When dealing with the relationship between the experiential self and the constitution of a personal identity, it will be seen that the self is the starting point for personal growth; despite always involving a passive dimension, it nevertheless exerts "self-preservation" (Husserl 1989, p. 265) and therefore does not cease to be an active agent. The self exerts functions, develops particular competences and has intrinsic motivations; in short, it is the centre of the faculties. For Husserl, this is only one dimension of self—that of *practical reason* (Husserl 2001b). However, even rational dispositions are influenced by passive moods (Husserl 1989). Thus, it is important to highlight a crucial point: the self is constantly and simultaneously active and passive; the sediments of ways of being and habits acquired are intertwined with the free will of subjectivity. Following the notions of the active and passive self, three central aspects may be identified with regard to Husserl's notion of passive geneses: there are active geneses that occur with the participation of the self and in rational cognitive acts; there is a dimension of passive geneses that promote a mutual influence between the active and passive selves, forming a bridge between passive and active geneses; finally, there is a dimension that is totally passive, in which associative networks of meaning creation occur without the active participation of the self (Husserl 2001a; Steinbock 1995). The space of pure passivity is that of "primordial constitution", because this occurs *prior* to a rational and thematic constitution on the part of the subject.

Passive "Unconscious" Geneses

If we accompany Husserl in his elaboration of the genetic method and its application in the analysis of the depth of temporal facticity, the active self and passive self, we enter into the domain of passive geneses which transport phenomenology to the unconscious dimension. "Thus, our considerations concern a phenomenology of the so-called unconscious" (Husserl 2001a, p. 201). Let us look at this in parts. The world of passivity leads to an obscure, latent, hidden dimension that is veiled from temporal awareness. The point to be stressed is not to sustain Husserl's "nil of vivacity" means the same of Freud's unconscious. Although Husserl referred several times to a recondite and anonymous dimension of self, a deep part of existence that is not immediately accessible, he always did so cautiously, placing the word in brackets, or using hedging devices such as "what was then called the unconscious" so that the reader could distinguish his own specific approach. But the aim here is not to set up a dialogue between Husserl and Freud, nor to clarify the differences between their theories. The aim is to make explicit the theory of Husserl's passive geneses, how this directly connects with inner time-consciousness theory and with the pre-reflective dimension of self, and how these together may offer an important contribution to existential phenomenological psychology.

The theory of passive geneses may extend the horizons of phenomenology and consequently to existential psychotherapy, as other authors have done it. For example, Heidegger, Sartre and Merleau-Ponty have all considered the covert dimension of human existence. Heidegger mentioned that *Dasein* is not only ontologically distant from itself, for even at the ontic level it is hidden (Heidegger 1962). Sartre claims that consciousness affects itself pre-reflectively even in bad faith (Sartre 1943) As for Merleau-Ponty, connected the aims of psychoanalysis with the phenomenological method, linking them with the notion that "all human acts have a meaning" (Merleau-Ponty 2002, p. 184). Later, he would claim that, although psychoanalysis and phenomenology had not followed parallel paths, they both pointed to the notion of *latency* (Merleau-Ponty 1982, p. 71). However, an attentive reading of Husserl's theory of passivity and concepts associated with it suggest that it is closer to a psychological language of phenomenological psychology, and therefore may be linked to existential psychotherapy.

Affective Zero-Consciousness

The primordial laws of the constitution of geneses, of their associative motivational laws, originate in inner time-consciousness (Husserl 2001a). As we have seen, all retention is always retention of a lived experience. A primordial impression occurs simultaneously with a transformation in the retentional chain and each retention is relegated further back into the past, implying that each experience included in a retention will gradually lose more of its "force". "Continuous retentional modification proceeds up to an essentially necessary *limit*. That is to say: with this intentional modification there goes hand in hand a *gradual diminution of prominence*; and precisely this has its limit, at which the formerly prominent subsides into *universal substratum*—the so-called "unconscious", which, far from being a phenomenological nothing, is itself a limit-mode of consciousness (Husserl 2001a, p. 217). Husserl describes the uninterrupted process of transformation of the retentional chain as a "clouding over" process (Husserl 2001a, p. 217) in which all experiences that are initially a primordial impression gradually lose their clarity, traces and salient features, causing their affective force to diminish. From the psychological point of view, it is fundamental to grasp not only the connection between lived experiences and time consciousness, but also that the retentions that gradually lose their salience are relegated to the "nil of the vivacity of consciousness", or to a space of "affective zero-consciousness". This passive dimension of consciousness is not a nothing of psychological life; the retentions of inner time-consciousness do not disappear. On the contrary, they form the subsoil, the background of lived experiences, which are permanently present as an experiential atmosphere of subjectivity. "This gradation is also what determines a certain concept of consciousness and degrees of consciousness and the opposition to the unconscious in the appropriate sense. The later designates the nil of this vivacity of consciousness and, as will be shown, is in no way a nothing" (Husserl 2001a, p. 216). Inner time-consciousness is the place of constant genesis; the meanings created by the self have a history. For Husserl, temporal awareness is a constant becoming (Husserl 2001a). Passivity is a subsoil that is being constituted throughout a person's development, a space for the creation of a cluster of personality features, of more or less sedimented habits, which are sometimes present in a totally passive and obscure form, but which nevertheless play a role in the being of subjectivity. One of the main aims of genetic analysis is to explain the constitution of meanings that were sedimented throughout the different phases of development, which Husserl calls *habitus*, meanings that are in part not immediately accessible to the self.

In short, genetic-phenomenological analysis proceeds from the assumption that the self does not have access to all the perspectives of lived experiences. Some are superimposed on others and some are sometimes more prominent than others, for reasons not immediately apprehended, while others are vague or peripheral, transformed or distorted in the retentional process, or, as we shall see below, by associative processes. The analysis of passive geneses places phenomenology before the deep life of the subjectivity (Steinbock 1995). Having arrived at this point, it now becomes possible to delineate a preliminary contribution to the question raised above concerning the way the self can collapse, a collapse that may be manifested in multiple ways. In the sphere of existential psychotherapy, Spinelli broaches the concept of *worlding* as an experiential process in which all subjectivity deals simultaneously with the ontological dimensions of existence and with the ontic strategies of being before the givens of existence (Spinelli 2007). Worlding also expresses how existence is a continuous process and in constant becoming, existence as it is projected outside itself. However, worlding-as-process necessarily has a structure that fuses into a worldview; i.e., the more or less rigid *sedimentations* that are gradually established along the personal development of the self, others and the world. This worldview includes the personal beliefs, self-vision, meanings, behavior, emotions and affectivity that the person has created in the interrelational space and upon which he bases himself when dealing with his existence. This worldview structure is complex but "attempts to maintain a structure that places greater value upon the continuation of being rather than upon the cessation of being" (Spinelli 2007, p. 32).

This assumption is directly in line with the self-preservation that Husserl speaks of and which was mentioned above. But the connection is closer; the worldview and worlding enunciate a basic characteristic of the experiential self which has already been evoked here and which is present in the flow of temporal consciousness—a streaming and a standing. As we have seen, inner time-consciousness and passive geneses form a theory about the way sedimentations are formed and transform into habits, some more rigid than others, and which are constituted in the experiential self. The first principle of existential psychotherapy is that the self is grounded relatedness. For this reason, uncertainty and existential anguish are two dimensions of human existence which arise from this presupposition, as everything that is developed is lived in the uncertainty of the intersubjective space. Inevitably, there will be tensions and conflicts that arise from one's own existential project, between worlding as process and the sedimentations of the worldview. These conflicts may result in different types of psychological manifestations and disturbances, and, in extreme cases, with the collapse of the self; according to the existential approach, tensions arise that are inherent to the experience of the givens of existence (Yalom 1980).

Phenomenology of Association, Intentional Motivations and Affective Allure

Husserl introduced the concept of *intentional motivation* as the essential law of personal self (Husserl 1989). In the world of subjectivities, of people, this implies intentional motivations, both intrinsic to each subject and intersubjectively between subjects. From the idiosyncratic perspective, there are motivations that are veiled from self knowledge, anld which inclusively interconnect in "associative motivation networks". These include sedimentations of cognitive acts, memories, and also apperceptions, non-thematized pre-reflective acts, sensorial acts, therefore a whole non-rational dimension of self. "By all means, there are hidden motivations. Even without our performing acts of belief, they enter into motivations. Examples of it are provided by the realm of *experience*, the infinitive field of motivations included in every perception, in memory, and (modified, however) in every phantasizing of a thing."

Apprehensions of things and of thingly nexuses are "webs of motivation" (Husserl 1989, p. 236). Husserl considered phenomenology of association (Husserl 2001a) to be a continuation of inner time-consciousness theory (Husserl 2001a). Not only are associative processes transmitted between and through previously established sedimentations, the associative laws of intentional motivations occur *without* any conscientialization of self (Husserl 2001a). These networks of associative motivations occur in progressive and regressive movements, influencing each other mutually in such a way that past experiences may flow into future expectations or present action, just as pre-reflective expectations (protention actions) may influence sedimentations or acquired habits (Husserl 1989). Much phenomenology of association highlights the fact that associative trajectories take place in the sphere of passive geneses; they are not previously defined or reflectively elaborated upon by the self, yet nevertheless retain their influence on it, either by remaining in the passive sphere or by articulating influences between the passive and active self (Husserl 1977). Thus, a motivational association may arise in the consciousness through an "affective allure": "By affection we understand the allure given to consciousness, the peculiar pull that an object given to consciousness exercises on the ego; it is a pull that an object given to consciousness exercises on the ego; it is a pull that is relaxed when the ego turns toward it attentively, and progress from here" (Husserl 2001a, p. 196). Between thought and feelings, cognition and emotion, the self has various experiences that simultaneously exert an allure upon it. Affection presupposes a *prominence*, a *contrast*, for either cognitive or affective reasons. A lived experience produces an affection in the self, which for its part will imply a "relief" of that same allure when the self reacts to it. However (and this is a particularly important point from the psychological perspective), even when the self does *not* direct all its attention, even when the self is not totally active in relation to that experience, the affection may even diminish in force. As Husserl said, there is relief in the sense that the attraction provoked a genuine effect in the self, even when "it remains in the antechamber of the self" (Husserl 2001a, p. 215).

Associative Reactivation and Passive Geneses

Finally, three aspects need to be mentioned that are crucial for existential psychotherapy. Firstly, passive geneses may be *reactivated* even when they have lost affective force and are in zero consciousness. Secondly, the importance of passive geneses does not have to do only with retentions (that is to say, with experiences of the past); equally important is research into protentions (i.e., passive expectations). Thirdly, all experiences lived in a particularly stream of consciousness, in a particular self, influence each other mutually. This is one of the reasons why phenomenology of association gives particular importance to the phenomenological investigation of memory (Husserl 2001a). Phenomenology of association also connects the first point mentioned (i.e., that associative processes can provoke reactivations of experiences, even those that are occult). Husserl uses the term "awakening", defined as follows: "by awakening we understand and distinguish two things: awakening something that is already given to consciousness as for itself, and the awakening of something that is concealed" (Husserl 2001a, p. 120). As we have seen, in first place, the primordial impressions that become retentions gradually lose prominence and are sedimented in zero consciousness. However, *what is sedimented is the original meaning of the lived experience.* Thus, an experience may be inactive in the consciousness but its meaning is implicit and is kept present, though in an occult form. Experiences of the lived present may reactivate retentions and passive geneses through an "associative awakening". There are many reasons why a particular retention may be reactivated, and these may be both cognitive and rational, and emotive and pre-reflective (Husserl 2001a). What is more, the associative process does not follow previously defined routes; the reactivations may "touch upon" different sedimentations that were not initially interconnected (Husserl 2001a). Associative recollections, which include the retentions upon which they are based, should be distinguished from traditional memory (Drummond 2003). This question emphasizes the existence of an extensive horizon in the experience of self, which, passively, continues to permit the elaboration of associations between past experiences, or future expectations, at an implicit pre-reflective level. This hidden experiential sea, for its part, may be reactivated, though it is not possible to anticipate how that will happen or the form that it will take in particular situations that occur. We should also remember that everything that has been said about retention (and in fact Husserl gives particular importance to the exploration of memory networks), the laws of passive genesis and associative reactivation processes also apply to protentions. Indeed, protention is presented as having priority for the updating of present experience, and is the temporal foundation of intentionality (Rodemeyer 2003). It is obviously important for the psychotherapeutic process, for as we know, the existential approach always emphasized the future dimension of lived experience and how this connects with and influences present experiences.

The Person

We have already plumbed the depths of the passive geneses of self. Now it is time to move upwards in the direction of Husserl's notion of the *person*. Inner time-consciousness, the experiential self and passive geneses form a theoretical triad that is fundamental for psychological and psychotherapeutic praxis. However, it would be incomplete if we did not consider the notion of the person, the relationship between the person and the other, and how the former is constituted intersubjectively. According to Husserl, intersubjectivity conditions must be fulfilled for a person to develop beyond basic selfhood (Husserl 1989). Basic ipseity implies growth and development in order to achieve the plenitude of a personal identity. The concept of person is phenomenologically and ontologically dependent on the experiential self (Zahavi 2005), but basic selfhood, while being a necessary condition, is not in itself enough to constitute a personal identity; it has to be developed within a social and cultural context, with the Other (Zahavi 1999). Genetic-phenomenological analysis involves describing and interpreting meanings that have become sedimented during the course of personal development, at its different phases, during its interaction with the family and with social and cultural environments. It also involves describing and making explicit expectations that are present in the associative networks of protention (Husserl 1989). In a surrounding world, the experiential self is situated as a basic ipseity that includes sensations, associations, passive geneses, and stimuli, which remain largely hidden, though they passively influence the activity of the active self, of the person. They influence its being-in-the-world, its thought, affectivity, behavior. The experiential self is the container of the obscure moods of the person (Husserl 1989). At the level of personal development, we not only consider a stream of abstract consciousness, or experiences flowing in the retentional chain (Husserl 1989, p. 290) but also the sedimented dispositions, traces of personality, affectivity, the meaning inherent in passive and active geneses and their idiosyncratic components as expressed through thought, the body, affectivity and the person's behavior. Genetic-phenomenological analysis has as its object of study the person, who has a history and a unique life. From the psychological and psychotherapeutic point of view, it considers the connection between the experiential self and the person, knowing that it is in the presence of a unique subjectivity. The person is the object of exploration, containing within himself an experiential self, the core of the lived experience. There exists a continuous two-way flow between the experiential self and the surrounding world, i.e., a bidirectional influence that is dynamic and constant between the dimension of the self, the person and the intersubjective space of the surrounding world. The interconnection, hiatus, contrasts, oppositions, cracks between these two worlds that are both an integral part of the existential project result, or may result, in conflict or in the loss of adequate self-preservation. A dramatic change in one of these dimensions, in the self or in the world, will necessarily influence the other (Stolorow 2009).

However, psychological disturbance, and in extreme cases, the loss of meaning, occur in the intersubjective space and are the result of disruptive interrelational processes. The sedimentations which are at zero consciousness may spontaneously unleash a reactivation in the self as a consequence of a confrontation between aspects sedimented in the experiential self and the experiences of the surrounding world. As mentioned above, in the process of personal development, there will certainly be a place for the confrontation between the structural dimension of self based on sedimentations and the process of becoming, which is the characteristic dimension of being in the world. There is a continuous two-way flux between the "inner" world of the self and the "outer" world of the surrounding environment. A dramatic change in one of the systems influences the other. This existential tension is what I call *paradoxical reversibility*. Change is an intrinsic part of the human condition. The matter has to do with cognitive and emotional abilities and resilience that each person has, from one moment to the next, to deal with the affective forces of the self, together with the challenges that are raised in the interrelational space. Sartre mentions the restlessness that characterizes the fatality of consciousness becoming spontaneously anguished (Sartre 1994a). Suddenly, sometimes for no apparent reason, the consciousness will become anguished; it is as if that anguish were a possibility that is always there. At these moments, the introduction of phenomenological reduction is not a learned or intellectual operation, but rather a way of achieving a true and authentic connection as the mode of being. The existential conflict may arise from an impact that is produced in the self as a result of its interactions with the surrounding world, and which may unleash dissociative processes (Spinelli

2007). The dissociation may involve the different strategies that the self develops in response to the challenge raised to one of the sedimented dimensions: for example, the suppression, negation or redirecting of existential tension, which can be translated into false beliefs or behaviors that are not in tune with an authentic way of being. In extreme situations, the conflict may lead to the fragmentation of self, the loss or annihilation of the sense of being a person (Orange et al. 1997). The concept of reactivation mentioned by Husserl may be understood in two ways from the psychological and psychotherapeutic point of view. On the one hand, the reactivations of associative networks intertwine sedimented meanings which, when confronted with the thematic horizon of mundane experiences, may unleash existential anguish. On the other, that which is defined here as *reflexive reactivation* is a psychotherapeutic objective, in the sense that it seeks to phenomenologically investigate the constitution of meaning in passive geneses, which in turn may only happen in the sphere of a privileged interrelationship space.

The Other

For Husserl, the constitution of the person always occurs with another, never on one's own. Personhood is intersubjectively constituted (Zahavi 2005). The self is constituted and may achieve development and personal subjectivity in its relationship with others and in the surrounding world that is common to different people. People are given as co-subjectivities in interrelationship and not as objects opposed in themselves. They exist and develop in personal associative networks, based on the surrounding world, and address each other in relationships of mutual influence and understanding. Relationships of mutual understanding are here understood in a broad sense, as they may involve disagreements; however, what is fundamental is that the surrounding world is an intersubjective space of interpersonal motivations (intersubjective motivations) (Husserl 1989) and of communication between subjectivities (Husserl 1989). The space of the surrounding world gives an ontological dimension to the development of subjectivity, and the relationship between the self and the other is a necessary condition for personal construction.

The subject develops in the relationship with the other. Although the face-to-face encounter is an important dimension of intersubjectivity, and makes it possible for a subject to access the thoughts, feelings and behaviors of another subject, it is also clear that experiences are intrinsically idiosyncratic. Through empathy I can access the experiences of another person, but that does not mean that I have access to exactly how that other person experiences them. As mentioned above, what distinguishes experience in the first-person perspective is that it has the quality of being intrinsically *mine*. In this sense, the other's perspective is totally inaccessible to me; I can have access to the other person's perspective only from the second- or third-person perspective. This difference, far from being a limitation or problem, is *constitutional* from the phenomenological point of view (Zahavi 2005). From the moment we gain access to the experience of the other, just as the other has access to his experiences in the first-person perspective, we are before the negation of alterity. Otherness will be dissipated. The intersubjective experience is never the same for two subjects, though it may be similar, and the appearance of a phenomenon to two subjects can never have the same fusional possibility as it has when two eyes belonging to the same subject observe a particular phenomenon (Zahavi 2005, 2007). This question does not mean that it is impossible to have access to the other, nor that we should confuse different types of access (first-person, second-person) with different types of certainty (Zahavi 2005). Different perspectives always have advantages and disadvantages and it is well-known that also in psychotherapy, this asymmetry is crucial to introduce alterity into a space which, at least in part, is also of development and knowledge. It is important to recognize two central aspects: firstly, there is a constitutional asymmetry between the first- and second-person perspectives (Zahavi 2005); secondly, the self may have access to the experiences of the other through a particular intentional experience that Husserl has written extensively about—empathy. As Husserl refers: "I can have a 'direct' experience of myself, and it is *only my intersubjective form of reality* that I cannot, in principle, experience. For that I need the mediation of empathy. I can experience others, but only through empathy. Their own content can be experienced only by themselves in originary *perceptio*. Likewise, my lived experiences are given to me directly, i.e., the lived experiences in their own content. But others' lived experiences can be experienced by me only mediately, in empathy" (Husserl 1989, p. 210).

To access my intersubjective space, I need the other; it is through the mediation of empathy that, through the other, I experience myself intersubjectively as a person. The self may in fact develop selfhood and constitute its personal identity, but that *project* is realized through interaction with the other in the space of the surrounding world, i.e., intersubjectively. My personality is constitutively inseparable from the interrelational space; existence cannot be apprehended exclusively through individuality. Although I have my own experience, in the first-person perspective, as totality—and the body plays a crucial role here—it is the other that I apprehend in first place as another, as a human being, and only at a second moment do I apprehend myself as a total person (Merleau-Ponty 2002). When I experience the other experiencing me as an other for him, when I live an experience in which the other can experience me as I can experience myself, there occurs a fundamental change and I apprehend myself as a person. Once more we should point out that personality is, according to Husserl, constituted intersubjectively. In fact, for the author, it is particularly relevant when my own experience is mediated by another and when I experience another having the experience of me (Zahavi 2005). A quotation from Zahavi is crucial to understand the pertinence of this point in the psychotherapeutic context: "Husserl elaborates this idea in his description of a special kind of experience of the Other, namely, the situation in which I experience the Other as experiencing myself. This 'original reciprocal coexistence,' where my indirect experience of an Other coincides with my self-experience, can be described as a situation where I see myself through the eyes of the Other" (Zahavi 1999, p. 160).

What is suggested is that this understanding of a type of particular experience with another has a direct resonance with the way the existential phenomenological psychotherapist conceptualizes the space of the therapeutic relationship as a *human encounter* (Spinelli 1997). For Spinelli, in that space, it is not the intervention techniques that are crucial but rather "*being with* the person" (considering the person's way of being as valid and with its own meaning), and "*being for* the person" (the attempt to understand the person's way of being in the sense of clarifying his beliefs, values, sedimentations, dissociations, etc.) (Spinelli 2007). The therapist provides the person with a particular experience of an "other," who, representing all others and the world, simultaneously offers the person the possibility of rethinking and reliving his being-in-the-world emotionally in a safe environment.

Alterity in the Self: Temporality, Corporality and Reflexivity

Temporality
The question to be highlighted here is that there exist three conditions of human experience that promote the constitution of an inner alterity

in the self: the temporal, the corporal and the reflective (Zahavi 2004, 2005). The possibility of gaining access to the intersubjective context, to the self of another, is something that makes part of the intrinsic structure of consciousness (Rodemeyer 2003). We shall not here repeat the arguments relating to *temporality*. Husserl's inner time-consciousness, expressed as the dynamic structure of primordial impression, retention and protention, places temporal consciousness in a constant dialectic between presences and absences. Temporal awareness is always beyond itself, projected in becoming. Consciousness never totally coincides with itself, for the temporal structure always leads to a time lapse in relation to itself. As Merleau-Ponty points out, the temporal structure of consciousness breaks the total coincidence in itself, draws the possibility of perspective and introduces the non-being of subjectivity (Merleau-Ponty 2002). Temporality is certainly the possibility of relating itself to itself, which makes possible interiority and selfhood, but just like temporality, subjectivity too requires an opening to the other as a way of getting out of itself, even so that it can constitute itself (Merleau-Ponty 2002). Sartre also emphasized that the subject's whole relationship with himself is always a relationship of duality. Presence to itself implies a permanently unstable temporal equilibrium between identities, cohesion of itself and the diversity of a synthesis of multiplicities (Sartre 1943). In subjectivity, the ontological grounds of consciousness imply a time lapse, which consists in being itself in the form of presence to itself, which never totally coincides, presupposing an internal fissure (Sartre 1943). Temporality is thus one of the conditions that enable subjectivity to intrinsically possess the possibility of encountering the Other, therefore, with access to intersubjectivity (Rodemeyer 2003).

The Body

Husserl developed an extensive theory of *corporality*, which, among other matters, stresses that the psychological world is connected to existence through the body (Husserl 1989). Psychological development and experience are given in an embodied subjectivity (Husserl 1977). Even the meaning of psychological experiences are, in part, dependent upon bodily processes, although joy and sadness are not lodged in the heart as blood is, nor are the sensations produced by touch only a matter of organic tissue (Husserl 2006). The body is the point zero from which all perceptive experience is realized; there exists only perceptual experience from embodied subjectivity, but that experience is not only affirmation of bodily existence, it is also the presupposition that the body is given to itself in an immediate form. Husserl distinguishes different types of bodily consciousness. In first place, I experience my body pre-reflectively, not thematically; the body is experienced as a unity, it is the subjective experience of the body (*Leib*). Later, an objective thematized experience of the body is acquired (*Leibkörper*) (Zahavi 1999). At the first moment, however, all perceptual and spatial experience is dependent on the kinaesthetic experience (Zahavi 1999). Unfortunately, an in-depth exploration of Husserl's theory of the body falls outside the sphere of this text. However, a brief note is necessary in order to highlight that corporality is one of the conditions for the presence of an inner alterity of self. One of Husserl's basic arguments is that the body has the unique particularity of being experienced with a *double sensation* (Husserl 1989, 1977; Zahavi 2005). When my left hand touches my right, there is simultaneously an experience of touching and of being touched; the body is both an object for itself and a living feeling body. The experience is reversible, because the possibility of the body touching itself and being touched places subjectivity concomitantly before its interiority and its exteriority. This experience is not only corporal; it is also a *double psychological experience*: "thus the body is seen at this level, as well as every specifically bodily process, every specific bodily member, and seen in its two-sidedness, at the same time in its physical externality and its animating internality... The experience of the body as body is therefore already a psychic or rather two-sidedly psychological experience" (Husserl 1977, p. 100).

Merleau-Ponty's theory of embodied subjectivity, which seeks to overcome the classic dichotomy between subject and object, is also well-known (Merleau-Ponty 2002). The body is not only an object for itself, it is also experienced; it is not merely exteriority of the psychological life, but on the contrary, existence is realized in the body (Merleau-Ponty 2002). But the embodied existence presupposes an experience of another, the experience of an alter-ego (Merleau-Ponty 2002). It is precisely because subjectivity is not transparent to itself and because it is embodied that the other becomes evident. There is an *internal* relationship between body-consciousness and another body-consciousness experienced *externally* (Merleau-Ponty 2002). Merleau-Ponty highlights a direct connection between bodily kinaesthesia and the psychological world, between bodily emotion and "psychic facts". For example, in a situation where an adult plays interactively with a 15-month-old child, placing one of the baby's fingers in his mouth as if he to bite it, he will find that the baby will also open its mouth, and despite never having recognized itself in the mirror and not having the same kind of teeth as the adult, it will feel that its own mouth is an instrument that can "bite". The baby feels this because it sees the adult on the outside and sees that his jaw is capable of the same intentions. This game also has for the baby an intersubjective meaning. The baby perceives the intentions through his body, while he perceives the body of the other and their intentions (Merleau-Ponty 2002).

One of the reasons why the self manages empathically to gain access to the other is because his own bodily experience of self intrinsically presupposes a game of ipseity and alterity; that is to say, the double bodily experience is an anticipation of the experience of otherness (Zahavi 2005). In Husserl, the body is a centerpiece for the constitution of psychic reality, the source and origin of our experience of alterity, and consequently, our experience of the other. The body is the centrepiece for ensuring one of the essential conditions for the constitution of a person—the intersubjective space (Husserl 2006). The body is also constituted intersubjectively through the other. For Husserl, the mundane object is that which is intersubjectively accessible. As mentioned, my body is not accessible to me in that mode. The body that I apprehend is the living body, not the object body. The body is not experienced as a mundane object, tactilely or visually, and it is given in parts, not as a whole. The first body that I access as a whole, as mundane object, is the body of the other, and through this I can constitute my own corporality (Zahavi 1999). There is a constitutional hiatus between the self and the other; for Husserl, the body as empathy exerts an essential condition for intersubjectivity: "for psychic being to be, to have *Objective existence*, the *conditions of possibility of intersubjective givenness* must be fulfilled. Such an intersubjective experienceability, however, is thinkable only through "empathy", which for its part presupposes an intersubjectively experienceable Body that can be understood by the one who just enacted the empathy as the Body of the corresponding psychic being" (Husserl 1989, p. 101). Consequently, phenomenological theory presupposes that an understanding of the self and the other, of intersubjectivity, will have to take account of the body. In both Husserl and Merleau-Ponty, corporality of subjectivity is one of the seeds of present alterity *in* the self.

Reflexivity

Finally, *reflexivity* is also a source of alterity in the self. Sartre, as we have seen, mentioned the importance of the pre-reflective consciousness. He connects reflection to time awareness, in such a way that it can transform the givens of pre-reflective non-thematic non-positional consciousness into self-consciousness (Sartre 1943). In order to clarify the connection between reflection and temporality, Sartre distinguishes two types of reflection: the pure and the impure (Sartre 1943). Pure reflection does not alter the pre-reflective givens of consciousness. It is a situation in which reflection is simple presence to itself, turning non-thetic consciousness into thematic consciousness, in keeping with lived experience. It does not add anything to pre-reflective experiences. Indeed, it is above all explicative, because it connects with what is already known. This, according to Sartre, is achieved in an ideal form through a *catharsis* (Sartre 1943). Impure reflection gives unity to psychological acts that are present in daily life. Through impure reflection, the temporality of consciousness is constituted and, in the process, objectifies the self's experiences. Reflection is considered impure because it transcends that which is presentified to the consciousness; it interprets it, transforming and objectifying what was present to the consciousness. There is a reflexive transformation of the original experience. Reflection is a tool intrinsically linked to Husserl's phenomenological method. It is also related with his inner time-consciousness theory. As an analysis of pre-reflective consciousness, inner time-consciousness theory is a starting point, beginning from the retention that reflection makes possible. Reflection, for its part, is what constitutes experiences as temporal objects. Retention makes it possible for the just-passed to be realized *through* retrospective observation (Husserl 1994). Reflection is always given in a temporal dissonance, as the reflective act is about something that has already happened. But what arises in the reflexive act is the *same* act that occurred in that something that has already happened, and it is the same act because it has been held in retention (Zahavi 1999). The retentional phase is pre-reflective consciousness of experiences without these being objectified. It is retention that makes it possible for reflexive consciousness to introduce a doubling between the act of reflecting and the act that is reflected upon. Pre-reflective consciousness does not apprehend its own experiences as object. There is no difference between the intentional experience and pre-reflective consciousness, and so the former cannot be understood as an object. Inner time consciousness enables this difference to be created; it makes it possible for the experience to arise reflexively, in a multiplicity of appearances through a temporal horizon.

But what happens when the experience is apprehended reflexively? According to Husserl, there is a *modification*, a *transmutation and* an *alteration* (Husserl 2001b). Reflection does not therefore have a merely reproductive action; it actually alters the primitive state of experiences of the pre-reflective consciousness. Reflection is not only a change of attention; it also gives rise to *new* cognitive acts and *transforms* experience (Zahavi 1999). It is the reflexive movement that enables consciousness (of) itself—self-knowledge. It is one and the same subject that reflects about the reflected act. Reflection allows us to distinguish perception itself from what is perceived (Husserl 1994). It is a consciousness of itself based in *alterity* and *difference*. This does not imply that we are speaking of a division in the self or that reflection places me before another self. Sartre mentions a sketch of duality in a reflexive self-presence. This dual dynamic becomes a *unity* in which the reflex is the reflector (Sartre 1994b). Husserl mentions that, when I reflect about myself, I am a subject that reflects and simultaneously I am an object that is being reflected about, that object that I designate as *I* (Husserl 1977). Reflective consciousness is distinguished from pre-reflective experiences because it introduces a type of fragmentation of self that is not experienced in lived experience. In this sense, reflection is characterized by having a component of *otherness* (Zahavi 2004). In reflecting about himself, the subject becomes a theme for himself. According to Zahavi, this movement is characterized by a certain *alienation, a fragmentation of self*, which brings implications (Zahavi 2005):

- Reflection is a precondition for self-critical deliberation; the first-person perspective, though necessary, is not enough to enable the subjectivity to deliberate, confront its experiences, eventually introducing alterations in its action;
- Reflection involves a kind of splitting of the self;
- Reflection, which is in part a fragmentation of the self, implies that there is always an anonymous non-thematic and unknown part to subjectivity.

Husserl emphasizes that reflexivity unveils the pre-reflective existence of the self. Reflection enables personal development, the exploration of personal characteristics, traces of personality (Husserl 1989). But reflexivity not only transforms the experience of subjectivity, it is the very condition for the intersubjective dimension of human existence. That is to say, reflexivity is one of the conditions for knowledge of intersubjective motivations present in the co-existence between subjectivities (Husserl 1989). However, and because this is not only a mirror to the experiential world, reflection represents both a loss and a gain. On the one hand, it is limited by the lived experiences, which are at its source; on the other, when experiences are represented thematically, they are not merely reproduced but modified. Reflection, in thematizing experiences, alters them and transforms them to different degrees. But it is precisely because reflection is not only a mirror of experiences that it can constitute something more in terms of self-understanding (Zahavi 2005). The relation of the subjectivity with itself is a relation based upon the temporal doubling existing in the self (Merleau-Ponty 2002). As we have seen, Sartre specifies that all *presence to itself* involves a duality, a separation at the core of consciousness (of) self, that is, of pre-reflective consciousness. That separation, an intangible fissure, is a *distance in space*, a *time lapse*, a *psychological difference—nothingness* (Sartre 1943, p. 113). The phenomenological tradition postulates pre-reflective consciousness not as a static identity but as *dynamic ipseity*, in possession of intrinsic temporal differentiation (Zahavi 2005). That is, an *ek-static* existence. It is from this differentiated unity present in the experiential life that reflection can constitute self-knowledge. Reflection, for its part, introduces an alterity, an otherness, in the self. To sum up, there is an internal *alterity* in the self, or (to use Husserl's paradigmatic expression) there is *transcendence in immanence* based on the *temporal structure*, the *corporal dimension* and a *reflexive differentiation*. Although these forms of internal alterity of the self are essential to the development of subjectivity, this does not have absolute control over them. As we have seen, temporality, corporality and reflexivity place the subject before a difference, a duality, a splitting of himself; that is to say, he is placed before an otherness in himself that he cannot control nor apprehend in its totality (Zahavi 2004). The being of consciousness consists in existing at a distance from himself (Sartre 1943).

Arguing that there exist different types of alterity, Zahavi claims that, from the phenomenological point of view, three are fundamental: "(1) nonself (world), (2) oneself as Other, and (3) Other self". (Zahavi 1999, p. 195). This triad of alterity is directly in keeping with the way Spinelli conceptualizes the notion of *worldview*, dividing it into three substructures: the self-construct; the other-construct, and the world-construct (Spinelli 2007). Although Spinelli does not broach the three sub-structures in terms of alterity, as Zahavi does, the theoretical connection is pertinent. This is one of the reasons why it is argued that the existential approach should not be considered only as an interpsychic vision of self. The basic forms of alterity of self are the three essential dimensions that form the object of phenomenological analysis in the psychotherapeutic context. What this exposition shows is that, even on the level of the face-to-face relationship in the therapeutic space, the self, the other and the world need to be investigated together in an integrated way: "according to our presentation, the concepts I and we are relative: the I requires the thou, the we, and the 'other'. And furthermore, the Ego (the Ego as person) requires a relation to a world which engages it. Therefore, I, we and world belong together; the world as communal environing world, thereby bears the stamp of subjectivity" (Husserl 1989, p. 301).

Double Reduction and Intersubjectivity

This chapter ends with a short note that identifies one more contribution from Husserl's phenomenology of intersubjectivity to existential psychotherapy and the face-to-face context. This note has been placed in epilogue position due to the fact that it brings together a number of the concepts that have already been discussed above. Two main ideas are emphasized. Subjectivity, for Husserl, is, from the outset, intersubjectivity (Depraz 2001). On the other hand, the notion of empathy (important for the face-to-face encounter) is, for Husserl, first and foremost a primordial, original and passive dimension of experience, and therefore prior to the notion of empathy as a way of understanding another. Empathy as *paarung* or coupling is an associative process between a living-body and another living-body, which experience a similar functioning of actions behaviors and kinaesthetic movements. It is a holistic experience of similar experiences through which a body-consciousness may be recognized in another through empathy (Depraz 2001). However, empathy is also a particular intentional experience which enables me to gain an understanding of another. But can phenomenological reduction exert a crucial role in empathy or is it restricted to a questioning self? (Husserl 2006). Can phenomenological reduction be applied in the intersubjective context of psychotherapy?

In first place, it is important to point out that, for Husserl, all human experience admits the possibility of *double phenomenological reduction*. For one, reduction makes experience in itself accessible to the immanent gaze; secondly, reduction may be performed upon the intentional content of experience (Husserl 2006). As far as it is possible to access memory, reduction may be performed a posteriori on the contents of the original experience, both on the experience that was effectively the object of attention and on the intentional experiential foci that were maintained in the experiential background. Double reduction emphasizes the importance of memory. Reduction may be performed *on* memories and may even be able to make explicit aspects, experiences, emotions, thoughts and desires that were present at the original moment of the experience in the background of the person's experience. Even "unconscious" dispositions may be object of phenomenological reduction, scrutinized through the person's memories (Husserl 2006). Memories are a particular interest, and the description and analysis of them forms a fundamental part of phenomenology. What Husserl says is that of the multiple experiences (cognitive, affective) that temporal consciousness has at any moment, the self focuses its attention upon the immediate and reflects only upon some. "Even 'unconscious' lived experiences are integrated in the context, which itself if given by way of perception and directly grasping consciousness, or else the context is supplemented through such 'unconscious' lived experiences. I recognize that I am experiencing various sensations and feelings, which right away I will not get hold of in reflection" (Husserl 2006, p. 97). But phenomenological retention may be practiced on any lived experience. At any moment we can, through reduction, focus our attention upon a second-plane experience that was only partially noted or which has lost its affective force in the retentional chain. Phenomenological investigation of memory probes contexts of simultaneity and of succession to try to understand how those phenomena are interrelated in the single stream of consciousness. While retentions and memories are often unclear or undetermined, they may nevertheless be clarified. The reactivation of a memory may in addition shed light upon another memory; it may relate and connect memories that were not initially connected and shed light upon their experiential value. The whole "stream of consciousness of retentions and memories is a field of experiential investigation in itself" (Husserl 2006, p. 72).

This process is valid for subjectivity, but could phenomenological reduction be transported to the intersubjective space and help to gain access to the other, to understand the other? As asked by the author: "Do we ever arrive at an *other* phenomenological I? Can the phenomenological reduction ever arrive at the idea of several phenomenological I's?" (Husserl 2006, p. 82). Husserl would say that it could. Through empathy, double phenomenological reduction is imported to the intersubjective space and applied in the face-to-face encounter with the other (Husserl 2006). Empathy is a particular empirical experience, and may also be the object of phenomenological reduction, the space of intersection, where a subjectivity may have access to the comprehension of another subjectivity. It is important here to mention some aspects that are particularly important for the therapeutic relationship and which constitute a reading of Husserl. What is affirmed is that, through empathy, it is possible to access the comprehension of another. However, Husserl constantly affirms that there is a law that reminds us that, even in the sphere of empathy, I do not have access to the same thoughts, emotions and experiences of the other. The crucial question is that the empathic experience may become fundamental precisely because there does not exist any total connection or fusion between two people. When phenomenological reduction is applied to empathy and to the face-to-face encounter, a person may get beyond his stream of consciousness and gain access to the experience of the other. Here there is shared access and an experiential connection is effectively given; two people "accommodate themselves to each other" (Husserl 2006, p. 162), influencing each other motivationally, in reciprocal comprehension of thoughts and emotions, which may in turn bring relief, and cognitive and emotional transformations. But the reason why empathic experience may be particularly powerful is because the independence between the people is never broken. The space of alterity is assured in the intersubjective encounter. It is precisely because there is independence between two autonomous selves, phenomenological reduction can produce significant experiential effects. The empathic connection exists because a primordial independence is maintained simultaneously with the interrelational unity between the subjectivities. In addition to constitutional alterity between subjectivities, two dimensions are crucial to promote that empathic space of bonding and differentiation: the objective time and space of the natural attitude. The question that Husserl seems to highlight is that experiences of the natural attitude function as *indices* from which those same experiences may be analyzed phenomenologically. It is because the face-to-face encounter takes place in the sphere of the natural attitude that reduction, when applied, is no longer only about the individual experience, but also about the natural attitude of the self and of the other person that is present in the face-to-face encounter. *Empathic reduction is co-reduction* (Husserl 2006). The natural attitude is a space from which experiences, through empathy, become indices of intersection between two autonomous experiential systems. In that space of intersection, the objective time of the natural attitude is a bridge for the two consciousnesses that live a mutual experience in the same Now. Sartre demonstrated in his phenomenological analyses of shame and fear that the gaze of the other is not received only as a spatializer but also as a temporalizer. Simultaneity presumes a temporal connection of two co-existences that are not linked in any other way, so that the gaze of the other attributes another dimension to the time of a subjectivity. At that moment, according to Husserl, there is an experience of *mirroring*, which, in the sphere of the therapeutic encounter, may be termed *experiential validation:* "any possible empathy is the 'mirroring' of each monad in the other, and the possibility of such mirroring depends on the possibility of a concordant constitution of a spatial-temporal nature, of an index for the respective constitutive lived experiences, which index extends into all I's" (Husserl 2006, p. 164).

Experiential validation presupposes an *affective reflexivity*. It is not only a cognitive or merely emotional process, but a harmonization of total co-existences in which both dimensions are inherent. But this experience of experiential validation is viable for two concomitant reasons: there is a profound empathic experience between two people and neither is the "victim of reduction" (Husserl 2006, p. 160) of the other; neither is dependent upon the meaning that is achieved by each of the individualities in the dyad; on the contrary, what is achieved is "in itself and for itself and conceived through its own being" (Husserl 2006, p. 164). This aspect has resonance with the notion of an *original experience of co-existence* when I experience the Other having an experience of me. For that reason, the existential approach has always insisted on the concept of *presence* as a central dimension that influences the therapeutic process, including the therapist. Through a complete human presence, the therapist is co-present in the relational field of the other and only thus is it possible to truly "see" the other. In this sense, the therapeutic space reflects the principle of constitution of self-development and of a personal identity. It is a continuous process of validation through a person that is in tune with the affectivity of another, which enables the emotional experience to be strengthened and consolidated, and for the latter to consequently develop. It is a space in which my indirect experience of the other coincides with my experience and through which I see myself through the eyes of the other. That gaze of the other may transform me. As Sartre mentions, through the gaze of the other, not only am I transformed, but there also occurs the total metamorphosis of the world. This chapter has focused above all on a theoretical component concerning a series of concepts, which require subsequent adaptation and integration into the praxis of existential psychotherapy.

References

Bernet, R., Kern, I., & Marbach, E. (1993). *An introduction to Husserlian phenomenology*. Evanston: Northwestern University Press.

Depraz, N. (2001). Husserlian theory of intersubjectivity as alterity. In E. Thompson (Ed.), *Between ourselves*. Thorverton: Imprint Academic.

Donohoe, J. (2004). *Husserl on ethics and intersubjectivity. From static to genetic phenomenology*. New York: Humanity Books.

Drummond, J. L. (2003). The structure of intentionality. In D. Welton (Ed.), *The new Husserl. A critical reader*. Bloomington: Indiana University Press.

Gallagher, S., & Zahavi, D. (2008). *The phenomenological mind*. New York: Routledge.

Heidegger, M. (1962). *Being and time*. Oxford: Basil Blackwell.

Heidegger, M. (1988). *The Basic Problems of Phenomenology*. Indianapolis: Indiana University Press.

Held, K. (2003). Husserl's phenomenology of the life-world. In D. Welton (Ed.), *The new Husserl. A critical reader*. Bloomington: Indiana University Press.

Husserl, E. (1970). *The crisis of European sciences and transcendental phenomenology*. Evanston: Northwestern University Press.

Husserl, E. (1977). *Phenomenological psychology*. The Hague: Martinus Nijhoff.

Husserl, E. (1989). *Ideas pertaining to a pure phenomenology and to a phenomenological philosophy: Second book*. Dordrecht: Kluwer.

Husserl, E. (1994). *Lições para uma fenomenologia da consciência interna do tempo*. Lisboa: Imprensa Nacional—Casa da Moeda.

Husserl, E. (1997). The Amsterdam lectures on phenomenological psychology. In *Psychological and transcendental phenomenology and the confrontation with Heidegger*. Dordrecht: Kluwer.

Husserl, E. (1998). *Ideas pertaining to a pure phenomenology and to a phenomenological philosophy: First book*. Dordrecht: Kluwer.

Husserl, E. (2001a). *Analyses concerning passive and active synthesis. Lectures on transcendental logic*. Dordrecht: Kluwer.

Husserl, E. (2001b). *Meditações cartesianas*. Porto: Rés.

Husserl, E. (2001c). *Logical investigations*. Oxon: Routledge.

Husserl, E. (2006). *The basic problems of phenomenology*. Dordrecht: Springer.

Merleau-Ponty, M. (1982). Phenomenology and psychoanalysis. Preface to Hesnard's L'Oeuvre de Freud. In K. Hoeller (Ed.), *Merleau-Ponty & psychology*. Atlantic Highlands: Humanities.

Merleau-Ponty, M. (2002). *Phenomenology of perception*. London: Routledge & Kegan Paul.

Mohanty, J. N. (2008). *The philosophy of Edmund Husserl*. New Haven: Yale University Press.

Montavont, A. (1999). *De la passivité dans la phenomenology de Husserl*. Paris: Presses Universitaires de France.

Orange, D., Atwood, G.E.,& Stolorow, R.D.(1997). *Working intersubjectively contextualism in psychoanalytic practice*. New York: Psychology Press.

Rodemeyer, L. (2003). Developments on the theory of time-consciousness. An analysis of protention. In D. Welton (Ed.), *The new Husserl. A critical reader*. Bloomington: Indiana University Press.

Sartre, J. P. (1943). *L'être et le néant*. Paris: Gallimard. Translated into English as *Being and Nothingness* (1953). Abingdon: Routledge.

Sartre, J. P. (1994a). *A Transcedência do Ego*. Lisboa: Edições Colibri.

Sartre, J. P. (1994b). *A Consciência de si e Conhecimento de si*. Lisboa: Edições Colibri.

Sousa, D. (2014). Validation in qualitative research. General aspects and specificities of the descriptive phenomenological method. *Qualitative Research in Psychology, 11*, 211–227.

Spiegelberg, H. (1994). *The phenomenological movement*. London: Kluwer.

Spinelli, E. (1997). *Tales of un-knowing. Eight stories of existential therapy*. New York: New York University Press.

Spinelli, E. (2001). *The mirror and the hammer. Challenging orthodoxies in psychotherapeutic thought*. New York: Continuum.

Spinelli, E. (2007). *Practising existential psychotherapy. The relational world*. London: Sage.

Steinbock, A. J. (1995). *Home and beyond. Generative phenomenology after Husserl*. Evanston: Northwestern University Press.

Stolorow, R. (2007). *Trauma and human existence*. New York: The Analytic Press.

Stolorow, R. (2009). Individuality in context. *International Journal of Psychoanalytic Self Psychology, 4*, 405–413.

Yalom, I. (1980). *Existential psychotherapy*. New York: Basic Books.

Zahavi, D. (1999). *Self-awareness and alterity. A phenomenological investigation*. Evanston: Northwestern University Press.

Zahavi, D. (2003). Inner time-consciousness and pre-reflective self-awareness. In D. Welton (Ed.), *The new Husserl. A critical reader.* Bloomington: Indiana University Press.

Zahavi, D. (2004). Alterity in self. In S. Gallagher, S. Watson, Ph. Brun, & Ph. Romanski (Eds.), *Ipseity and alterity. Interdisciplinary approaches to intersubjectivity.* Rouen: Presses Universitaires de Rouen.

Zahavi, D. (2005). *Subjectivity and selfhood. Investigating the first-person perspective.* Cambridge: The MIT Press.

Zahavi, D. (2007). Self and other: The limits of narrative understanding. In Daniel D. Hutto (Ed.), *Narrative and understanding persons.* Cambridge: Cambridge University Press.

CHAPTER 3

Existential Psychotherapy: The Genetic-Phenomenological Approach

In this chapter we will present a model for existential psychotherapy. We will define its theoretical underpinnings, which will in turn provide the framework for a psychology-based psychotherapeutic practice. We shall seek to show how the existential approach can easily draw connections between its theoretical and practical underpinnings and empirical research, and thereby promote successful psychotherapeutic interventions. This chapter will accordingly seek to connect the issues dealt with in Chap. 1, on research into psychotherapy, with the theoretical dimensions discussed in Chap. 2, where we identified the concepts and theory of the genetic-phenomenological approach.

The world of psychotherapy is still riven by divisions which bring no benefit to the field. It is also our belief that a series of misconceptions exist *within* existential psychotherapy. These are partly responsible for existential psychotherapy's status as an outsider in the world of psychotherapy, excluded from mainstream research and consequently held back from achieving political, academic or social influence. Let us look first at some of the features of this approach and sketch the historical background, which will then allow us to address the misconceptions to which we would like to draw attention. Existential

---

This chapter has some parts based on a original paper: Existential Psychotherapy. The Genetic-Phenomenological Approach: Beyond a Dichotomy Between Relating and Skills. *Journal of Contemporary Psychotherapy*. 45:69–77.

© The Author(s) 2017
D. Sousa, *Existential Psychotherapy*,
DOI 10.1057/978-1-349-95217-5_3

psychotherapy[1] has traditionally focused on issues of *being* rather than *doing*, promoting *understanding* rather than *explaining* (Spinelli 2007; May et al. 2004), and preferring *description* over *interpretation* (Spinelli 2007). The essence of existential therapy is found in the notion of *presence*, which is to say that presence can emerge and be experienced in the *human encounter* between the client and the therapist (May et al. 2004; van Kaam 1958). Rather than put forward a set of new therapeutic techniques, existential psychotherapy has sought, since its foundation, to present an analysis of human existence. A therapist who wanted to read existential handbooks as texts of therapeutic techniques would be disappointed (May et al. 2004). Several factors may have contributed to this scenario. Historical reasons: the approach was characterized at one point of the twentieth century as a critical alternative to psychodynamic and behavioral models. Theoretical reasons: existential psychotherapy does not advocate application of the medical model of psychotherapy. The basis of this approach is not focused on identifying diagnosis, nosological categories, symptoms, or the ill side of the individual, but rather the whole individual, in his human existence that encompasses all dimensions of being in the world. Practical reasons: rather than focusing exclusively on a medical perspective, in which the therapeutic goal is centered on healing, the therapist does not apply a set of techniques that would bring about remission of the symptoms or the disease. Scientific reasons: the existential-phenomenological tradition has criticized the scientific context that has granted the natural sciences a monopoly over the epistemological decision-making process, regarding the definition of what is valid scientific knowledge. Cultural: existential phenomenology has criticized the danger inherent in the excessive technologization of human beings. Summarizing, to explain the techniques of existential psychotherapy might mean adhering to a medical model, and manualization of the existential approach would amount to losing its most important specific feature—the human dimension. In addition to these aspects, connected more to criticism of psychotherapy techniques, the approach has also taken issue with the type of scientific research which is carried out in psychotherapy. The authors believe that measurement of human activities and feelings is always limited and biased. Hence, existential psychotherapy has been aloof and critical concerning the empirical research conducted in psychotherapy, and this, in our view, has had negative consequences (Sousa 2004). As a result of this stance, existential psychotherapy is poles apart from evidence-based practice, and consequently sidelined from the main debates and decision-making centers in psychotherapy. Certain authors have even argued that the future of existential psychotherapy is uncertain, some even anticipating that its global importance is set to dwindle over the decades ahead (Norcross 2016).

The issues referred to above which characterize existential psychotherapy are strong points, and a valuable contribution to the psychotherapy community. We have no wish to repudiate the historical and theoretical legacy of the existential approach. One of its great strengths, in our view, is the epistemological roots of the approach. Existential psychotherapy was born under the influence of existential phenomenology. This field of philosophy is extremely fertile and has contributed decisively to how we see mankind. But if we regard these features as positive, what are the misconceptions we believe to exist in the world of existential psychotherapy? In the first place, the existential approach should not be presented as a philosophical approach. The approach is based on an existential-phenomenological epistemology, but is not distinguished from other therapeutic models for being philosophical—all models have philosophical roots—since its theoretical principles are rooted in psychology and psychotherapy. So the approach is based on psychological constructs which, in turn, sustain an existential psychotherapy which meets the standards of a *bona fide* therapeutic intervention. Secondly, existential psychotherapy is not based only on what are called relational interventions, nor should it be presented as an anti-technical approach. On the contrary, it makes use of relational stances *and* specific technical interventions, as we shall demonstrate here. At a practical level, the dichotomy between "being qualities" and techniques is not present, as both are present and influence each other. Thirdly, existential psychotherapy should incorporate in its practice the main contributions and knowledge yielded by scientific research, as these have proved to be particularly useful and effective, irrespective of the psychotherapist's theoretical approach. In addition, not only does participation in scientific research in no way contradict the epistemological roots of the existential approach, but also conducting research is a fruitful way of questioning our actual knowledge of existential intervention. Alongside clinical experience, it is a way for us to keep learning on an ongoing basis. One of the risks which any theoretical field may run is when it turns into an ideology. Scientific research is just one of the ways in which we can question our convictions and apparent certainties. In addition, research has already shown that it is useful in producing theoretical and practical knowledge which in the last instance benefits the clients of psychotherapy. Finally, as will be clear, since its founding the approach has advocated theoretical and practical principles that are in line with the latest research findings in psychotherapy. Fourthly, we believe that the theory and practice of existential psychotherapy are fully in keeping with the assumptions of evidence-based practice. We should distinguish clearly between a position that defends empirically supported treatments and the defense of evidence-based practice. As we saw in Chap. 1, the two positions are not synonymous, meaning that we defend the usefulness of a practice which is based on empirical evidence. We are in agreement with other practitioners of the existential approach who defend the idea that the underpinnings of the existential approach are in keeping with the criteria of evidence-based practice (Hoffman et al. 2015). Fifthly, the practice of existential psychotherapy is in keeping with the main factors (cutting across the different theoretical models) that contribute to therapeutic change, as we will argue in this chapter. Although one of the main concerns of existential psychotherapy is to defend an ethical stance (Cooper 2007), we believe it is more important to demonstrate and argue that in reality the approach already reflects and includes the main factors of psychotherapeutic effectiveness. The ethical issue is already quite clear. The entire existential stance is based on deep respect for human subjectivity. In addition, we should be careful when we refer to this, as we may unwillingly imply that other approaches lack the same concern. The values of humanism are actually regarded as a common factor in psychotherapy (Wampold 2012).

Taking into consideration all the aspects mentioned above, this chapter aims to (1) summarize the theoretical underpinnings of the genetic-phenomenological approach (presented in the previous chapter); (2) summarize the principles supported by scientific evidence (presented in the first chapter) that will be integrated in the genetic-phenomenological approach of existential psychotherapy; (3) present and define the relational stances and the therapeutic techniques of the genetic-phenomenological approach; (4) exemplify how to carry out case conceptualization using the genetic-phenomenological approach; and (5) give practical examples of case conceptualizations and the application of the approach taking in consideration all the aspects mentioned in the previous points.

EXISTENTIAL PSYCHOTHERAPY: THEORETICAL UNDERPINNINGS

The theoretical underpinnings of the genetic-phenomenological approach were presented in the previous chapter. However, in order to follow the aims of this chapter and to help the reader, a summary of the key concepts is presented:

(1) *Intentionality.* This means that every conscious act, be it a perception or the recollection of a fantasy, has a meaning or particular significance (Husserl 1977). Intentionality implies an intrinsic relationship between consciousness and the world. One cannot be separated from the other. For phenomenology, any phenomenon is an intentional experience. The focus of phenomenological investigation, to go beyond an empirical and causal point of view, is to find the meaning of the human experience. Because we are in the world, we are condemned to give meaning to our existential project (Merleau-Ponty 2002).

(2) *inner time-consciousness* theory is an explanation of the prereflective structure of consciousness (Husserl 1989) which is in turn one of the main areas in therapeutic work. Inner timeconsciousness is the prime space for constituting of identity. Albeit in a unity, there is a connection between stream of consciousness, experiential self and identity.

(3) *experiential self/narrative identity.* The perspective on the prereflective structure of consciousness means that all and any experience in a first-person perspective immediately implies a basic awareness of self (Husserl 1994; Zahavi 1999). This basic selfhood does not yet mean self-awareness that needs to be developed through a narrative identity.

(4) *Passive geneses* are like subsoil where meanings which were sedimented throughout the different phases of development maintain their influence on the self. Inner-time consciousness and passive geneses form a theory about the way sedimentations are shaped and transformed into habits. These meanings can reflect ways of being or behaviors that are reasonably flexible, or more rigid and profoundly sedimented, and hence resistant to change (Spinelli 2007). Existential conflict can arise in two ways: from reflective confrontations with the givens of existence; because the worldview is dissonant with lived experiences, and is always submersed

in the uncertainty inherent to the development of the life-project in each relational context (Yalom 1980).

(5) *Existential angst*. Associated with the concepts just described, this is psychological suffering, or the associated disorders found in human life, which are an intrinsic possibility of human existence. Angst is inherent to the human condition (Kierkegaard 1980; Heidegger 1962). If on the one hand, we are beings that construct meaning in our life, on the other, we face a constant openness to the uncertainty of the very meanings we establish in the existential dimensions, as those meanings are in permanent becoming and are established in an interrelational space. The meaning of human existence is dependent on intersubjective relational contexts. Angst is not seen exclusively as a disease, but an integral part of our human essence. Existential angst is simultaneously a possibility of personal transformation, but is also, a source of psychological suffering and of limitations to individual freedom.

(6) *Interrelatedness*. Everything that is constructed about us, about others, or the world, is grounded in relatedness (Spinelli 2007). This implies that, to reflect on any aspect of existence or to arrive at any conclusions about it, one must begin in inter-relatedness. As such, any divide, such as I-thou, I-world, mind-body, is (simply) an abstraction and a form of expression of being-in-the world of a particular person. The relational backdrop (intersubjectivity) that permeates all human existence is actually the prime matter from which all subjective experiences are constructed. The existential approach assumes an intersubjective perspective on human development. By going beyond only the uniqueness and individuality of beings (the intra-psychic dimension), phenomenological investigation identifies the relational context (the inter-psychic dimension) as primary.

(7) *The givens of existence*. Existential psychotherapy assumes that human existence is characterized by several general dimensions (ontological), although these are given their unique and specific lived expressions by each subjective being (ontic). Existence extends itself until the end of time (temporality) and is always situated within a context (spatiality). Existence presupposes an intrinsic conflict between facticity (limited conditions), finitude

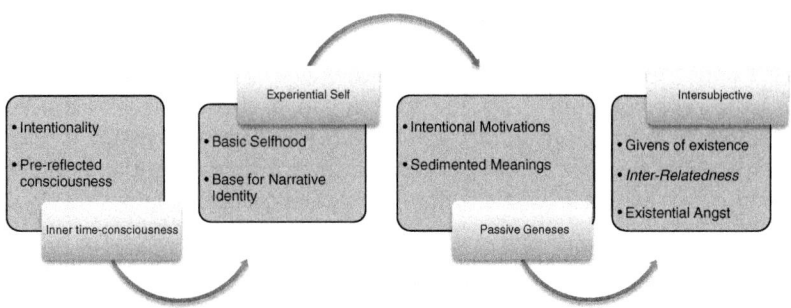

Fig. 3.1 The genetic-phenomenological underpinnings

(death), and the freedom to choose between the various possibilities inherent to the development of a life-project. Existential psychotherapy sees human subjectivity as intrinsically free to make choices, where each individual is responsible for the way he/she is in the world, and for the relationship established with him/her and others (Fig. 3.1).

Theses concepts are methodologically framed by Edmund Husserl's static and genetic methods. Below we will present the relational stances and the specific techniques framed by the genetic-phenomenological underpinnings and methods. First, a summary of key principles from research is presented.

INTEGRATION OF THE PRINCIPLES OF SCIENTIFIC EFFECTIVENESS IN EXISTENTIAL PSYCHOTHERAPY

As already stated, *principles supported by scientific evidence* (defined in Chap. 1) are integrated in existential clinical practice. Without pretending to be exhaustive, we shall set out briefly the principles of scientific effectiveness to which we are referring, in order to be able to demonstrate, in the following sections, how they can be integrated into existential intervention, and how they are in keeping with its theoretical and practical underpinnings. For an in-depth exploration of these concepts, to be integrated into existential psychotherapy, the reader may consult Chap. 1.

The Theoretical Rationale

Existential psychotherapy makes it possible to provide an explanation for the problems, questions and suffering that clients bring to psychotherapy. As we have seen, one of the common factors in psychotherapy, and possibly one of the most crucial, is that of the psychotherapist presenting an explanation that fits the patient's complaints (Wampold 2012). Existential psychotherapy not only presents a convincing theoretical rationale but also combines a series of therapeutic actions which the patient feels as having a healing effect. We don't mean by this that the existential approach follows a directive course. In the sense of "giving" the answers to the patient. What it does mean is that the approach has a theoretical model that offers a framework for a series of answers to the patient's issues. The way in which these answers will be found depends on a number of factors, in particular the patient's characteristics and the relational dynamic established in the therapeutic process. As we have seen, one of the most crucial factors for any human curative context is for it to present an explanation for the person's problem, for this explanation to be consistent with its theoretical rationale and philosophical grounding, which in turn inform a series of practices which are also consistent with the rationale and which are felt and accepted by the patient (Wampold 2012). Existential psychotherapy considers these aspects and, on top of this, making use of one of its fundamental practices (the phenomenological method), it strives to ensure that the explanation developed in conjunction with the patient is above all accepted by the patient and in keeping with his worldview. More important is that the scientific basis of explanation is acceptance of the explanation by the latter (Wampold and Imel 2015).

The Real Relationship and the Therapeutic Alliance

Scientific research has shown that the therapeutic alliance and, in particular, the real relationship are among the strongest predictors of good therapeutic outcomes (Zilcha-Mano et al. 2016; Gelso 2014). The relational dimension is one of the cornerstones of the existential approach. The concept of the real relationship presupposes that for human beings it is fundamental to have an experience of belonging. This need is fundamental to our development. The fact that we are beings for whom a real relationship is crucial to our development as people has implications in the therapeutic context. In this context, the creation of a real relationship is a necessity. Likewise, it is argued in existential psychotherapy that everything we know about ourselves, others and the world "emerge[s] through an irreducible *grounding of relatedness*" (Spinelli 2014, p. 8). This concept also has implications for how the psychotherapist positions himself in the therapeutic relationship, both from a theoretical point of view, and also in practical terms. If there is anything that existential psychotherapy has proclaimed loudly since its founding, it is the creation and primacy of a real and genuine relationship between therapist and patient. Questions of how to manage ruptures and cracks in the therapeutic alliance have perhaps received less attention in the literature of existential psychotherapy. As we have seen, negotiation of ruptures in the alliance is one of the most important skills in psychotherapeutic processes (Safran et al. 2014).

Consensus on Aims and Level of Collaboration

At the start of the psychotherapy, it is of paramount importance to define the aims of the psychotherapy with the patient, and also that a consensus be reached on these between the patient and the therapist. Research has confirmed that the consensus on aims and also the level of collaboration have a direct impact on therapeutic outcomes. Both should be confirmed and negotiated over the course of the therapeutic process, along with the level of the therapeutic alliance, as these dimensions are highly dynamic and fluctuate over the course of psychotherapy (Lambert and Cattani 2012; Tryon and Winograd 2011).

Expectations

Like the consensus on aims and the level of collaboration, monitoring of patient expectations is a crucial aspect that the therapist should take into account. Positive and realistic expectations are associated with better therapeutic outcomes (Constantino et al. 2011). Expectations are important at several levels. They play a particularly important role in creating optimism and hope in the process of change for the patient. It is important, in turn, for the psychotherapist to be able to monitor the patient's expectations, not only so he can adjust the intervention, but also to assess whether the patient really believes that the intervention will be useful in overcoming his obstacles, and also to assess his level of motivation in the psychotherapy.

Feedback and Monitoring

Asking for patient feedback and monitoring the psychotherapeutic process reduces the dropout rate and promotes better psychotherapeutic outcomes (Lambert 2015; Lambert and Shimokawa 2011). There appear to be advantages in seeking feedback through objective measures, but psychotherapists can conduct monitoring and request feedback directly from patients, even informally at their sessions. One of the central aims of feedback is to have direct access to the patient's subjective perspective on the therapeutic process, finding out what is going well and, above all, what is not so positive for the patient from his own perspective. This point combines particularly well with the existential approach which lays great stress on the patient's involvement in the phenomenological method. This method is focused on a first person perspective. However, seeking feedback and monitoring the therapeutic process are specific actions that involve know-how which is also specific on the part of the psychotherapist.

The Psychotherapist's Interpersonal Skills

Research into psychotherapy has confirmed that one of the most important factors is that psychotherapists have good interpersonal skills (Anderson et al. 2016). Empathy is the relational factor which has received the most study, and contributes decisively to the variance in therapeutic outcomes (Elliot et al. 2011). Patients have systematically referred to the importance in psychotherapy of feeling safe, listened to, validated, support, understood and that they are not being judged by the psychotherapist. It is important to consider the ongoing development of therapist's interpersonal skills and that therapists should combine humility with a convincing and credible attitude (Rønnestad 2016; Chow et al. 2015).

Common Factors and Stages of Change

Common factors are essential for psychotherapists, irrespective of their technical model, and are no impediment to the application of specific interventions. Common factors, divided into support, learning and action factors (Lambert 2013), provide an essential foundation of factors that promote the success of the therapeutic process (Wampold et al. 2016). Common factors and specific techniques interact with each other (Norcross and Lambert 2011). Stages of change—pre-contemplation, contemplation, preparation, action and maintenance—can be regarded as points of reference in patients' therapeutic journey, irrespective of the therapist's theoretical model (Norcross et al. 2011).

The Active Client and the Psychotherapist's Responsiveness

Research has systematically shown that the patient is primarily responsible for the process of change (Bohart and Tallman 2010). This finding is definitively compatible with the principles of existential psychotherapy. Since the outset, this approach has argued that the patient is the agent of his own life and therapeutic process, locating the therapist as someone who is "side-by-side" with the patient (Spinelli 2007). The idea of the active client is even more vital when the psychotherapist is able to be responsive and capable of adapting the intervention to the characteristics of the patient's person (Stiles 2013). It is essential not to be restricted to diagnostic categories, and to consider above all the client's potential and personal characteristics (Beutler et al. 2016); The ability to supplant the reductive vision of the diagnosis, considering the patient's personal characteristics, and the psychotherapist's ability to be responsive, have been cited as two of the most important attributes for therapeutic interventions (Stiles 2013; Norcross and Wampold 2011; Stiles 2009). As already mentioned, existential psychotherapy encourages neither a medical-style perspective nor attempts to centre the intervention on the basis of an assessment of the diagnosis, meaning that the active patient and responsiveness are two concepts completely interconnected with phenomenological-existential theory.

AIMS, RELATIONAL STANCES AND THERAPEUTIC TECHNIQUES

A model in psychotherapy can be defined as a unified theory, or a set of theoretical assumptions about what is needed to promote change, and includes an insight into personality and individual development (Anderson et al. 2009). The therapeutic technique is a well-defined procedure implemented to achieve a specific task or objective, and skill is defined as the competence or ability to do something (Cooper 2008). The techniques can be operationalized according to their type and content (interpretation, paradoxical intervention), by the way they are implemented (level of empathy, congruence) and quality (moment of application, suitability to the client's need) (Hill 1995). The rationale of psychotherapy is that the therapist, on the basis of a theoretical model, applies specific techniques informed by the model, in order to promote therapeutic change. Some authors argue that existential psychotherapy is a philosophical, not a psychological method, and that it is an anti-technical approach (van Deurzen and Adams 2011). Techniques and skills are an obstacle to a true understanding of the human being; so the approach is based solely on a set of "attitudes" (van Deurzen 1995, p. 14). However, this position may result in methodological eclecticism (Walsh and McElwain 2001), leading to a lack of specificity about the know-how of the approach, or in adopting interventions that are inconsistent with the theoretical principles of existential psychotherapy (Spinelli 2007). Other authors argue that, maintaining the primacy of being over doing, the approach does not reject systematization of know-how and of therapeutic practices. The "being qualities", not excluding specific therapeutic postures, maintain the latter in perspective, not assigning them primacy in the conduct of the therapeutic process (Spinelli 2007; May et al. 2004; Schneider and May 1995). Our approach will be in support of this position and will refute the idea that existential psychotherapy is an anti-technical or a philosophical method.

Aims and Goals

Existential psychotherapy based on genetic-phenomenological approach, focuses on the analysis of meaning and existence. It assumes that: (a) based on the concept of intentionality, human beings have inherently the need to construct meaning from their existence; (b) people have the ability to choose freely and take responsibility for their existential project; (c) the confrontation with the givens of the existence and the construction of life, inevitably leads to challenges, limitations and dilemmas; (d) personal construction takes place primarily in the intersubjective space of relations with others and with the world.

The focus of existential psychotherapy is on the *interrelation dynamics* that are established between the client and therapist. The existential therapist's main goals are to:

- Facilitate a more accurate and authentic attitude towards one's experience of being and to make choices;
- Facilitate the processes of meaning-making in the face of one's existence;
- Promote self-strength and self-knowledge;
- Enhance the ability to confront the dimensions of existence;
- Identify and engage with existential angst;
- Improve reflection and self-awareness about the worldview (beliefs, emotions, thoughts, experiences);
- Increase consciousness about interpersonal processes;
- Increase personal responsibility for the existential project (accept freedom, limits and personal autonomy);
- Help to identify solutions and resolutions taking into consideration the client's request;
- Promote in the client the capacity to develop a more adaptive way of dealing with the questions, problems, complaints brought to therapy, regardless of whether it implies thoughts, emotions or behaviors;
- Explore with the client the essence (what I am) of existence (how I am) and personal identity (who I am) (Spinelli 2007, p. 61).

Despite the setting of aims in existential psychotherapy, there is another factor that takes precedence: the patient's request. It is the patient who should originate the psychotherapeutic intervention, which should accordingly consider what is most important to the patient. The theoretical model and the psychotherapeutic model should adapt to the patient, and not the other way around. There is a whole specific dynamic concerning the setting of therapeutic aims, which we shall address in detail. For example, the patient himself may be confused about the aims, and the psychotherapist may be able to help in clarifying them. However, the first principle is a phenomenological principle *par excellence*: starting out from the person and his own perspective.

Relational Stances and Therapeutic Techniques

Existential psycotherapy is defined in dichotomous versions, regarded as descriptive, or more interpretative, and as being phenomenological in nature, or conversely focusing on analysis of existence (Cooper 2003). We believe this is equivocal and raises more questions than it answers about the approach (Sousa 2015). Our perspective on existential psychotherapy advocates the combined application of static-phenomenological (descriptive) and genetic (hermeneutic) methods. The methods are linked to each other dialectically, and fit specific relational stances and techniques. The notion of *leading clue* is the bridge that nudges the psychotherapist to position himself/herself in a more descriptive (phenomenological) or more genetic (hermeneutic) manner, at a given moment in a session or in the therapeutic process. With relational stances, we have above all included actions that bring out the potential of the psychotherapist's relational and interpersonal abilities. Their focus is on the person's intentional experience. This is to say that the focus of the interventions is on the *how* of subjective experience. With the genetic method, more specific psychotherapeutic interventions may be seen, focusing on the origin of meaning of the client's experience. Here, more than understanding the *how* of experience, it is a matter of understanding the *why* and the root of the intentional meanings. From a conceptual point of view, the experiential self has ontological precedence over the narrative identity. This derives and develops from the experiential self. However, the experiential self and personal identity are closely connected. With the application of the static and genetic methods in existential psychotherapy, we are considering both dimensions simultaneously, that of the experiential self and that of personal identity. The relational stances and the therapeutic techniques will first be presented and defined schematically (Fig. 3.2; Tables 3.1, 3.2). We will then offer a number of clarifications and comments.

There is no assumption that the relational stances and therapeutic techniques presented above are unique to the approach. Interpretation, for example, is used and conceptualized by different therapeutic models. Our aim is to define the interventions and make explicit how they are framed in the theory and practice of existential psychotherapy. Some of the therapeutic interventions mentioned have already been proposed and defined in the existential literature. However, we defined some specific therapeutic techniques that are completely in line and fit with the

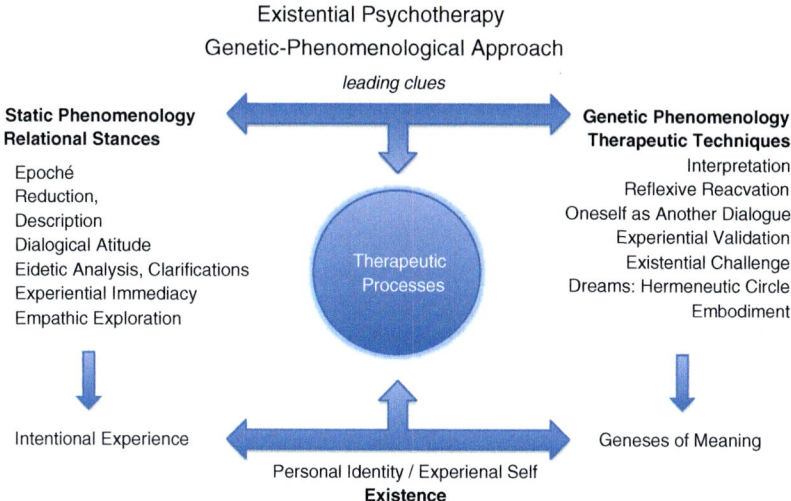

Fig. 3.2 Relational stances and therapeutic techniques

theoretical underpinnings of the genetic-phenomenological approach. Those are the cases of the relational *epoché*, experiential validation, oneself as another dialogue, and reflective reactivation. Another aspect we would like to highlight is that the way that relational stances and therapeutic techniques have been presented is for conceptual purposes. In fact, within the therapeutic process, the genetic and the descriptive, the relational stances and techniques intertwine one another and are mutually inter-dependent. We then add some comments about the interventions of the genetic-phenomenological approach, linking up with examples of research conducted in existential psychotherapy (Sousa et al. in press; Sousa and Vaz, in press; Alegria et al. 2016; Correia et al. 2016; Oliveira et al. 2012).

Since its founding, existential psychotherapy has always laid stress on the concepts of presence and encounter (van Kaam 1958), to highlight one of the pillars of the intervention: the genuine human relationship between the psychotherapist and the patient. It is our understanding that the descriptive phenomenological method, in conjunction with other relational practices, provides a space which is fundamental for establishing a strong therapeutic alliance. As we have seen, research has repeatedly drawn attention to the real relationship and the therapeutic alliance

Table 3.1 Existential psychotherapy: Relational stances (static phenomenology)

Relational stances	Description and aims
Phenomenological method (Static) *Epoché* Phenomenological reduction	Therapist *attempts* to suspend all his/her theoretical, personal and cultural assumptions. Identifies and avoids a judgmental attitude towards client. The aim is to help to develop openness in the therapist to focus on the client's meanings. The suspension of assumptions is a pre-condition for phenomenological reduction To focus exclusively on the intentional experience of the client, and the meanings associated with subjective experience. The main aim is to fully understand the client's worldview, his own perspective about self, the other and the world
Description leads to: *relational epoché*	Without preconceptions, discover the client's worldview, the meanings constructed and the sedimentations; understand the inter-relational contexts and recognize existential conflicts and paradoxes. Identify central issues (anguish, guilt, affection etc.). Discover if the narrative is integrated and connected to the client's experiential world. Since the goal is to have access to the person's world, the therapist promotes essentially, if possible, descriptive questions. Also, asks the client to describe his experience rather than give explanations. In many cases clients come to therapy because their own answers have failed. Sometimes clients acknowledge that, other times, without being fully aware maintain the same kind of answers. So the main goal of phenomenological descriptions is to reach a full understanding of *how* the beliefs, thoughts and behaviors are working or not working for the client rather than why The application of these three dimensions constitutes what we have defined as *relational epoché* (Sousa 2015). In *relational epoché* the therapist aims to create a time/space where the client *experiences* (cognition/emotion): a real/human relationship; understood; trust; accepted; listened; secure and support
Client's request/ goals and tasks	To clarify the goals and issues brought to therapy by client. To clarify aims and tasks defined by both client and therapist. Also, the therapist will check and ask about the client's expectations and level of motivation with regard to the therapeutic intervention. Depending on all these aspects the therapist will need to delineate different therapeutic strategies at the outset. It is very important that from the outset the therapist should monitor the level of collaborations between him/herself and the patient. At the end of the first session or at one of the initial sessions a therapeutic contract should be established

(continued)

Table 3.1 (continued)

Relational stances	Description and aims
Real relationship	A real relationship based on mutual trust and genuineness provides the foundations for a setting where the client is accepted and protected, in a safe yet challenging relational space. This relationship goes beyond the I-it (subject—object relation) towards the I-Thou (relationship between *people*) (Buber 1970). The constitution of a real relationship is a crucial step towards the establishment of a therapeutic alliance and the therapeutic process
Experiential immediacy	The therapeutic relationship and experiential immediacy (Spinelli 2007) are fundamental dimensions for access to the client's inter-relational contexts and the way he/she positions him/herself. The focus of existential psychotherapy is always on the client-as-is-relationally-present. The experience of the therapeutic here-and-now, is based on the conscious experience of the client, as he/she is relationally present. The relationship will be in many aspects the driving force of the therapeutic process. It provides the client with a real, live, human experiential laboratory-like experience before the therapeutic gains are transposed to other contexts in life. The *epoché* applied in the experiential immediacy presupposes that the therapist will be in a position of total acceptance of the client, so without having a morally approving or disapproving attitude, but always trying to *stay* with his/her way-of-being, just as he/she presents him/herself (expectations, perceptions, beliefs, angst etc.). Because the therapist isn't focused on problem-solving, the phenomenological stance on relational immediacy is the first challenge to the client's worldview
Active listening	The therapist tries genuinely to listen to the subjective, personal experience of the client without trying to change or propose alterations to the client's world-view or behavior. This procedure will in turn promote in the client the profound experience of actually being heard. The therapist may adopt an attitude of *active waiting*. In this case, the therapist may become aware of the client's difficulty in verbalizing or exploring certain issues in therapy. The main goal is to try to follow the client's timing. The feeling of being genuinely heard is identified by clients as being the first experience of acceptance and of personal change. Sometimes active listening provides a space in which the client can overcome personal obstacles. The client can verbalize whatever is able to express and experience the comfort of the therapist that respects his time and doesn't try to impose a specific pace

(continued)

Table 3.1 (continued)

Relational stances	Description and aims
Dialogic attitude	The dialectic of question and answer focused exclusively on the life and experience of the client helps to open up horizons (Gadamer 2003) in the client's discourse and beliefs. The dialogue is characterized by being dynamic and mutual. The question in this context takes the lead, the primacy. The dialectic of question and answer in the therapeutic space fosters a growing questioning of the self of the client, which is perceived as both challenging but also as a process of self-knowledge and discovery. The dialogic attitude is characterized by not being previously established. There is a dialectic dialogue, an undefined construction process, in which the two actors did not previously set a course. The therapist assumes a position of *un-knowing* (Spinelli 2007), a curious and genuine openness to the client's way of being. Still causing uncertainty, this situation promotes the client's feeling of involvement in the therapeutic process and his/her own effort in it. Makes it possible to create openness to possibilities about thoughts, beliefs, emotions and behaviors. The dialogue is often preceded by active waiting by the therapist
Reformulations, clarifications, and eidetic variation	In a way that differs from free dialogue, the therapist will intervene using clarification and rephrasing what was heard, trying to clarify and simplify significant issues found in the client's narrative. This makes it possible to distinguish what is essential from what is secondary. The client becomes engaged in the main issues of his own discourse and lived experience, while the excess detail that sometimes blurs or simply brings "noise" to the communication and self-awareness is set aside. Reformulations and clarifications help to create meaning from and with the content that is expressed by the client. It is like looking at the same content with different spectacles. This allows the clarification of paradoxes or contradictions in the client's discourse and a feeling in the client of being understood. He/or she feels understood by the other (therapist), which in turn, often brings about a rupture or a split from all other relational experiences lived before by the client. The eidetic analysis conducted with the client aims to help the essential dimensions of a given experience and to leave aside merely contingent factual variations

(continued)

Table 3.1 (continued)

Relational stances	Description and aims
Empathic exploration	Empathic exploration is a way of exploring in a deep way thoughts, emotions, and behaviors that are seen as problematic to the client. Empathic exploration has a particular resonance with the client's emotions and affects. The therapist reflects and communicates understanding of the client's emotional world. The therapist can thus clarify and synthesize using different words for the emotional content that is presented in the client's narrative, and can put into words the emotional content that isn't specifically identified by the client but is present implicitly. The empathic dimension, built upon relational security, permits the client's contact with his whole being, naming and bringing to light all of his/her feelings and emotions, even those felt as hard to deal with
	Clients may share experiences that have never been revealed, or they may find a new and liberating space for experiences that have never been shared before

The beginning of the therapeutic process focuses on three essential dimensions: the use of the *descriptive phenomenological method* (implies *epoché*, phenomenological reduction and description), clarification of the *goals and tasks* and the *client's request*, and the establishment of a *real relationship*. The establishment of a therapeutic contract (with goals/tasks) gives the therapeutic process a framework. The descriptive phenomenological method is a central dimension throughout the therapeutic process, coordinating with other techniques and practices. The relational stances are understood as central pillars of the therapeutic process, they are not specific techniques but general principles that are tailored to each particular situation, the moment in the psychotherapy, and what the client brings to therapy. The relational competencies are dependent on the clinical judgment of the therapist, and are based on its validation or non-validation, the context and relational network of meanings that is established between the client and therapist. The relational stances have a holistic nature, influence each other, intertwine and form connections with each other, and must not be construed as techniques for specific and isolated application

Table 3.2 Existential psychotherapy: therapeutic techniques (genetic phenomenology)

Therapeutic techniques	Description and aims
Reflexive reactivation	Phenomenologically, reflection upholds the distance between original and spontaneous experience, and the way it is integrated and apprehended in the worldview. Reflection is not a mere reproduction of experience, it brings along new reflective operations, new changes, and transformations relating to the lived experience. The therapist aims to promote a reflective self-awareness. It creates a suspension of the client's natural attitude, enhances insight, self-understanding and self-knowledge. It rests on the difference between the lived experience of natural attitude, and reflection on that same lived experience. It allows the patient to move beyond self-awareness towards self-knowledge, with another. Reflective reactivation associates ideas, lived experience, and memories. It increases the client's feeling of actively participating in the therapeutic process, while promoting self-knowledge. Reflexive reactivation may be promoted in several ways but one of the main aims is for the client to move from a pre-reflexive consciousness to a reflexive consciousness and therefore to be able to be more aware of his own thoughts and emotions. The reactivation of reflexive consciousness brings to the fore many aspects of the experiences, thoughts and memories of which the client is not fully aware
Experiential validation	Experiential validation is a cognitive and emotional process where there is a synchrony between two co-existences (client/therapist). It is a deep empathic experience between two people. It is an *original experience of co-existence* where one experiences the other, and as this last one, is experiencing me. The client feels validated, emotionally and cognitively reaffirmed, and this promotes the creation of a stronger foundation for personal identity. It encourages the client's self-acceptance of hidden issues that are typically unrecognized, guilt-ridden or seen as being worthy of criticism. Validation does not come specifically from the therapist as a direct affirmation, but comes from the inter-relational dynamic created in the therapeutic space. It is also necessary for the client to take action and integrate this experience. Experiential validation can occur through verbalization, through body language or even in silence. It promotes greater authenticity in the client, concerning him/herself

(continued)

Table 3.2 (continued)

Therapeutic techniques	Description and aims
Oneself as another dialogue	Through client or therapist verbalizations, the clients may become open to the unveiling or challenging of aspects of their self that are somehow present in their existence, but in an implicit way. The therapist may present possibilities ("As if a part of you was angry" or "as if a part of you says you're behaved badly", or even "more than betraying others, I have betrayed my values"). The therapist can offer a client-to-client dialogue (C—"There is a part of me that wants to fight for the family, but another part of me is very unhappy in this context" T—"Ok, if each of those dimensions were to talk to one another, what would they say to each other?" The goal is to create a distance between different parts of self, to encourage their acknowledgment, and promote a dialogue between these different dimensions of self that are often only present in a pre-reflected way. It helps the client recognize sources of anguish, promotes coherence, self-integration and a new recognition of oneself
Interpretation	Interpretation is always preceded by a *structure of comprehension* (Heidegger 1962) of the act in itself, the client's lived experience. Interpretation is above all else an *openness of possibilities*. It promotes articulation between the client's experience in a way that sometimes has never been done before, and exposes new meanings. Interpretation arises from the narrative and the client's experience. The therapist may give back insights or connections based on what was shared by the client, either from the present session, or from issues that have been presented before. Interpretation enables the client to reflect about his way of being in the world, and confronts him with personal issues that may be dissociated, thereby carrying further the exploratory process of therapy. When used, the interpretation that is meaningful for the client causes an impact on his relational and emotional world

(continued)

Table 3.2 (continued)

Therapeutic techniques	Description and aims
Existential challenge	Therapists challenge, sometimes quite directly, the client's assumptions, beliefs and sedimentations regarding his worldview. The first goal is not to offer alternatives or solutions but to increase the client's responsibility in order to attain a greater awareness of his beliefs and emotional experiences, which in turn, may lead towards occasional behavioral changes, deeper change of sedimentations or even some general change in the worldview. Existential psychotherapy makes it possible to challenge assumptions that are rigid, un-reflected or unquestioned regarding the client's way of being. It allows clients to confront their personal obstacles and resistances. Challenging existentially enables the client to question deeply, review and engage more directly with dilemmas, conflicts and existential tensions. It upholds responsibility and contextual freedom so the client may assume and own his existential project. The existential challenge is often experienced in the therapeutic relationship. Like interpretation and reflexive reactivation, existential challenge is often a pre-condition for the client to move from a pre-contemplative or contemplative stage to a more active phase. It sometimes helps the clients to review his beliefs and to move toward new solutions in their lives
Embodiment focus	Existential-phenomenology stresses that consciousness is always embodied. The psychological world is connected to existence through the body (Husserl 1989; Merleau-Ponty 2002). The body is not only an object for itself, nor is it merely exteriority of the psychological life. On the contrary, existence is realized in and through the body. Therefore, to address the issues of consciousness it is always necessary to consider them through and with the body. Existential therapy focuses as well on the expression of emotions, feelings, and behaviors, including those experienced as disorders, as lived through and inseparably connected with the body. Existential therapists invite their clients to describe the incarnational focus of their experience and to consider where it is located in a felt sense. Their aim is to assist clients in developing a more connected, or "owned", relationship with their experience via their embodied investigations. Existential theory argues that this investigation of embodiment via the phenomenological description of a felt meaning will enhance a greater awareness and connectedness to one's lived experience and in that way encourage a movement toward integration

(continued)

Table 3.2 (continued)

Therapeutic techniques	Description and aims
Dreams: Hermeneutic circles of existence	Dreams are valued and are generally treated as analogies of the relational dimensions of the client's existence, but eventually as an analogy of the therapeutic process. The exploration of dreams is initiated with the phenomenology of dreams. The client is asked to recall and describe the dream, its contents, objects, spaces, etc. Secondly, the dream is integrated within a hermeneutic circle that is present for both the client and the therapist, where both interact in order to create meanings that connect with the client's experience and often with the therapeutic process. In this phase, the dream is suspended and created between client and therapist like a spiral of meanings, articulated within the narrative and the lived experience of the client. This increases self-awareness, insight and has a powerful effect in terms of increasing the client's attention towards all the details and dimensions of his/her existence. However, in keeping with a phenomenological principle the client is not requested to bring their dreams. It is the client who will decide if makes sense to work with dreams in therapy

The genetic method enables a therapist to the use of therapeutic techniques. These are not applied in a manualized form but in conjunction with the relational stances. The use of an interpretation can be preceded by an empathic holding or descriptive phenomenological method. The relational stances are a constant background of the therapeutic process. The techniques are embedded with more specific goals. For example, after performing over a set of sessions a descriptive investigation of the sedimentations of the client's worldview, the therapist can introduce existential challenges to those beliefs, aiming at improving the client's awareness. Sometimes that it can happen within one session. The therapist will follow the concept of leading clues to decide which kind of therapeutic strategies makes sense to follow in a given moment. It is worthwhile to highlight that the reason to present the relational stances and the therapeutic techniques is this form is exclusively conceptual. At the practical level there are completely intertwined. An interpretation can be made with all the empathy, a challenge may be raised within a context of security, and so forth as two of the most important factors in therapeutic processes, with a direct impact on outcomes (Gelso 2014). In qualitative research into significant events in psychotherapy, from the patient's perspective, the dimension that patients pointed to most was the establishing of a "real and trusting relationship" with the therapist (Sousa and Vaz, in press). All the clients used similar expressions, such as those voiced in particular by this patient: "We developed a quite, quite good relationship (...) I don't question that he's there for me and that I can trust him" (Sousa and Vaz, in press). But patients also stressed that the real and genuine relationship with the therapists entailed "reassurance, support and safety". In conjunction, these factors helped clients to feel the safety and trust they needed to carry through the psychotherapeutic procedures, to create positive expectations and to establish a good level of collaboration with their psychotherapists. As stated by one of the research participants: "I did feel safe, yeah, really... express myself, and that I could go through those hives and, no, yeah, that was a real, real positive" (Sousa and Vaz, in press). In another qualitative study of existential psychotherapy, the creation of an authentic relationship between therapists and patients was regarded by the latter as one of the most important factors in the therapeutic process (Oliveira et al. 2012). In the same study, patients also pointed to a good level of collaboration with the therapist as one of the most important dimensions (Oliveira et al. 2012). The data yielded by these research projects into existential psychotherapy highlight again one of the most frequent findings of research into psychotherapy: the need for a good level of collaboration between patient and therapist (Lambert and Cattani 2012; Tryon and Winograd 2011), based on a genuine, trusting relationship. But it is important to note that, without prejudice to the level of collaboration, creating hope, expectations and creating meaning, existential psychotherapy underlines the concept of *presence* as being at the centre of all these effective dimensions (Schneider 2015). In other words, the experience of presence is an essential condition, a basis, for establishing this and other fundamental conditions for constructing an appropriate therapeutic space. No less important, from the start of the process, existential psychotherapy promotes active involvement by the client, considered to be an essential common factor (Bohart and Tallman 2010). One of the most important common factors! Since its origin, the existential approach has advocated something that research has consistently emphasized: clients are not dependent variables where the independent variables are applied, they are not diagnoses where techniques are applied (Bohart and Tallman 2010). The phenomenological method promotes what I call *relational epoché* (Sousa 2015). Together, client and therapist form an experiential space framed in time and space where it is impossible to create a single, unique world, different from the outside world, that allows the client to be in an emotional and reflective safe space, distinct from that he/she usually inhabits naturally. *Relational epoché* seeks to contribute to create seven fundamental dimensions of the therapeutic process, where the client should feel: a real/human relationship; understood; trust; accepted; listened; secure and support (Sousa 2015). With these therapeutic stances, the existential approach is fully in line with the common and relational factors mentioned in the literature as the main relational competences of the therapist (Norcross and Wampold 2011).

In another study, the Psychotherapy Process Q-Set (PQS) was used to analyze recordings of 48 sessions of psychotherapeutic processes following an existential orientation which took place over one year (Alegria et al. 2016). PQS is an instrument with 100 items divided into three sub-categories: (a) attitudes and actions of the therapist; (b) attitudes, behaviors and verbalized experiences of the patients; (c) environment and atmosphere where the session occurs and the nature of the interaction between the client and the therapist. The ten most characteristic items identified by order of importance were: (1) therapist emphasizes patient feelings in order to help him or her to experience them more deeply; (2) therapist is sensitive to patient's feelings, attuned to the patient, empathic; (3) therapist clarifies restates or rephrases the patient's communication; (4) patient's interpersonal relationships are a major theme; (5) patient's current or recent life situation is emphasized in the discussion; (6) dialogue has a specific focus; (7) therapist communicates with the patient in a clear coherent style; (8) therapist accurately perceives the therapeutic process; (9) patient talks about feeling close to someone or wanting to feel close to someone; (10) therapist is confident or self-assured (vs. uncertain or defensive); (Alegria et al. 2016). Several aspects of these findings may be in keeping with the general data from psychotherapy research and with interventions based on the genetic-phenomenological approach. Attention is drawn, in the first place, to psychotherapists focusing on patient's subjective experience, and the fact of the psychotherapist being particular empathic. As stated above, empathy, one of the factors most closely associated with psychotherapy outcomes, is a fundamental characteristic of the real relationship. Moreover, empathy is the relational factor most closely studied, accounting for approximately 9% of the variance in therapeutic outcomes (Elliot et al. 2011). The relational practices in the static method, such as experiential immediacy, empathic exploration and relational epoché, are designed above all to provide an empathic space for the patient and the security he needs to explore his emotional dimensions (Sousa 2015). These findings also attach importance to the interventions of the psychotherapist. Several of the 10 items address the therapist's interventions, and the last refers directly to the importance of the psychotherapist being confident and assured. As we have seen, the qualitative meta-analysis highlights the main characteristics of the therapist, as highlighted by clients; are felt as being careful, empathic, caring, supportive, are highly understanding and attentively listening and validating their patients' experiences (Levitt et al. 2016). In addition therapists are perceived by patients as being competent and credible (Wampold 2011). In addition, the findings also refer to the importance of therapists reformulating, clarifying and communicating coherently and clearly with clients. As already stated, the genetic-phenomenological approach includes reformulations and clarifications in the static method as one of the types of intervention that most facilitates the patient's ability to express himself.

Several studies have pointed out that existential psychotherapists make use of relational-style interventions, but also others of a more directive and interpretative nature. In a recent study, which includes developing an observational grid of existential practices, in which 32 sessions of existential psychotherapy were analyzed, the five types of interventions most commonly used by existential psychotherapists were: (1) relational practices; (2) hermeneutic interventions; (3) other practices; (4) phenomenological practices; (5) directive/confrontational interventions (Correia et al. 2016). The intervention most commonly cited in the dimension "other practices" was reformulations. The researchers expressed surprise at their finding that reformulations were more frequent than the actual application of the phenomenological method, and that hermeneutic interventions were ranked as the second most highly used type of intervention (Correia et al. 2016). However, these findings are consistent with the framework proposed above by the genetic-phenomenological approach. They are findings which also support what the empirical evidence has stressed: the interdependence between common factors and specific factors, the interrelation between more supportive, exploratory and relational interventions and interventions of a more challenging, interpretative and directive type (McAleavey and Castonguay 2013; Norcross and Lambert 2011; Wampold et al. 2010). In one of the studies of significant events in existential psychotherapy, clients refer to the importance of having had a process that provided a "release from personal experiences" (patient: "I kept feeling as the rest of the session went on that I just kept getting lighter and lighter, like there was just an unburdening feeling") but they also felt that their beliefs were being "challenged and deconstructed" (patient: "Yes, a challenge, a different point of view, statement, sometimes a mirroring, sometimes a mirroring just with a, trigger words… I feel quite challenged") (Sousa and Vaz, in press). In another study, looking at significant events in existential psychotherapy, which gathered descriptions of significant events from the patient's perspective, session by session, using HAT (Helpful Aspects of Therapy), the results were grouped into three main categories: intervention by psychotherapists, experiences in therapeutic space and impact on the patient (Sousa et al. in press). In the "therapist intervention" dimension, the type of psychotherapy actions most often highlighted by patients were: *feedback* ("the therapist having given me very clear feedback on what we had talked about helped me to develop a different perspective"); *challenge/confrontation* ("when the therapist confronted directly my usual stance wherever I am, both personally and professionally, it's like 'I'm just passing through' without really getting involved"); questioning/reflexiveness ("when the therapist asked me what I could so as not to feel so frustrated and angry"). These were the three types of therapist intervention that patients valued most highly and felt were most useful. In addition to these, *giving meaning* ("the therapist completely understood the central dilemma in my life and took an objective view"), *validation* ("it was the therapist telling me it was OK to have ambivalent or contradictory feelings") and *active listening* ("because the therapist listens to me very attentively and tries to understand") were the other three types of interventions by their therapists that patients valued most highly (Sousa et al., in press). Other researchers arrived at a more unexpected finding, that patients preferred therapist's directive interventions (Watson et al. 2012). These therapists, who had existential/experiential training, were particularly well equipped to intervene on a relational basis. However, the patients highlighted their more directive interventions (Watson et al. 2012). In addition to considering relational dimensions, research data on existential psychotherapy has shown that patients also value interventions in which the therapist gives feedback, makes suggestions, asks questions and advances other points of view. In other words, in addition to interventions of a more phenomenological or relational nature, the therapists also intervened in a more directive and interpretative way. All these researchers appear to be in some way surprised when they are confronted with what is commonly stated in the literature of existential psychotherapy, with regard to the dimension relating to the therapist's interventions. These studies, which are fundamentally centered on the patients' perspective, appear to suggest something which has long been regarded as part of the essence of psychotherapeutic processes: the ongoing dialectic between validation and challenge. Patients systematically undergo processes which lead to experiences of validation of their experiences and of themselves, and also experience moments when they are challenged and forced to rethink their beliefs, habits and perspectives of self. What we argue is that in the genetic-phenomenological approach these two essential dimensions, which occur through different types of intervention, make an equal contribution to the psychotherapeutic process. Even the phenomenological method (static), although based on a descriptive research, is a challenge to the client (Spinelli 2007). Description promotes issues and challenges beliefs and assumptions (thoughts, emotions, behaviors) partly immersed in a pre-reflective level in the experiential self. So whilst patients who have undergone existential psychotherapy stress the humanized, real and trusting relationship that made them feel validated and respected, they also value the fact that their therapists challenged them by questioning their personal beliefs and ways of being (Sousa et al., in press; Sousa and Vaz, in press; Correia et al. 2016). These data fit with the suggestion that, in the existential clinical context, consideration be given to dialectic use of the two phenomenological methods: static and genetic (Sousa 2015; Husserl 2001). With the static method, the therapist, through *epoché*, phenomenological reduction and description of his patients' experiences, is able to help his patients feel validated and succeed in other aspects essential to therapeutic processes: a human relationship, with trust, in which the patient feels listened to, understood and accepted, in a space felt to be safe and supportive (Sousa 2015). With the genetic method, the therapist introduces challenges and re-thinking of beliefs, as well as other types of therapeutic intervention, such as oneself as another dialogue, interpretation in the sense of opening up other meanings concerning the patient's experience and reflexive re-activation (Sousa 2015). Both methods function through mutual interdependence and are used at the right moment in the session or therapeutic process. This suggestion that the static and genetic methods are both applicable is consistent with two aspects highlighted by the literature on psychotherapy: (a) the need for the therapist to be responsive and to adapt to the person of the patient, rather than the patient adapting to the therapist's theoretical model, (b) the existence of a deep synergy between the human relationship and specific techniques (Beutler et al. 2016; Sousa 2015; Norcross and Lambert 2011). One of the reasons for the applicability and dialectic use of the static and genetic methods has to do with the need for the therapist and patient to construct a rationale for the issues which the latter has brought to the psychotherapy. The introduction of more interpretative, directive, reflexive or challenging interventions, carried out and based on a human relationship, allow people to create and transform meanings about themselves and their existence. The psychotherapist's success will depend on how far the patient believes in the rationale introduced by the therapist (or his model) (Wampold 2015b). In order for this to be achieved, and depending on the patient's characteristics and the context of the therapeutic process, the existential psychotherapist will have to be able to make use of specific therapeutic interventions and not base himself exclusively on the relational dimensions (Sousa 2015).

A final note on some of the interventions proposed by the genetic-phenomenological approach, in particular, reflexive reactivation, oneself as another dialogue, experiential validation and interpretation. In one of the studies mentioned above, concerning significant events in existential psychotherapy, the most important categories from the patients' perspective (1) awareness raising; (2) verbalization; (3) identification/exploration of new meanings; (Sousa et al., in press). The patients said that their increased self-awareness was what they valued most in psychotherapy ("I felt it helped me to a better understanding of myself, and that makes me feel more secure"). Secondly, the possibility of being able to verbalize, in part, many experiences which are or were felt to be difficult and painful was regarded as one of the valuable experiences over the course of the therapeutic process ("Having agreed to 'open up' and talk about emotions and issues I have felt since I was very little"). In the third place, the fact of having been able to formulate and explore new meanings about themselves, their most significant interpersonal relations, and about their way of being in the world ("I understood that I want to control everything, I even want to control my child's future. This was new for me") (Sousa et al., in press). Although this data clearly needs to be corroborated by further research, they shed some light on the theoretical rationale presented here and on how it relates directly to the type of therapeutic interventions. As we have seen, there has to be consistency between the rationale and the psychotherapeutic interventions. From a theoretical point of view, one of the generic aims of existential psychotherapy, albeit not exclusive to this approach, is to raise patients' self-awareness. The way in which self-awareness is raised derives from the different types of psychotherapeutic interventions, taking into consideration the stage of change, personal characteristics and the patient's relational stance. But the fact is that many patients highlighted an increase in self-awareness as one of the most important direct impacts, just as, in another study of existential psychotherapy, "self-knowledge and personal growth" was one of the most important impacts of existential psychotherapy (Sousa and Vaz, in press). The patients cited aspects such as: "therapy helps a lot, in that sense, and to know yourself better" or "look for my life and understand that why I am doing things, and how I am capturing it, so sort of grow really…" or "so I think it has been a growing environment". This aspect is particularly important. Let's look at the connection with the theoretical model (see Chap. 2). Experiences which occur, from moment to moment, are experienced by the person, although they stay at a pre-reflexive level in the temporal stream of consciousness (Husserl 1989; Zahavi 1999). It is only when reflexivity is introduced, in other words, when the subject reflects on his own experience, that this becomes an object for the subject. It is only at this moment that a difference occurs between the object and intentional consciousness (Husserl 1989). Reflection is a tool intrinsically linked to Husserl's phenomenological method. Pre-reflective consciousness does not apprehend its own experiences as object. There is no difference between the intentional experience and pre-reflective consciousness, and so the former cannot be understood as an object. Reflection enhances transformations, as mentioned above, does not therefore have a merely reproductive action; it actually alters the primitive state of experiences of the pre-reflective consciousness (Husserl 2001). Reflection gives rise to *new* cognitive acts and *transforms* experience (Zahavi 1999). It is a consciousness of itself based on *alterity* and *difference*. That is why the interventions such as reflexive reactivation, another as oneself dialogue and interpretations aim to promote an internal alterity, helping the client to gain some distance from himself. Sartre mentions a sketch of duality in a reflexive self-presence. This dual dynamic becomes a *unity* in which the reflex is the reflector (Sartre 1994). Husserl mentions that, when I reflect about myself, I am a subject that reflects and simultaneously I am an object that is being reflected about that object that I designate as *I* (Husserl 1977). In this sense, reflection is not only a mirror rather characterized by having a component of *otherness* (Zahavi 2004). So it makes sense to express *reflective self-awareness* as a therapeutic task and goal in existential psychotherapy. Reflexive reactivation, one of the techniques proposed, is also linked to inner time-consciousness and the passive geneses theories. Experiences of the lived present may reactivate retentions and passive geneses through an "associative awakening" (Husserl 2001, p. 120). In a stream of consciousness, in the experiential self, in the unity of a subjectivity, all experiences influence each other mutually. However, this process can be enhanced in the therapeutic process too. The importance of reflexivity in the psychotherapeutic process is something that has been stressed by authors subscribing to different theoretical models (Rennie 2010). The importance of reflexive reactivation is not necessarily an exclusive feature of the existential approach. What we want to underline here is how reflexivity is conceptualized theoretically in the genetic-phenomenological approach, how it can be viewed from the perspective of psychotherapeutic strategy and, lastly, how it contributes to therapeutic aims. So research appears to confirm that the theoretical rationale of the genetic-phenomenological approach has repercussions for intervention and, more importantly, on the therapeutic impacts and gains experienced by clients. In one research project, which involved 30 therapists from different theoretical approaches and 121 patients, it was concluded that the most important dimension was "raising self-awareness" (Castonguay et al. 2010). The authors point out that the therapeutic process provides opportunities for patients to obtain for themselves clearer perspectives on their experiences, whether cognitive, emotional or behavioral (Castonguay et al. 2010). This increase in self-awareness arises from previous activities, such as being able to talk about life events, experiencing a safe space, being able to symbolize and narrate their experiences, which appear to have an impact on patients and which in turns leads them to explore new meanings (Castonguay et al. 2010). As we have seen, both these dimensions—verbalization and exploration of meanings—were also crucial in the study of significant events in existential psychotherapy (Sousa et al., in press). In general, patients rated significant events as extremely useful or very useful, which underlines the importance assigned to these critical moments and the inter-dependence between the different factors. For example, verbalization was essential for reflexivity to be able to permit awareness raising, which in turn led to further exploration of the meanings of self. The consistency of these findings with those obtained in other psychotherapy research appears to suggest the vision of the contextual model (Levitt et al. 2016; Ekroll and Rønnestad 2016; Watson et al. 2012; Castonguay et al. 2010). The contextual model argues that different theoretical approaches, which have a convincing theoretical rationale for the patient's problems, and a series of therapeutic interventions consistent with this theoretical rationale, will in general be effective and will generically lead to the same outcomes (Wampold and Imel 2015). As can be seen in Fig. 3.3, both the principles of psychotherapeutic effectiveness, based on psychotherapy research, and relational stances and psychotherapeutic techniques contribute equally to existential intervention in the genetic-phenomenological approach.

Case Conceptualization

One of the reasons why a theoretical model is fundamental is because it gives the psychotherapist a framework in which to understand the issues that his clients bring to the psychotherapy. It is also through the

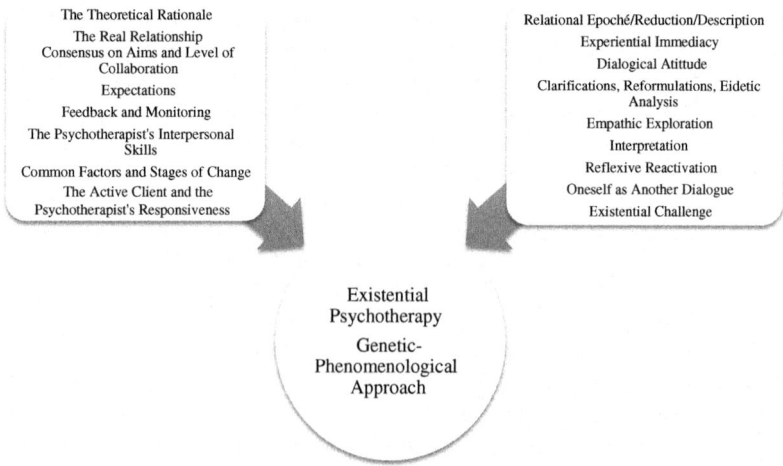

Fig. 3.3 The interdependence of the psychotherapeutic principles based on research and the relational stances and the therapeutic techniques of the genetic-phenomenological approach

theoretical model that a psychotherapist will delineate a psychotherapeutic strategy for the patient's issue. Case conceptualization allows the therapist to make a theoretical reading of the clinical case and to plan his psychotherapeutic intervention. So below we present how cases can be conceptualized, from an existential point of view. But our interest here is not just in conceptualization from a theoretical point of view. The aim is to describe how the psychotherapist can seek to follow the criteria of conceptualization, *as he progressively intervenes* in the therapeutic process. So we will look at theoretical aspects, but also at the psychotherapist's intervention, in order to demonstrate how conceptualization can take place over the course of the intervention. The genetic-phenomenological approach uses the following criteria in conceptualizing cases:

(1) **Identification of the client's request**. The first aim is to listen carefully to the reasons that led the person to seek psychotherapy. Listening to the request is fundamental and demands a great deal of attention from the psychotherapist. The person may arrive with a very specific and concrete request: "I've come here because I feel very, very anxious. "This", and I don't know what it is, has never happened to me before. It's like I can't feel well anywhere. When things get bigger I get really scared... they told me at the hospital that these are panic attacks. I've come here because I want to stop feeling this". In this case, although there may be other important issues for the psychotherapy, the patient may above all be interested in resolving situations of anxiety and not wish to embark on a therapeutic process for other aims. The psychotherapist focuses on the request. What exactly does the person want from the psychotherapy? Sometimes, the psychotherapist may uncover other issues of importance to the therapeutic process and to the person's actual well being, and can give this feedback before closing the therapeutic contract. However, there appear to be two particularly important aspects. The first is to respond to the person's request, and the second, in the event of identifying other aspects associated with the request, is that these issues should be clear for the patient. Provided they are addressed and clarified, other dimensions, which may be implicit in the request and important to it, can therefore be reflected in therapeutic goals and included in the dynamic which will establish the level of collaboration between the patient and the psychotherapist. In other

circumstances, the person's request might be vaguer. For instance, the person could say "I've always thought about having psychotherapy... it would occur to me from time to time... but I always put it off. I don't know why... but this time I decided to get in touch and book and appointment. I think a malaise has taken hold for a long time". This "malaise" which has "taken hold for a long time" could be the line of exploration which the psychotherapy would pursue. However, at first sight, the request is not apparently as explicit as that in the previous example. In any case, it will be important for the psychotherapist to listen carefully to the person, to seek to form a picture of the person and to focus on his narrative. Not infrequently, one to three sessions may be needed before the psychotherapeutic contract is closed. When this happens, one of the goals is to allow both the patient and the psychotherapist to reach together a sound understanding of whether the psychotherapy makes sense, and if so, with what goals. In any case, it appears to be important that the psychotherapist should give the patient feedback at these early stages. For several reasons. It is important for the client to know how the psychotherapist has understood what the patient has said and expressed. It is important, probably, that patient to understand whether the psychotherapist will provide him with a path forward for his issues and problems. These aspects can be misunderstood from an existential point of view. The approach is based on a fundamental assumption: people are themselves capable of freely making choices about their existence. The idea is not to overrule or to disagree with this goal. Indeed, one of the important tasks of the existential psychotherapist it to make it possible for the person to make his own choices freely. However, the question is that it may be important for the person to establish trust and even realistic hope that he will find on the way to these answers. So a person who is experiencing a moment of heightened vulnerability may need a stance of greater support from the psychotherapist. Depending on the patient's emotional moment, the psychotherapist should assess the type of feedback he can and it is appropriate to give to that particular person, at that specific moment. For some people, in certain circumstances, it is important to feel they will have the support they need to find answers again. In any case, it seems always to be important that the client should receive this feedback that provides a framework for the person's request, that explains what the psychotherapist understood about the patient's issues, which clarifies how far the psychotherapy can provide help for the issues the person has brought, and that explains how this help can be offered in the context of psychotherapy. In discussing the request, and when it is formulated between the patient and the psychotherapist, aspects are involved which are crucial to the whole psychotherapeutic process: reaching consensus on psychotherapeutic goals and tasks, management of the patient's expectations, and even those of the therapist, and assessment of the client's expectations concerning the psychotherapy. Clarification of the person's request should be provided within the framework of a psychotherapy contract, which also deals with practical and logistical issues (duration of the therapy, frequency of session, payment, rules on cancelling sessions, etc.).

(a) **Description and focus on the existential narrative**. The psychotherapist focuses on the person's narrative, on how he addresses the issues that he brings to the early sessions. At the start, depending on the person's request and the therapeutic goals, the psychotherapist may focus on one or other aspect in particular. However, the phenomenological principle par excellence is that the "phenomenon manifests itself to itself, starting from itself". This principle, transposed to psychotherapy, implies that as far as possible the person should be able to manifest or express himself, starting from his own meanings. In other words, the first aim of the existential psychotherapist is to *describe* the person's subjective existence. In this case, the phenomenological method (static), using *epoché* (suspension of the psychotherapist's beliefs) and phenomenological-psychological reduction, acts out precisely to gain access to the person's existential narrative, as far as possible, *from the person's own perspective*. This phenomenological stance on the part of the psychotherapist, who seeks to promote a descriptive dialogue, is combined with other relational dimensions and with other psychotherapeutic interventions. And above all, despite the phenomenological principle, the psychotherapist should not be inflexible in the stance he takes. For example, at a second session, a patient says: "you know, I've been thinking.... I'm not sure... you seem really young (allusion to the psychotherapist's age)... and I don't know if this is the right moment to start therapy..." If the psychotherapist followed the rule of the phenomenological method—in which the main aim is to describe the person's subjective experience—he might say: "What's it like for you to feel that I look young?" However, the psychotherapist decided to say: "Maybe what's worrying you is not my age. Maybe you're thinking whether I'll be able to understand you and whether you can trust that I will really be able to help you resolve the issues you told me about last week". Many other interventions would be possible. What the example seeks to illustrate is that although his first principle is the description phenomenological method, the existential psychotherapist should still regard this as a principle, and not as a rule. If he feels that at a given moment, even at the start of the psychotherapeutic process, it is more important to convey something to the patient in a different, non-descriptive way, he should do so. In the example given, he assigned priority to confronting the patient with what appeared to be her (legitimate) concern, relating to the psychotherapist's abilities. So knowing that it is fundamental to establish a good therapeutic alliance at the start of a psychotherapeutic process, the existential psychotherapist will not focus rigidly on his method, but will take in the personal characteristics and the relational style of the person before him, while he seeks to centre himself in the patient's existential narrative. In other words, although the existential narrative (i.e., in essence, the issues that the patient brings to the sessions) lies at the centre of the therapeutic dialogue, it is the psychotherapist's responsibility to adjust and adapt to the patient's relational style. Someone who may be more anxious may need the psychotherapist to provide more interventions of a supporting nature, instead of merely introducing descriptive issues. Someone else may prefer to use the psychotherapeutic space differently, and feel that he needs the psychotherapist to listen more than to intervene, given that the patient feels that he is himself coming up with answers, as he verbalizes his issues before another. In order to reach a better understanding of the patient's relational style, the psychotherapist may introduce feedback requests, even at the initial stages of the therapeutic process, in order to monitor the sessions and the psychotherapy. We have here an interrelation between the principles of existential psychotherapy and the principles of psychotherapeutic effectiveness. In this case, it is proposed that the psychotherapist may request feedback directly from the patient, concerning the psychotherapy. Even informally, without a form feedback system, the psychotherapist can ask "How have the sessions been for you?", "Is there something in the sessions you feel has helped you most?", or "Is there any aspect you feel has not gone so well in the psychotherapy?" The questions may be these or others, depending on what makes sense to the psychotherapist. However, it is important, from the first sessions onwards, to monitor the therapy and the level of collaboration between patient and psychotherapist. So in general the psychotherapist focuses on the existential narrative, without however ceasing to consider other important dimensions in the therapeutic process.

(b) **Gathering information on intentional meanings, sedimentations (self, other, world) and leading clues**. One of the main aims of focusing on the existential narrative is to identify intentional meanings, sedimentations of the person's worldview, and what we call leading clues in the psychotherapeutic space. From a conceptual point of view, as stated in Chap. 2, the sedimentations present in the self/the persons identity divides into sedimentations of: self, other and world (Zahavi 1999; Spinelli 2007). So by using the person's narrative, the psychotherapist will be able to identify the main sedimentations and intentional meanings. Sedimentations refer to thoughts, emotions and behaviors. For instance, the person may say "since childhood I have closed myself off in my own bubble. It was easier for me. Sometimes it was like I tried to come out ...but I soon wanted to be back in the bubble...I didn't feel well..." This part of the narrative provides indications on a sedimentation in the "world" dimension of his worldview. This possible sedimentation also points to a genetic point of view, i.e., to a historic character, concerning person development. As the person concerned is an adult aged 38 years, the person's description appears to point to a characteristic which has solidified. Sedimentations can be more or less rigid. This type of assessment is important for the psychotherapist because, once again, it will provide clues to the intervention strategy. It is not uncommon for sedimentations which have crystallized more to be difficult to change, and they may require ongoing therapeutic intervention, or more interpretative and less exploratory types of intervention. Clearly, there are no pre-set rules for the issue we are addressing. Not least because more important than the type of technique are the personal characteristics of the patient. What we wish to stress, above all, is that different psychotherapeutic interventions may be required depending on the degree to which the sedimentation is consolidated. At the same time, leading clues may be gleaned from the narrative. These serve basically two functions: (a) they tell the psychotherapist whether he should conduct the therapeutic process in a more descriptive or relational manner or else introduce interventions of a more hermeneutic nature or using therapeutic techniques with more specific aims (genetic-phenomenological method); (b) they are clues to sedimentations or intentional meanings in the person's narrative which may not be addressed at that moment in the session or the therapeutic process, but which the psychotherapist feels it is important to address in due course. In relation to item (a), we should clarify that the use of the leading clue, as information telling the therapist to move from a more descriptive to a more hermeneutic mode, is above all a conceptual form of presenting both phenomenological methods. At a practical level, as in many other circumstances and interventions in psychotherapy, the therapist takes these decisions in the moment, as if he were thinking about these issues, without however occupying his thought with these issues. It is something experiential—which includes the psychotherapist's cognition and emotions—rather than exclusively rational. Sedimentations are one of the central aspects in case conceptualization in the existential approach. An understanding of the sedimentations of the worldview permits the psychotherapist to reach an understanding of the being-in-the-world of the person before him. It is important to make connections between the reading of sedimentations and the request and psychotherapeutic goals, and to adjust the psychotherapeutic strategy in keeping with the dynamic between these factors. In this aspect of conceptualization, it is therefore very important for the psychotherapist to identify, in the existential narrative, as much information as possible that allows him to identify the person's main sedimentations. Rather than focusing on pre-set existential theme, the psychotherapist continues here to focus on the narrative described by the subject. This may contain themes which are called existential:

isolation or loneliness, finitude, responsibility for making choices, freedom of being, feelings of guilt, etc., But the psychotherapist's prime concern will not be to identify existential topics in the person's discourse. The issues may, or may not, arise explicitly or implicitly in the narrative. The central aim is to identify the themes, the most important issues that arise *from* the person's narrative. So the logic of phenomenology is paramount, and takes precedence over the application of a pre-set hermeneutic grid, even if based on ontological dimensions or the main existential dimensions, which all human beings have to deal with. By ontological dimensions we understand the aspects of existence that all individuals have to deal with, irrespective of how they do this. For instance, we all have to deal with death. Finitude is an *ontological* dimension. The way in which each of us, idiosyncratically and uniquely, deal with death is called the *ontic* way of dealing with death. In existential psychotherapy, these dimensions can crop up in the psychotherapeutic process. This is only natural, and the existential psychotherapist can clearly be more suited or sensitive to these issues, and detect their implicit or pre-reflexive presence in the patient's life experience. But what we want to stress is that the psychotherapist's aim is to identify the intentional meanings which are most important to the patient, in view of the therapeutic goals and the course of the psychotherapy, and not necessarily to be on the look-out for existentialist themes. Two crucial aspects should be stressed concerning sedimentations. First, they form "associative motivation networks", and second, they are largely to be found at a pre-reflexive level (Husserl 1989). On the one hand, sedimentations exert influence in regressive and progressive movements, in which past experiences may influence present behavior, or expectations, even when implicit, may reactivate or influence past sedimentations (Husserl 2001). On the other hand, this mutual influence between sedimentations and the vast dynamic that occurs in this network of intentional meanings, which are part of the experiential self, occur largely without the person being really aware of this (Husserl 2001). Following a chronological logic in the psychotherapeutic process, it is highly likely that some of the common factors (Lambert 2013) most frequently present at the start of the psychotherapy will be the common factors providing support (see Chap. 1). So although the psychotherapist is focused on the existential narrative and on identifying sedimentations, he will also take particular care with interventions that promote and take supporting common factors into account, as these appear to be truly important, irrespective of the theoretical model. In the first place, creating a real and genuine relationship, in which the patient feels the psychotherapist as a empathic and caring person, who doesn't make value judgments and accepts the patient just as he is. One of the supporting common factors is that the patient should feel psychological and emotional relief at the early sessions and that his isolation should be mitigated. Even if the patient's problems persist and there is an awareness of a road still to be travelled, it is a hopeful sign for the psychotherapy that the patients are at the same time able to feel a certain relief. On the other hand, one of the common factors is the patient feeling a structure and organization, transmitted by the therapeutic setting, which often contrasts with the meaninglessness, distress and lack of answers, often relational, which patients feel when they arrive at psychotherapy. It seems crucial for the patient to feel these dimensions, to experience the psychotherapy as a space where trust and safety are absolute, and also that the therapist, whilst being felt to be empathic, should convey a sense of credibility and capability, of someone able to help.

(c) **Identify areas of existential tension, distress and conflict.** Together with collecting information, through narrative and identification of sedimentations of intentional motivations, recognition of existential tensions, distress and conflicts will help to complete an important phase in conceptualization. As consistently stated by authors in existential psychotherapy, rather than a treatment to cure illnesses, the therapeutic process consists of confronting the person with his own existence. Once again, the psychotherapist's sensibility will be important. In many cases, the patients will verbalize the tensions present in their lives. Amorous relationships may be an example. A patient seeks psychotherapy because, apparently, she has decided to separate from her husband, although she is not able to do so. Aside from other factors, and even considering the need to assess the specific request, in this case an area of tension clearly emerges from the patient. In other circumstances, the patient is not always clearly aware at the time of existential distress or conflicts. At these times, it may be important for the psychotherapist to help to identify these tensions and to return this issue to the patient, at the opportune moment. For example, a man seeks psychotherapy because he senses extreme tension at work. His co-workers and boss single out his personal characteristics as the reason for his team, as a whole, failing to achieve their goals in the projects on which they work. When asked later in the session about other areas of his life, he broaches the affective dimension and his relationship with a female partner of several years' standing. After a number of more descriptive questions from the psychotherapist, and careful listening to the patient's narrative, the patient is presented with the following intervention: "listening to you speak about your relationship, the image that comes to mind is that you're always the centre of attention. And the centre of attention appears to be a permanent and continuous assessment of yourself and your behavior. Does this chime with what you feel in the relationship?" When the psychotherapist finished the intervention, the patient was weeping in a way that pointed to something important: "Yes, it's true, I feel that my partner is always judging me. She is very critical and she too is always finding fault with me, as if I were doing everything wrong.... sometimes I wonder whether it's right.. if she's not overdoing it..." Then the psychotherapist asks: "You said she *too* is always being critical. Is there someone else who also is?" The patient smiled, still with tears in his eyes, and said: "yes, me". Of course, several interventions would be possible in this small excerpt. What matters most here is that, as from this point in the session, it was possible to identify another area of tension and distress for the patient, despite it not being mentioned at the start, of included in the patient's express request. Following on from this, the issue of the relationship, but perhaps even more broadly, the way this man perceived himself, became part of the exploration and psychotherapeutic work, by mutual agreement between the psychotherapist and the patient. The psychotherapist's second intervention (descriptive phenomenological question) was intended to clarify whether a given characteristic, that of being over-critical, was part of the patient's way of being. On this point, we also have an example, of what was said about sedimentations and how they connect with each other in a network of intentional associations. So in this case it was important to clarify whether the criticism that this patient felt in intersubjective space, in both the professional and personal domains, was felt as something he felt in the behavior of others, or on the contrary whether a highly critical assessment of himself is part of one of the base sedimentations of the self. The answer to these questions will lead the psychotherapist to decide between different goals and types of intervention. In some situations, existential conflict areas as all but impossible to eradicate, from the patient's perspective they are something natural they are used to living with. The psychotherapist's aim, in this case, is not to bring about immediate change. He seeks instead to help the client gain awareness of these tensions. For many patients, it is hard to change. Even though the client may be suffering, the idea of change means venturing into unknown territory. At difficult moments in life, it seems preferable to stick to what we know makes us suffer, rather than enter unfamiliar territory, not knowing what it may hold. In addition, people know how to live with the limitations and advantages of the intentional meanings they developed over the course of life. Changing some of these knots of meaning sometimes has broader and deeper impacts on the person. Whilst these changes may be beneficial, it also appears important to respect the time and motivation needed by the patient himself to decide what changes to make, and when. Accordingly, over the course of the therapeutic process the psychotherapist will assess the stage of change that the patient has reached (pre-contemplation, contemplation, preparation, action, maintenance) (Norcross et al. 2011). The trans-theoretical model of change may be a resource, added to the level of existential change, described in the next section, and to the other information on the client (personal history, request, sedimentations, etc.). The patient does not follow a linear course over the different stages of change, just as he may be at different stages of change, depending on the issue or the psychotherapeutic goal addressed. So a given patient may more easily be at a stage of preparation and change for a given issue, and at the same time, in other psychological dimensions, still be at the pre-contemplation phase. On the other hand, moving from one stage to another is often far from linear, involving false starts and retreats. It is important that the psychotherapist pay careful attention to these vicissitudes and, if necessary, he should explain to the patient that this process is only natural. Lastly, different types of change and different types of common factors can overlap in stages of change. For example, it may be likely that the introduction of common factors of action, which include interventions where the psychotherapist encourages the patients to adopt new behaviors, may be counterproductive for a patient at the pre-contemplation or contemplation stage. It seems to be good clinical practice to adjust the intervention to the patient's stage of change, specifically concerning the psychotherapeutic goal.

(d) **Describe how the patient perceives himself and how he situates himself in inter-relational processes**. In many circumstances, existential conflicts and distress is connected to interpersonal relationships. For the existential psychotherapist, self is interrelational grounding (Spinelli 2007). Accordingly, a preliminary phenomenological exploration involves describing how the person positions himself in the different interrelational arenas of his life. How does the person appear in his own narrative? How does he describe himself in the different relationships he establishes with the most significant people in his life? What patterns may be present in the different relationships he has had over his life? On the interrelational issue, the actual relationship with the psychotherapist plays an important role. Because in any psychotherapy, it is essential to create a real relationship and a consistent therapeutic alliance. But from an existential point of view, because our development as persons is grounded in relatedness, it is necessarily the case that all reflections, and all the knowledge we have of ourselves, others and the world, is existentially uncertain (Spinelli 2007). The meanings we have created, our beliefs, what we hold to be truths about the world, all this can at any moment change, be different and be open to question, or even collapse (Spinelli 2007; Husserl 1977). Existence entails permanent incompleteness. Although the human being understands himself and needs to create meaning about his existence, grounded in the interrelational dimension, he has in this very capacity to create meaning the paradox that these meanings are incomplete or transitory. From an existential point of view, the static-phenomenological method assigns primacy to an experiential immediacy between the psychotherapist and the patient, precisely because of the place he places on the concept of relatedness.

The relationship established in the psychotherapeutic process will provide a unique arena in which both persons involved can feel and experience the client's way-of-being in relationships. We may look again at the example cited above of the patient who mentioned that his partner was very critical of him, but that he too, the patient, was often self-critical. At a certain point in the second session he said: "do you know what I'm thinking? That you surely don't want a patient like me..." In this situation, the client has initiated a description, concerning the critical view he judged the psychotherapist to have of him. The appearance of interrelational dynamics, also with the psychotherapist, is one of the areas of psychotherapeutic intervention which is clearly not an exclusive feature of the existential approach. However, existential psychotherapy lays stress on this particular and unique dynamic which is established with the patient, so as to be able to use it as a starting point for addressing issues brought by the client to the psychotherapy. An important aspect relating to the interrelational dynamic of the therapeutic space has to do with managing cracks and ruptures in the therapeutic alliance (Zilcha-Mano et al. 2016; Safran et al. 2014). Attention should also be drawn to an aspect of the existential approach which links up directly with one of the principles of psychotherapeutic effectiveness: considering the person who sought psychotherapy as an active client (Bohart and Tallman 2010). A balance is maintained between a possible positioning of the patient who may appear in a more fragile state in the psychotherapy, and a realistic view of the client's characteristics, abilities and skills for dealing with his issues. Researchers in psychotherapy have been particularly mindful of one fact: the client's contribution to the success of the psychotherapy is greater than that of either the specific of intervention or even the therapeutic relationship (Norcross and Wampold 2011). Several patient factors contribute decisively to the psychotherapy: his engagement, the natural ability of individuals to overcome obstacles, the reflexivity that transforms experience on the basis of its verbalization, integration of therapeutic gains in the patient's life, and social support (Bohart and Tallman 2010). Existential psychotherapy has always emphasized the intrinsic ability of people to carry out their own changes or transformations. In this sense, one of the aims of psychotherapy is to give (realistic) positive feedback on the client's abilities, gains and efforts, not least because he will be the party primarily responsible for any changes which may take place during the psychotherapeutic process.

(e) **Assess the client's expectations, level of motivation and goals for psychotherapy.** The concept of the active patient is closely connected to a common and crucial aspect in psychotherapy. The patient creating positive and realistic expectations about the psychotherapeutic process. Creating the belief that the intervention will help the person find an answer to the issues that he has brought to the psychotherapy appears to be fundamental for the client's intrinsic processes (his engagement, motivation, etc.) to function to the full. In turn, expectations are fostered by introducing a convincing rationale which gradually helps the patient to assimilate new meanings and new answers for the problems he is experiencing (Wampold 2015a). So it is important for the psychotherapist to monitor how the patients perceive the psychotherapy. What are his expectations? What would be like to have resolved when the psychotherapy is over? What is more important for the patient? What does he expect to find in psychotherapy? Many clients have implicit expectations about what they do or do not expect from psychotherapy. These are expectations concerning the process, and concerning the role they will have in the psychotherapy. They also have expectations about the outcomes of the psychotherapy (Constantino et al. 2012). These expectations are often not clearly stated by the patient, which means it may be particularly important for the psychotherapist to ask and provide information about expectations of the process (how the psychotherapy will go) and about the outcome (what is expected to happen and what outcomes they will work together to achieve). One way of assessing expectations involves asking the client questions, leading him to provide the psychotherapist with clues as to how much he believes in the usefulness of the psychotherapy. For instance, a patient says: "I've been to see two psychotherapists in the past... I don't think it went well... one of them used to tell me to do breathing exercises, but the fact is that it never helped me to overcome this issue of panic attacks and anxiety. I was on medication for years... I think I came here out of desperation... when they talked to me about seeing a psychotherapist I know I've already tried it and it didn't work... but look, the medication has also not helped to make things better". The client's discourse appears to point to a degree of ambiguity. On the one hand, it expresses a certain reluctance in the real possibility of the psychotherapy being a help, given that in the past the patient felt that the therapeutic intervention was not efficacious. On the other hand, he has decided to seek out another psychotherapist, partly because he believes that the problems remain unabated and the medication is also not working. This is highly important information for the psychotherapist who should pay it careful attention. From this short excerpt the psychotherapist can at least raise the possibility that he is dealing with a patient who may be prepared to try out a therapeutic process but who still has reservations which will naturally have an impact on his expectations and on his level of motivation. Among other things, two factors, for example, may ensue in this case. The psychotherapist having the implicit concern to foster the belief that the psychological explanation for his anxiety is plausible and credible; and seeking to introduce a degree of relief early on in the psychotherapeutic process. These two therapeutic goals may help to reduce the ambiguous feelings about psychotherapy and help to engage the patient more in the process. The issue of expectations is directly tied up with introducing the theoretical rationale. This may play an important role in managing expectations, because if the client feels that convincing "answers" to his tensions and distress are being introduced in the therapeutic process, he will more easily create positive expectations, which will in turn lead to increased engagement with the therapeutic tasks. So the assessment of motivation level and expectations will have direct impacts on the psychotherapeutic strategy. The psychotherapist will necessarily have different types of interventions, depending on whether he is dealing with a highly motivated patient or, on the contrary, a client with little belief in the psychotherapy. It is no less important to make a connection between the question of expectations and the therapeutic gains felt by the client at the start of the therapeutic process. Apparently, therapeutic gains which occur early on in the psychotherapy encourage positive expectations and a better level of patient engagement. Meta-analyses have highlighted that judicious management of expectations reduces the dropout rate and boosts positive therapeutic outcomes (Constantino et al. 2012).

(f) **Defining a plan for psychotherapeutic intervention**. The intervention plan should set out to respond to the request and the patient's goals, to his personal characteristics and the dimensions agreed in the therapeutic contract. As we have broadly stressed: psychotherapy is a process of collaboration between the patient and the psychotherapist. It therefore seems important for the psychotherapist to monitor the level of collaboration on an ongoing basis. Data collected on intentional meanings, sedimentations, existential tensions and distress, and also the clarification of the request and the timeframe established for the psychotherapeutic intervention, are crucial for the psychotherapist to be able to define the therapeutic strategy. Clear goals for both persons involved is a crucial aspect. Findings from meta-analyses show that when the level of consensus on goals is high, the success rate increases (Lambert and Cattani 2012). It should be possible for the client to understand the therapeutic tasks, which should be consistent with the rationale introduced and the goals. If it is established that the main goal of the therapeutic process is to help the patient referred to above to deal with her anxiety and panic attacks, then it may be useful for the psychotherapist to clarify what steps and therapeutic tasks they are to undertake together in order to achieve this. For instance, will it be important at the first sessions to undertake a phenomenological description of the anxiety crises? If so, the psychotherapist can inform the patient: "at these first few session, something I'm going to ask you is to describe to me in as much detail as possible the situations in which you have felt these moments of anxiety. Don't worry too much about explaining, just tell me how you experienced these situations, how these events were for you. These descriptive moments will help us identify important aspects which might go unnoticed and will help us understand what is happening". Without going into theoretical–practical niceties, which are of little import to the patient, the psychotherapist introduces information on the therapeutic tasks, but also informs the client of the rationale and the reasons for these tasks. It is important to stress that "tasks" does not necessarily mean practical and/or behavioral actions. In the example given, *describing* the emotions may be a therapeutic task. As we have seen, introducing a rationale is fundamental. The theoretical rationale should fit in with the patient's worldview. So although the answers discovered in psychotherapy are often challenging, different or even confrontational in relation to the person's worldview, this rationale will nonetheless be accepted if it can in some sense be accommodated by the person's beliefs. This is one of the reasons why the psychotherapist seeks constantly to bear in mind the patient's personal characteristics. The psychotherapist is required to have an understanding of the intervention strategy, to communicate it in simple terms to the patient and to ensure that the patient is engaged. In establishing the psychotherapeutic strategy, a combination of factors will necessarily be considered: what are the goals of the person's request? What stage of change has the patient reached in relation to the different aspects of the therapeutic goals? What is his level of motivation and engagement? What type of relational stance has been established in the therapeutic dyad and what timeframe has been defined for the therapeutic process? What type and degree of sedimentations and tensions have been identified in the existential narrative? What type of existential change is being worked towards (see process of change in the following section)? Like the therapeutic relationship and process, the definition of the psychotherapeutic strategy may fluctuate. Rather than avoiding fluctuations, it appears crucial to recognize that they exist and to address and deal with them in the therapeutic relationship. On this point as in many aspects of the therapeutic process, the psychotherapist's interpersonal skills and responsiveness are particularly important (Goldberg et al. 2016; Stiles 2013). Adapting the intervention to the patient (Owen and Hilsenroth 2014), without however ceasing to follow a stable and credible psychotherapeutic course that provides an organizational framework, appears to be crucial to the progress in psychotherapy (Beutler et al. 2016).

The genetic-phenomenological approach is based on the "Psychotherapeutic Process Form" (see attachments), in which the psychotherapist can note the main issues in the case conceptualization, from an existential point of view. The psychotherapeutic process form is based on the case conceptualization fundamentals as described above, and so includes issues specific to existential psychotherapy (narrative of existential project, identification of sedimentations, existential conflicts, leading clues) and dimensions related to the principles of psychotherapeutic effectiveness (goals and tasks/therapies, feedback and monitoring, expectations, relational stance, common factors, stages of change).

Process of Change

The existential approach considers that change is a natural process in the course of personal development. Changes occur for intrinsic reasons (relating to the individual) and extrinsic reasons (life and factual circumstances of the intersubjective milieu) which, when combined, result in a process which is inevitably dynamic, and often unpredictable. This process is constant over the course of life with moments which, sometimes, can entail situations of greater complexity and/or psychological suffering. In many circumstances, people undergo processes, both positive and negative, which eventually have a delayed impact on their psychological life. It is not uncommon for people to arrive at psychotherapy, after many years of accumulating situations which are painful to them. So while change is something undeniably present in people's lives, it is no less true that these changes can be experienced in very different ways, and can often be difficult or even devastating. The process of existential development contains a number of paradoxes. One of these has to do with the fact that human beings are able and need to make sense of themselves, others and the world. The meanings they discover have an organizing function, but at the same time they are always uncertain and can be called into question (Heidegger 1962; Spinelli 2007). In many cases, instead of accelerating change, it may be important for the psychotherapist to provide a still space for *being*. Spinelli (2007) has stressed that for many people, although it may be difficult, it is important that they agree to stay still, so as to be able to describe and clarify properly their thoughts, emotions and behaviors. Psychotherapeutic change can be conceptualized at three distinct levels from an existential point of view (Husserl 1989; Spinelli 2007):

Level 1—Level 1 changes do not alter the sedimentations identified in any of the three central dimensions—self, other, world—but they bring about changes in attitude and/or behavior. If sedimentation is identified in the self dimension, this same sedimentation may remain unchangeable, but still allow the person to adapt behaviors and attitudes in relation to the other two dimensions. For example, if the person's perception is: "I'm someone who always lives with fear". A level 1 change would presuppose that the person could say: "I'm still someone who is afraid, but I can now find ways of doing things that I was previously afraid of" (sedimentation maintained, but with change of behavior).

Level 2—At this level the change takes place *in* the actual sedimentation: The change brings about *de-sedimentation* or a change in this sedimentation, so the person experiences a more significant change. At this level of change, the alteration in sedimentations is confined largely to the construct with which it is associated. For example, if someone says "I feel that other people don't like me" (sedimentation in the dimension "other", without impacts on the subject's other beliefs and ways of being). A change in this sedimentation might lead the person to say: "today I feel that I have people in my life who are really interested in me. I don't feel the same emptiness and I can manage to feel that I'm part of other people's lives".

Level 3—Changes at this level not only take place in one of the dimensions (self, other, world), but also have an impact on the structure of the person's worldview. These are deeper changes, which occur with an impact on the basic self and on the narrative identity, with greater repercussions on the interrelation between the person and the world. So for example, a person who used to say "I'm someone who always lives with fear" could now make a different assertion: "there are things I understand differently and today I am able to feel capable and not afraid". However, this change in the dimension "self" may have implications for the individual in other psychological areas. He might say "because I'm no longer afraid all the time, I can today feel a different fullness in my relationship with my partner. I live things with others in a different way". In this case, the person may have made deeper changes with impacts in different dimensions of his worldview (self, other, world). In addition, the changes made were not in behavior. Although the transformations have an impact on attitudes and behaviors, they are experienced by the person through a cognitive and emotional perspective. His experience changes.

Level 1 and 2 changes are more likely to occur in psychotherapeutic processes in which people's specific issues and problems are identified, without the aim of altering the system of their worldview. In other words, without altering the sedimentations of the experiential self with impacts on the narrative identity. At level 1, the focus is more on changing attitudes and behaviors, and shifts at level 2 towards altering the sedimentations of one of the constructs, whilst sharing the level 1 focus on changing attitudes. Level 3 changes have wider structural implications and the therapeutic aims involved are in a certain sense more ambitious. The process of existential change (Spinelli 2007) is interrelated with the different factors mentioned in the case conceptualizations.

NOTE

1. In this text whenever we use the term "existential psychotherapy" we considered that this is an existential-phenomenological psychotherapy. For simplicity we use the first term.

REFERENCES

Alegria, S., Carvalho, I., Sousa, D., Correia, E. A., Fonseca, J., Pires, A. S., & Fernandes, S. (2016). Process and outcome research in existential psychotherapy. *Existential Analysis, 27*(1), 78–92.

Anderson, T., Olges, B. M., Patterson, C. L., Lambert, M. J., & Vermeersch, D. A. (2009). Therapist effects: Facilitative interpersonal skills as a predictor of therapist success. *Journal of Clinical Psychology, 65*(7), 755–768.

Anderson, T., Crowley, M. E. J., Himawan, L., Holmberg, J. K., & Uhlin, B. D. (2016). Therapist facilitative interpersonal skills and training status: A randomized clinical trial on alliance and outcome. *Psychotherapy Research, 26*(5), 511–529.

Beutler, L. E., Someah, K., Kimpara, S., & Miller, K. (2016). Selecting the most appropriate treatment for each patient. *International Journal of Clinical and Health Psychology, 16*, 99–108.

Bohart, A. C., & Tallman, K. (2010). Clients: The neglected common factor in psychotherapy. In B. L. Duncan, S. D. Miller, B. E. Wampold, & M. A. Hubble (Eds.), *The heart and soul of change: Delivering what works in therapy* (2nd ed., pp. 83–111). Washington, DC: American Psychological Association.

Buber, M. (1970). I and Thou. New York: A Touchstone Book.

Castonguay, L. G., Boswell, J. F., Zack, S. E., Baker, A., Boutselis, M. A., Chiswick, N. R., ... Holtforth, M. G. (2010a). Helpful and hindering events in psychotherapy: A pratice research network study. *Psychotherapy Theory, Research, Practice, 47*(3), 327–344.

Castonguay, L. G., Boswell, J. F., Constantino, M. J., Goldfried, M. R., & Hill, C. E. (2010b). Training implications of harmful effects of psychological treatments. *American Psychologist, 65*(1), 34–49.

Chow, D., Miller, S. D., Seidel, J. A., Kane, R. T., Thornton, J. A., & Andrews, W. (2015). The role of deliberate practice in the development of highly effective psychotherapists. *Psychotherapy, 52*(3), 337–345.

Constantino, M. J., Arnkoff, D. B., Glass, C. R., Ametrano, R. M., & Smith, J. Z. (2011). Expectations. *Journal of Clinical Psychology: In Session, 67*(2), 184–192.

Constantino, M. J., Ametrano, R. M., & Greenberg, R. P. (2012). Clinician interventions and participant characteristics that foster adaptive patient expectations for psychotherapy and psychotherapeutic change. *Psychotherapy 49*(4), 557–569.

Cooper, M. (2003). *Existencial therapies*. London: Sage.

Cooper, M. (2007). Humanizing psychotherapy. *Journal of Contemporary Psychotherapy, 37*(1), 11–16.

Cooper, M. (2008). *Essential research findings in counselling and psychotherapy: The facts are friendly*. London: Sage.

Correia, E. A., Sartóris, V., Fernandes, T., Cooper, M., Berdondini, L., Sousa, D., Pires, B., Fonseca, J. (2016). The practices of existential psychotherapists: Development and application of an observational grid. *British Journal of Guidance & Counselling*. Retrieved from doi: 10.1080/03069885.2016.1254723.

Ekroll, V. B. S., & Rønnestad, M. H. (2016). Processes and changes experienced by clients during and after naturalistic good-outcome therapies conducted by experienced psychotherapists. *Psychotherapy Research*. Retrieved from doi:10.1 080/10503307.2015.1119326.

Elliott, R., Bohart, A. C., Watson, J. C., & Greenberg, L. S. (2011). Empathy. *Psychotherapy, 48*, 43–49.

Gadamer, H.G. (2003). *Truth and Method*. New York: Seabury Press.

Gelso, C. J. (2014). A tripartite model of the therapeutic relationship: Theory, research, and practice. *Psychotherapy Research, 24*(2), 117–131.

Goldberg, S. B., Hoyt, W. T., Nissen-lie, H. A., Nielsen, S. L., & Wampold, B. E. (2016). Unpacking the therapist effect: Impact of treatment length differs for high- and low-performing therapists. *Psychotherapy Research*. Retrieved from doi.org/10.1080/10503307.2016.1216625.

Heidegger, M. (1962). *Being and time*. Oxford: Basil Blackwell.

Hill, C. (1995). Therapist techniques, client involvement, and the therapeutic relationship: Inextricably intertwined in the therapy process. *Psychotherapy: Theory Research, Practice, Training, 42*, 431–442.

Hoffman, L., Vallejos, L., Cleare-Hoffman, H., & Rubin, S. (2015). Emotion, relationship, and meaning as core existential practice: Evidence-based foundations. *Journal of Contemporary Psychotherapy, 45*(1), 11–20.

Husserl, E. (1977). *Phenomenological psychology*. The Hague: Martinus Nijhoff.

Husserl, E. (1989). *Ideas pertaining to a pure phenomenology and to a phenomenological philosophy: Second book*. Dordrecht: Kluwer.

Husserl, E. (1994). *Lições para uma fenomenologia da consciência interna do tempo*. Lisboa: Imprensa Nacional—Casa da Moeda.

Husserl, E. (2001). *Analyses concerning passive and active synthesis. Lectures on transcendental logic.* Dordrecht: Kluwer.

Kierkegaard, S. (1980). *The concept of anxiety.* Princeton: Princeton University Press.

Lambert, M. J. (2013). *Bergin and Garfield's handbook of psychotherapy and behavior change.* Hoboken, NJ: Wiley.

Lambert, M. J. (2015). Progress feedback and the OQ-System: The past and the future. *Psychotherapy, 52*(4), 381–390.

Lambert, M. J., & Cattani, K. (2012). Practice-friendly research review: Collaboration in routine care. *Journal of Clinical Psychology: In Session, 68*(2), 209–220.

Lambert, M. J., & Shimokawa, K. (2011). Collecting client feedback. *Psychotherapy, 48*(1), 72–79.

Levitt, H. M., Pomerville, A., & Surace, F. I. (2016). A qualitative meta-analysis examining clients' experiences of psychotherapy: A new agenda. *Psychological Bulletin, 142*(8), 801–830.

May, R., Angel, E., & Ellenberger, F. H. (2004). *Existence.* New York: Aronson.

McAleavey, A. A., & Castonguay, L. G. (2013). Insight as a common and specific impact of psychotherapy: Therapist-reported exploratory, directive, and common factor interventions. *Psychotherapy, 51,* 283–294.

Merleau-Ponty, M. (2002). *Phenomenology of perception.* London: Routledge & Kegan Paul.

Norcross, J. (2016). *The face of 2025. The future of psychotherapy.* In Personal Communication presented at the International Conference of Psychotherapy—The Challenges of the Future, of the ISPA—University Institute, Lisbon, Portugal.

Norcross, J. C., & Lambert, M. (2011). Introduction. Evidence-based therapy relationships. In.

Norcross, J. C., & Wampold, B. E. (2011). What works for whom: Tailoring psychotherapy to the person. *Journal of Clinical Psychology: In Session, 67*(2), 127–132.

Norcross, J. C., Krebs, P. M., & Prochaska, J. O. (2011). Stages of change. *Journal of Clinical Psychology: In Session, 67*(2), 143–154.

Oliveira, A., Sousa, D., & Pires, A. (2012). Significant events on existential psychotherapy: The client's perspective. *Existential Analysis, 23*(2), 134–157.

Owen, J., & Hilsenroth, M. J. (2014). Treatment adherence: The importance of therapist flexibility in relation to therapy outcomes. *Journal of Counseling Psychology, 61*(2), 280–288.

Rennie, D. (2010). Humanistic psychology at York University: Retrospective: Focus on clients' experiencing in psychotherapy: Emphasis of radical reflexivity. *The Humanistic Psychologist, 38,* 40–56.

Rønnestad, M. H. (2016). Is expertise in psychotherapy a useful construct? *Psychotherapy Bulletin, 51*(1), 11–13.

Safran, J. D., Muran, J. C., Demaria, A., Boutwell, C., Eubanks-Carter, C., & Winston, A. (2014). Investigating the impact of alliance-focused training on interpersonal process and therapists' capacity for experiential reflection. *Psychotherapy Research, 24*(3), 269–285.

Sartre, J. P. (1994). *A Consciência de si e Conhecimento de si*. Lisboa: Edições Colibri.

Schneider, K. (2015). Presence: The core contextual factor of effective psychotherapy. *Existential Analysis, 2*(2), 304–312.

Schneider, K. J., & May, R. (1995). *The psychology of existence. An integrative, clinical perpsective*. New York: McGraw-Hill.

Sousa, D. (2004). A short note underlying reflection on psychotherapy research. *Existential Analysis, 15*(2), 194–202.

Sousa, D. (2015). Existential psychotherapy. The genetic-phenomenological approach: Beyond a dichotomy between relating and skills. *Journal of Contemporary Psychotherapy, 45*, 69–77.

Sousa, D. & Vaz, A. (in press). A descriptive phenomenological exploration of significant events in existential therapy. *Journal of Humanistic Psychology*.

Sousa, D., Tavares, A., & Pestana, A. (in press). Eventos significativos em psicoterapia existencial. In A. M. Feijoo & M. B. Lessa (Eds.). *Fenomenologia e práticas clínicas II*. Rio Janeiro: IFEN.

Spinelli, E. (2007). *Practising existential psychotherapy. The relational world*. London: Sage.

Spinelli, E. (2014). An existential challenge to some dominant perspectives in the practice of contemporary counselling psychology. *Counselling Psychology Review, 29*(2), 7–14.

Stiles, W. B. (2009). Responsiveness as an obstacle for psychotherapy outcome research: It's worse than you think. *Clinical Psychology: Science and Practice, 16*, 86–91.

Stiles, W. B. (2013). The variables problem and progress in psychotherapy research. *Psychotherapy, 50*(1), 33–41.

Tryon, G. S., & Winograd, G. (2011). Goal consensus and collaboration. *Psychotherapy, 48*(1), 50–57.

van Deurzen, E. (1995). *Existential therapy*. London: Society for Existential Analysis.

van Deurzen, E., & Adams, M. (2011). *Skills in existential counselling & psychotherapy*. London: Sage.

van Kaam, A. (1958). Existential foundations of psychology. Pittsburgh, PA: Dimension Books.

Walsh, R. A., & McElwain, B. (2001). Existential psychotherapies. In D. J. Cain & J. Seeman (Eds.), *Humanistic psychotherapies: Handbook of research and practice* (pp. 253–278). Washington: American Psychological Association.

Wampold, B. E. (2011). *Qualities and actions of effective therapists.* American Psychological Association. Retrieved from https://www.apa.org/education/ce/effective-therapists.pdf.

Wampold, B. E. (2015a). Humanism as a common factor in psychotherapy. *The handbook of humanistic psychology: Theory, research, and practice*, (2nd ed., pp. 400–408) (e-book). Thousand Oaks, CA: Sage.

Wampold, B. E. (2015b). How important are the common factors in psychotherapy? An update. *World Psychiatry, 14*, 270–277.

Wampold, B. E., & Imel, Z. E. (2015). *The great psychotherapy debate: The evidence for what makes psychotherapy work* (2nd ed.). New York: Routledge.

Wampold, B. E., Imel, Z. E., Laska, K. M., Benish, S. Miller, S. D., Flückiger, C., ... Budge, S. (2010). Determining what works in the treatment of PTSD. *Clinical Psychology Review, 30*, 923–933.

Wampold, B. E., Frost, N. D., & Yulish, N. E. (2016). Placebo effects in psychotherapy: A flawed concept and a contorted history. *Psychology of Consciousness: Theory, Research, and Practice, 3*(2), 108–120.

Watson, V. C., Cooper, M., McArthur, K., & McLeod, J. (2012). Helpful therapeutic processes: Client activities, therapist activities and helpful effects. *European Journal of Psychotherapy and Counselling, 14*(1), 77–89.

Yalom, I. (1980). *Existential psychotherapy.* New York: Basic Books.

Zahavi, D. (1999). *Self-awareness and alterity. A phenomenological investigation.* Evanston: Northwestern University Press.

Zahavi, D. (2004). Alterity in self. In S. Gallagher, S. Watson, Ph. Brun, & Ph. Romanski (Eds.), *Ipseity and alterity. Interdisciplinary approaches to intersubjectivity.* Rouen: Presses Universitaires de Rouen.

Zilcha-Mano, S., Eubanks-Carter, F., Muran, J. C., Hungr, C., Safran, J. D., & Winston, A. (2016). The relationship between alliance and outcome: Analysis of a two-person perspective on alliance and session outcome. *Journal of Consulting and Clinical Psychology, 84*(6), 484–496.

CHAPTER 4

Practical Applications and Clinical Case

This chapter provides further examples of how psychotherapy can be conducted, in the genetic-phenomenological approach. In the therapeutic dialogues, the type of psychotherapeutic intervention is indicated in brackets and underlined. Comments will also be added between dialogues, in order to explain to the reader aspects to which special attention is drawn. However, it should be noted that these examples are recalled in retrospect, and their fundamental characteristic is their simplicity. In other words, they smooth over both the complexity of the dialogue as it actually happened and also the complexity of the therapeutic processes. They are dialogues and short excerpts, which in these examples, rather than highlighting aspects of the existential approach, focus on dimensions to be found in the principles of therapeutic effectiveness. In the second part of this section we will present a clinical case, where we will have recourse to the testimony of a patient concerning her experience of existential psychotherapy. In this case, we interviewed the patient and sought to drawn connections between her testimony and theoretical aspects of the genetic-phenomenological approach, presented in Chap. 2. In this case we sought to made a deeper reading, from a theoretical point of view. In both sections, the names of any people and places have been fictionalized.

© The Author(s) 2017
D. Sousa, *Existential Psychotherapy*,
DOI 10.1057/978-1-349-95217-5_4

VIGNETTE 1

First, a small excerpt is presented from two sessions with the aim of exemplifying the concept of *leading clue*. The therapist can use clues from the client's speech to change his/her position, for example, to move from a more descriptive mode to a hermeneutic one. The therapist may be more focused on exploratory interventions, or conversely, challenge or interpret sedimentation of the experiential self. A leading clue can be a word, an expression, a memory, essentially aspects that arise in the client's narrative that the therapist retains for himself/herself and that can lead to a change in the therapeutic positioning. Sometimes this change occurs at other moments of the process. In the example presented below, the therapist makes a more interpretative intervention, based on a leading clue, which had appeared in the previous session. In the first excerpt, the client mentions the feeling of being inferior and this is synonymous with not being able to define herself as a person. The client also speaks of the criticism she felt and that lead her to refrain from showing others a thesis she is writing. This situation is repeated in other circumstances of her life. For the therapist, the connection "feeling inferior—define oneself as a person—show oneself", served as a leading clue for a genetic type of intervention. For the leading clue to arise and later for hermeneutic intervention to take place, there was prior experiential validation and use of descriptive phenomenology, demonstrating the interdependence between both phenomenological methods.

Client: I feel worse for not being able to move on with things.... And I shouldn't even be here...in this city...

Therapist: How so? (<u>descriptive phenomenological question</u>)

C: I'm sharing a rented place with my brother, he often says that I shouldn't be here that I don't need to be here to write my thesis... that I am spending my parent's inheritance money... deep down that I am spending his money... (silence)...

T: ... How do you feel when you brother says that to you? (<u>empathic exploration</u>)

C: I feel bad, but if I were in my parents' house it would be very hard too... I would feel like I was suffocating... my relationship with my father is very difficult... he has a very particular character; we basically don't have a relationship.

T: it is like you are not able to be well, neither there or here... (<u>experiential validation</u>)

L: Yes. And I can't move on with my thesis, I always think it's all wrong.... But maybe it was always this way...

T: How was it always this way? (<u>descriptive phenomenological question</u>)

C: I always felt I was worse than others, that I wasn't able to do things well

T: What do you mean with "I always felt this way"? (<u>empathic exploration</u>)

C: I think my brother wasn't doing it on purpose but he was always saying I didn't know how to do things, he criticized me... I, I went on living things that way, it seemed like I was always making an effort to do things... then I became close to my cousin and she was very critical... but even before... when I went to university I was already like that... I always felt inferior (<u>leading clue</u>) it seemed everyone told me how I should be... even to define myself... as if I couldn't define myself (<u>leading clue</u>)... now it has been harder... it is always hard to go home over the weekends, it only gets worse...

Somewhere in the following session, a small part of the dialogue picked up on the same topics.

Client: I'm still doing badly on my thesis...

Therapist: How's that going?

C: I don't know, it's hard for me... I always think others are going to see things.... That they'll criticize...

T: Showing the thesis is showing *yourself*, it is like if you defined yourself in front of others... (<u>hermeneutic intervention based on the leading clue from the previous session</u>).

In this short example we have several aspects related to theoretical issues, but also to the psychotherapeutic interventions. Firstly, we should point to the psychotherapist's exploration of an issue in the here-and-now of the client, who was experiencing enormous difficulties in completing an MA dissertation. But in the narrative, this difficulty appear entangled with other aspects of the patient's self. One of the patient's sedimentations present had to do with a very high degree of self-disparagement. According to her, this seems to have been present over the entire course of her development. This issue, if confirmed, points to the need for the psychotherapist to assess the *level* of sedimentation. A more genetic type of sedimentation, in the sense of having been part of the person's experiential self for a long time, might suggest a more deeply rooted characteristic of the person, meaning it would be more difficult to change or even to address. This short example is intended to show the connection which may exist between the behavior which the person recognizes as her own, although it may also bring malaise, and a psychological characteristic. So the patient has difficulty not only in presenting the dissertation but also in being with others, in inner freedom, without feeling (self-)criticism. The example also shows how the concept of leading clue can help the psychotherapist in two ways. It can serve, rather intuitively, as a way of following the patient's dialogue and gradually intervening in a more descriptive and relational way, or in a more interpretative way. It can also point the psychotherapist to address issues or intervene at other moments in the same session, or at different moments in the psychotherapeutic process. In this case, at the following session, the psychotherapist eventually effected a hermeneutic intervention linking the behavior (not showing the dissertation) to the patient's fear of showing herself to others (sedimentation self-other).

VIGNETTE 2

Right at the start of the first session the following dialogue occurred:

Therapist: Do you want to tell me what brought you here?

Patient: Yes...I have a problem that I would like to know if you can help me to resolve... I don't think this has to do with me directly but the fact is that affects my life. It's a situation that arises in the course of my relationship with my wife but with implications for me. I have had problems of premature ejaculation. And I want to know if you resolve this problem...

T: OK...can you tell me a little more about the premature ejaculation. When did it start to happen, how did it happen for you...? (descriptive phenomenological question).

C: Before we have intercourse, during foreplay I ejaculate. That's it.

T: I understand, ejaculation occurs even before intercourse starts. Is that it? (Clarification). (At this moment the psychotherapist was feeling the patient's difficulty in maintaining the dialogue and giving shorter, closed answers).

C: Yes, that's it.

T: Ok. Is there anything you can tell me about this issue that you think is important?

C: No. It's a frustrating situation for me. And for my wife. She also feels frustrated. Of course. But I don't think this is a problem of mine…

T: It's not your problem…(therapist paraphrased, in order to encourage the client's narrative)

C: No. I think this might have to do with me and with my wife. The fact is we get on fine. Our relationship works well. Except for this.

At this point in the dialogue offers a number of important clues for the psychotherapist. Some of these clues were confirmed at a later stage. Although the patient has sought psychotherapy because of premature ejaculation, he appears to articulate the possibility that the "problem" isn't his. Although this needs to be understood more clearly—what can it mean that the premature ejaculation that occurs with him is not his problem?—it points to a possibility: the patient is at a pre-contemplation phase on this point. Because, despite seeking psychotherapeutic help, he has come up with the belief that the problem isn't his own. The issue isn't in him. At the same time, there appear to be clues to a somewhat closed relational stance, and a degree of avoidance in the therapeutic dialogue. Another important aspect has to do with the patient saying: "I want to know if you resolve this problem…". Might the patient be taking a rather passive stance, in which his expectation is that the psychotherapist can resolve this matter for him? What might he expect from the psychotherapy? What does he think about how it functions? The patient's expressions, sometime just a single word, are leading clues to which the psychotherapist pays careful attention, in order to conduct the intervention in the moment. Another leading clue is the whole verbal and body language used by the patient, and *how* the narrative arises. The discourse is important not only as regards its content but also in the way (*how*) in which it is presented.

Therapist:	Have you tried to find help before coming here?
Patient:	Yes. I took pills and saw several doctors. But it didn't work. Nothing's changed.
Therapist:	And help from psychotherapy?
Patient:	No. I came here because a friend I really trust insisted on it. To tell the truth, I don't know if this can help. I want to know what you can tell me. I don't much believe that this can help because I'm completely fine and I don't know how this can have to do with the way I think. I'm not even convinced the problem's mine and then the doctors themselves see this as a physical problem.
Therapist:	Right. We'll talk in a while about these aspects and about psychotherapy itself. But tell me, what do you think you would like to find here, what do you think your expectations are?
Patient:	That you can tell me what I can do and how I can get over this. Specific things…

In this part, several important aspects come to the fore. His expectation of psychotherapy appears to be low. His level of motivation does not appear high and the patient presents a discourse that locates in the psychotherapist the possible capacity "to resolve the problem". In addition, the patient sees no great validity in an expectation of a psychological explanation for the problem. All these points are extremely important for the psychotherapist to be able to adjust his interventions to the particular individual. So during the first session, the patient said he didn't expect to be in sessions for long, that it didn't make sense to him, and what was more because he didn't know whether they would really be useful.

Psychotherapist:	From what you've told me at today's session, I understand that the most important thing for you is to find out specifically how to overcome the problem of premature ejaculation. Is that it?
Patient:	Yes, that's it.
Psychotherapist:	OK. So see if this makes sense. I would suggest that we do a series of sessions, during which we could look together at practical issues relating to premature ejaculation. In particular, specific things you can actually try in practice. For example, we known that

	in premature ejaculation, one way of delaying ejaculating is at the moment of intercourse to squeeze the base of the penis. Is that the sort of "specific things" you mean you're looking for?
C:	Yes, it is.
T:	Right. Sometimes these situations can be related to aspects of your life or your way of being. It can also happen that at first sight this doesn't make sense to you and that you can't at first see what aspects these are. What I would suggest to you is that in the sessions we could alternate between moments when we look at specific aspects, like I just mentions, and others when we would start to explore other aspects of your life and yourself. The reason why we do this is to be able to understand what might contribute to the question you bring here, in the event of it being more connected with your issues. Does that make sense to you?

At these moments in the session the psychotherapist seeks to adapt to the client. On the one hand, he sought to adjust the intervention to the request and, above all, to the patient's expectations and beliefs. The psychotherapist sought to respond to the request for practical tips on premature ejaculation. But he sought to introduce another type of therapeutic tasks, for which the patient appeared to be less motivated, in particular, in order to be willing initially to explore the reasons that might be contributing to this facet of his life. It also became clear that he was relatively unreceptive and little disposed to believe in the validity of a psychological explanation for his problem. In addition, he showed some reluctance in acknowledging what issues of his own might be at the root of the problem. All these aspects of the patient's narrative at the first sessions provide very important clues for the psychotherapist about his expectations, the request and the level of collaboration from the client at this initial stage. So all these dimensions are like initial goals to be worked on. The aims for the intervention will include increasing his belief that the psychological explanation can be useful and to increase the level of collaboration, so that the intervention can in turn be more effective in relation to the main goal of the psychotherapy. In these situations, the objectives break down into several parts which will be worked on simultaneously. In this case, for instance, introducing specific suggestions for the patient to try our new strategies for premature ejaculation, alternating with more descriptive and exploratory moments looking at the characteristics of the person, his life story, his affective and other significant relations, his relationship with his wife, etc., could be one of the ways of starting the intervention. At the same time, it is important to establish deeper trust in the psychotherapy and in the therapeutic alliance. It may also be very important for the client to feel some initial therapeutic gains. If this happens, it might help him accept more easily the relevance of undergoing psychotherapy. These aspects do not mean that the psychotherapist simply does what the patient wants, or that the psychotherapist conducts interventions or psychotherapy with which he does not identify. What it does mean is that there is a breadth of intervention, in which the psychotherapist, when responsive and adapting the intervention to the specifics of the patient, can more easily achieve more satisfactory therapeutic outcomes. For the psychotherapeutic contract, the solution proposed to this patient was a compromise. We knew he didn't want to spend much time in psychotherapy. The therapist suggested a psychotherapy which could last 3 months with weekly sessions. It was not actually said that the problem would be sorted out in this time. But this at least was the compromise requested by the psychotherapist for them both to be able to see whether the psychotherapy would really be useful, without involving great investment (of time and money) on the part of the patient. It was also said to the client that we would speak for around 4 h each month (one session a week), to seek to resolve a problem which according to him he had had for more than 15 years. Putting the issue in perspective helped the patient to accept the contractual timeframe for the psychotherapy. These 3 months were later extended, and in total the patient underwent an intervention which lasted around 6 months. It was a therapeutic process which, for a large part of the early stage, required the psychotherapist to much more proactive in his intervention that he probably is with other patients, in view of the characteristics of this patient. It seemed to be crucial that the patient should experience improvements relatively early—roughly in the second month of the intervention—in order for his belief in the process to alter and allow him to agree to continue the therapeutic process until it yielded more satisfactory outcomes.

VIGNETTE 3

A woman started psychotherapy because she felt that her relationship with her husband had ended. Although this situation has been going on for several years, she was expecting her husband to make a move, and to make up his mind. When the therapeutic contract was closed, it was established that missed sessions would be charged normally, unless the patient gave 48 h' notice. It was also said that the sessions would last 50 min, and that if Louise were to arrive late one day, the therapist would not be able to extend the session time, and it would end at the same time as usual. These were two of the various issues addressed when the therapeutic contract was agreed. At the early sessions, Louise seemed to be highly engaged in the psychotherapy. Above all, she expressed relief and hope.

Client: It's doing me good to come here... just the fact of talking to you is helping. I don't even want to talk about these things any more with my (female) friends or even with my parents. It's good to talk to someone not involved... it seems that a weight is gradually lifting...

Therapist: You feel you have kept things to yourself for a long time... you're feeling relief because you feel you can talk about some of the things that have worried you for some time (<u>reformulation</u> of the patient's feelings)

C: Yes... but it's not just that...

T: No?

C: Last week, when I left here, I felt something I hadn't felt for a long time. Hope. I was hopeful again that something might happen for the situation to change.

Louise used the early sessions to look back over recent years and, at the same time, to address situations in the present with her husband. Sometimes, the psychotherapist felt that Louise seemed less willing at this early stage of the psychotherapy to address what held her back from talking to her husband to discuss and agree on a separation. However, that was her aim. But when she broached the possibility of thinking about her relationship whether she thought it was really over, even from an affective point of view, her answer was extremely direct. "Yes." This was not even open to discussion. Only how to arrange the separation. All the same, Louise appeared to have an attitude of expectation. Her husband should take the initiative.

Therapist: Louise, so for you, it's clear you feel that the relationship
             has ended? (dialogic attitude)
Client: Yes, of course, I haven't even thought about it for years.
             We don't have anything to do with each other. We're two
             friends who live in the same house. That's all. And we
             have 4 children together. Which is quite a lot and we have
             a story together that for me ended several years ago. I'm
             really tired of this situation. Why doesn't he do anything?
             Why not leave if I've already told him I don't love him?
Therapist: You would like him to take that initiative…
Client: But I've made it quite clear to him several times…
T: Right…Louise, tell me something, do you feel that you
             to have space to talk about this issue? I mean, are there
             moments when you can talk and can say to each other what
             you are feeling and thinking?
C: No, we don't talk about anything. We talk about every-
             day things. That's all. We don't have conversations about
             anything else, nothing intimate, and we don't even sleep
             together… I want him to make his mind up. To leave.
T: Have you ever spoken directly with him about your want-
             ing this?
C: No…
T: Is there any reason you think could help you broach the
             matter instead of waiting for your husband to take the ini-
             tiative?
C: No… I don't know. I think he should have realized.

After only a few sessions, she arrived late for the next session. She also
seemed less motivated and rather on edge. The therapist perceived this but
decided not to address it at the session. The next week, she sent a message
to the psychotherapist, a fess minutes before the time booked for the session. Saying she felt ill and would not go to the session. The next week,
Louise went to the session but arrived 20 min late. The psychotherapist
again felt that Louise was rather tense at the session, which was shorter, as
it ended at the usual time. This time, the therapist sought to broach the
matter of this possible tension, but Louise said it was nothing special. She
was annoyed because she had had to leave her two younger children at a
friend's house in order to come to the session, she had been rushing about
all day, she was tired and everything "was left to her". She felt no help

from her husband, even in practical things. Although the psychotherapist tried to explore the patient's tension a little more, he felt that Louise was unwilling to explore it further. At the end of the session, Louise paid the session and also the previous session, which she had missed. At the next session, Louise again arrived slightly late.

Therapist:	Louise, I would like to share something with you to see if we can talk about it. I have felt that perhaps the sessions are being rather different for you.
Client:	Different, how?
T:	Different from the first ones, where you felt more relief and hope as a result of coming here. Maybe the session or I, we may have changed something in a way that doesn't make so much sense to you. Or perhaps something has happened which has left you uncomfortable...
C:	No... I don't think anything has changed...
T:	Maybe I upset you because despite being ill and warning me, you still paid the session...
C:	You didn't upset me!
T:	Yes... how did you feel about it?
C:	You didn't upset me. But I would never do that! I mean, I was ill, wasn't I? I don't care about the money, but I would never do that.
T:	I understand, Louise. For you, its not the question of the money for the session that matters, but the fact that I accepted it...
C:	Yes!
T:	I understand, Louise. For you, it's as if I didn't care about you. In a certain sense, it's as if you felt that I was not con cerned about you, or was not taking care of you... you were of course ill and couldn't come... and all I could think about was the question of the payment for the session...
C:	(Louise is emotional, lowers he head) Yes... I think I would never do that... how is it possible? I know that's what we agreed but I was ill!

The dialogue described here was in reality slightly longer. In other words, at the start the psychotherapist was more exploratory and questioning in his interventions, trying to see if Louise would express for herself the unease she appeared to be feeling. When this failed to happen, the psychotherapist chose to put a possibility to her. That Louise might be upset with the therapist. Despite initially saying she wasn't, she went on to say she couldn't understand how the psychotherapist could charge for the session in those circumstances. From that point on it was possible to address in greater depth what had happened between Louise and the psychotherapist. The therapist's central aim at that moment was to reveal and understand how Louise *felt*. To accept her disappointment, her subjective experience, and not to make her feel bad for feeling what she was feeling. We both knew that we had agreed that sessions would be charged if the patient failed to given 48 h' prior notice. But at that moment, that was not the issue, which was rather how Louise felt what this meant that the psychotherapist would be in relation to her. The tension that arose in the therapeutic alliance also made it possible to build bridges with what Louise might feel in other relationships and how she was experiencing the therapeutic space. So it was possible to conduct a dialogue about how Louise had experienced the sessions at first, and how a slight change in the direction of the dialogue (broaching possibilities that preventing Louise herself from taking the initiative in the matter than was annoying her most) could also have contributed to a disconnection or a lesser feeling of connection between Louise and the psychotherapist. These issues were addressed at the next two sessions. After these sessions, there was increased integration between the psychotherapy goals and how Louise and the psychotherapist worked together on them. At a later stage, it even became possible to use humor on the question of paying for the sessions. But above all, it seems that from that moment in the process, there was a new engagement in the therapeutic dyad, which also made it possible to open up new avenues of psychotherapeutic exploration.

It seems important to stress that, at particular moments that are not previously anticipated by either member of the dyad, tensions, cracks and disconnections appear in the therapeutic relationship, which can become turning points or breakthroughs, or lead to new dynamics in the therapeutic process. There are basically three interrelated aspects to this question. In first place, there seems to be a silent process that is constructed implicitly and imperceptibly by both clients and therapists, and which unleashes centrifugal movements of approximation and distancing in which relational tensions are experienced. Secondly, as those relational tensions emerge, they create an eruption in the dynamic of the therapeutic relationship, producing different types of effects. When those effects are addressed and resolved some positive impacts can occur, like: the unblocking of impasses in the therapeutic process; the deepening of trust in the therapeutic relationship; the development of a new dynamic; an increase of awareness of important subjects; and the reinforcement of the client's individuality. These three interrelated processes do not necessarily unfold in a gradual linear fashion; there may be advances and retreats, and they may also be dependent upon spontaneous or unforeseen actions. Clients go through gradual subliminal periods of processing and pre-reflexive organization of cognitive and experiential processes without being aware of it, though, from a particular moment in the therapy, they become more receptive to the therapeutic intervention and revise their personal theories. If we assume that negative processes, relational ruptures and strains will inevitably occur in the course of the therapeutic process, one of the therapist's most important skills is knowing how to deal with and repair ruptures in the therapeutic alliance. Once more, there arises the assumption of interdependence between the relational and technical factors. Another crucial aspect has to do with the importance of negotiation between therapist and client, something that is on going throughout the therapeutic process and goes beyond the consensus concerning the therapeutic goals. It also considers emotional, pre-reflective processes underlying the relational process between the two people: "At a deeper level, it taps into fundamental dilemmas of human existence, such as the negotiation of one's desires with those of another, the struggle to experience oneself as a subject while at the same time recognizing the subjectivity of the other, and the tension between the need for agency versus the need for relatedness" (Safran and Muran 2000). A set of theoretical and practical principles have been proposed to conceptualize and identify skills that the therapist could develop in order to deal with ruptures in the therapeutic alliance (see Chap. 1). This might be developed within the specific sphere of the existential approach.

Vignette 4

Above (case conceptualization section), we gave the example of a patient who sought psychotherapy because of the problem related to anxiety and panic attacks. Her panic attacks were something she live with for more than 10 years. The way she dealt with this matter involved basically taking medication. She took medication which provided a degree of momentary amelioration, sometimes during 2 or 3 months, but then the anxiety and panic attacks returned "to torment her". The psychological support she had in two instances, both very short-lived because she had not found them useful, had not helped. In her thinking, the panic attacks had no explanation, although the assumption arose that they were a medical issue, despite feeling enormously fed up at taking medication for years on end with no satisfactory resolution. One of the issues present for the psychotherapist had to do precisely with how the patient could stick to the therapeutic process and what sort of therapeutic contract it would make sense to establish.

Therapist: You told me just now that the psychological support you sought was not very satisfactory for you. Is that so?

Patient: Yes, that's it...

T: What's it like for you coming here and being here to consider the possibility of starting psychotherapy?

C: Yes...like I said, I think that when they told me to go to a psychotherapist again, I thought, well, there's not harm in trying, to see what happens... and I'm really tired of taking medication. You know, I'm a woman, even at work I like to be focused on aims, I like to see results and things happening.

T: for you it's important that we manage to get results here too and that you feel that what we do together might really bear fruit and that Lucy can feel this.

C: Yes, that's very important. When I put my mind to something, I take it seriously. I don't like to mess around.

T: I understand, Lucy. Look, I would like us to talk at least once or twice more, if you agree, before we come to agreement about a possible psychotherapy we could undertake together. In other words, we could book a session next week, and carry on talking about the things that brought you here, and also about psychotherapy. It is also important for you to have time to think how you felt here with me, if any of the aspects we talked about made sense for you. But apart from that, how you felt. That's important. Then, I would also like to give you some more practical information about how you can process the psychotherapy, so you can reflect during the week on what might make more sense to you. And next week we would talk.

At this moment, it was the psychotherapist's concern not to put pressure on the patient, to be able to clarify with her the issues involved in undertaking a psychotherapy. He was mindful of the Lucy's possible doubts as to the real usefulness of psychotherapy, but in this excerpt another important issue also emerged: Lucy said that when she gets involved in things she does so assertively and with motivation. This appeared to be an important thing to know. If we managed to find a good basis for starting the psychotherapy, then we could take advantage of this *personal characteristic* of Lucy's. What followed from this dialogue was that the psychotherapist provided some information on psychotherapy. We were in June, and the psychotherapist knew that he would interrupt the sessions for the whole month of August, so he felt he should provide this information so that, in the event of her starting a psychotherapy, Lucy would be aware of this factor right from the start. The psychotherapist also felt it was important to share another aspect with Lucy.

T: Lucy, you told me that what you feel are panic attacks and very great anxiety. How do you understand this? Do you have or have they given you any information about panic attacks.

C: No one told me anything about this. The doctor only told me that the medication should help, his specialty is neurology, and what e told me is that these are things in our brain

T: Right. Very often peaks of anxiety and panic attacks are related to aspects of our life which are, shall we say, under tension inside us, even if we're not aware of them. For example, just now you told me about a situation in which you went to a shop with your husband. In the shop you went to a lower floor and when you got there you suddenly began to feel very anxious, and to feel trapped or stuck. And feeling that you wanted to get out quickly,

C: Yes, that was it…

T: In a certain sense, it's as if that tight space, it was at that moment Lucy who has things inside her, that don't have space to manifest themselves, or which are under tension, in conflict, when haven't yet found resolution. This is what happens in many situations of anxiety and panic attacks. What we have to do together is find out what these tensions are. Tensions are often related to aspects of our life which we even regard as, shall we say, natural. But once we have discovered them, and Lucy has found how to deal with them, you'll see that the anxiety and panic attacks will gradually diminish.

The psychotherapist's second concern had to do with providing some information on the question that Lucy had brought as her main concern, the panic attacks. It is common in these situations of anxiety peaks and panic, for it to be very important that people have specific information that begins to contribute to a "logical" explanation for what is happening to them. Very often, panic attacks come out of nowhere, without warning. Apparently, the person's life is fine and suddenly they feel acute anxiety. In addition, it is not uncommon for people not to have information that helps them deal with these difficult moments. So although Lucy had been dealing with panic attacks for several years, she appeared to have no information that could help her. In addition to this information being able to put the patient's mind at rest, it could also start to introduce something more important: trust and hope in the actual psychotherapeutic process, factors which we know were not particularly robust.

The next week, Lucy's feedback about the first session was positive. In her own words, she said she had "felt empathy" with the psychotherapist, and that she had found herself thinking during the seek about many things which they have talked of at the previous session. The therapeutic process started, agreement was reached on its terms, and also that there would be two sessions a week for about 2 months, as in August there would be none while the psychotherapist was away, The process would continue after August for the time need to achieve the outcomes sought by Lucy. This point tied in with the personal characteristic of Lucy mentioned above. She likes to make a commitment when she decides to do something. So the therapeutic process got off to a positive start, insofar as despite Lucy's (natural) misgivings, she was in fact motivated, and a good level of collaboration was maintained. She attended every session and her motivation was palpable. She asked the psychotherapist to give her "homework", things she could do or think about during the week that could contribute to the process and help her get better. At the early sessions, however, Lucy would bring examples of the present in which she still felt the peaks of anxiety. The therapeutic dialogue focused on this aspect and continued to work towards a rationale to explain what Lucy was feeling. In other words, this was a search for the potential reasons related to aspects of Lucy's life and her characteristics (sedimentations), which might be contributing to this anxiety. The analogy of Lucy' tensions which were expressed in closed spaces was maintained from session to session. Alongside this psychotherapeutic strategy, the central aim of which was to help Lucy identify a credible and plausible explanation for her experiences, Lucy was gradually provided with tips as to how she could deal with moments of anxiety. For example, by introducing these same responses that Lucy and the therapist were gradually building at the sessions, at the actual moment in which she felt the anxiety. This strategy appeared to be starting to bear fruit. But something was getting in the way.

Patient: There's something that's bothering me... although the things we have been talking about make sense, others perhaps a bit less, but there's one thing I've been thinking...

Therapist: Do you want to share it with me?

C: Yes... it's that if what we've been talking about here makes sense, then that means that I'm a weak [person]. I've never seen myself like that...

T: Lucy, can you tell me a little about this? What do you mean "I'm a weak person".

C: Well, for example, one of the things we've talked about is that maybe the fact that I feel I don't want to disappoint my parents is really creating a very great pressure in me, that I feel I'm responsible for my sister and that I have to take care of her and even her children and that this is also weighing.... things that have been that way for years...

T: Yes...

C: Then that means to me that I'm weak. For me, for the way I see things, it's natural to live with these things. For the way I think things are, if that is having an impact on me it's because I'm not a strong person.

The example provided by this excerpt is particularly important. For the psychotherapist, it was an example of something broached in several parts of this text, and which is considered as particularly relevant: the answers that the patient finds in the psychotherapy will have to accord with his worldview. This issue is many-sided and obviously depends on a number of factors, including the characteristics of self. In many circumstances, some of the sedimentations are changes so that the person can accommodate new meanings concerning his understanding of himself, others and the world. In other situations, it is not so much a question of making these changes to the worldview, but of the actual "answers" being given or constructed in a way which can be accepted by the person. Lucy saw herself as a woman capable of resolving everything.

A businesswoman, with her own family business, she felt she could deal with everything. She felt this was only natural. She felt that she took care of the business, the house, her children, but also of her parents' main expectations, and how her parents expect that she will end up as primarily responsible for "everything going better", including her sister. So although some of the questions that we were exploring in psychotherapy were beginning to make sense, this point seemed to crop up as an obstacle. "But does that mean then that I'm not the strong person I always thought I was?" It was as if the questions that Lucy was raising, exploring and even assigning a meaning to at the sessions would be stopped in their tracks by this way she had of perceiving herself. Subsequently, it seems that Lucy eventually found ways of overcoming this obstacle, partly reformulating what she felt appropriate to demand of herself and what she felt that others could legitimately demand of her. So it was not a question of her being less strong or capable, and perhaps it was even not fair for her to bear a series of burdens which didn't belong to her and which ended up causing her distress even when she didn't realize this. Lucy was capable of sorting out her issues. As the weeks passed, things gradually got better. She started to bring examples of where normally panic attacks used to occur, for example when she took a lift, but which now didn't happen. She actually got stuck in a lift, without becoming anxious. She came back after the August break, but fundamentally things were resolved in here view. She only seemed to have one minor misgiving, "aren't I perhaps being too optimistic?" Everything had been going well since July, from even before the break for August. The psychotherapist gave her positive feedback, told her she had good reason to be optimistic, that she hadn't only identified aspects that worried her, but had also found new resources to deal with her issues when they arose. Lucy came back for three more sessions—which is what was arranged between her and the psychotherapist—but then the psychotherapy ended. For her, it had been enough.

CLINICAL CASE

This clinical case is based on a set of interviews conducted by the author with clients and therapists about significant events that occurred in existential psychotherapy. In this section our aim is to show how the conceptualizations presented in Chap. 2 can be applied to a clinical case. The quotations in the clinical case, are from one of the clients, who underwent an existential intervention. Marie was married with three children, and was in a very anguished state when she began psychotherapy. She suffered from panic attacks and had a "complete inability to cope with life". She had never before experienced anything similar and indeed her self-perception was of a woman able to perform various roles (wife, mother and professional) in an active and committed way. She was even a "natural talker." However, she suddenly found herself overwhelmed by a devastating sense of anguish, which caused her to close herself away at home, unable to go to work and be with others, and profoundly distressed. How could Marie suddenly have got into this state? It all began on the day of the terrorist attack on the Twin Towers in New York on 11 September 2001. She had awoken that morning "with a feeling of real dread", though she did not know quite what was worrying her. She felt that it was somehow related with her daughter, who was starting or finishing college on that day, she couldn't quite remember. As it happened, her daughter phoned that morning, but this left her even more anxious. Although the daughter spoke about the incident in New York, Marie did not pay much attention at first. However, she soon realized the seriousness of the situation and decided to go home, because she did not want her younger son to witness such terrible events on television while he was alone. In fact, she was in the kitchen with the television on, and saw the towers collapse at exactly the same moment as her son came in from the back garden. Marie describes it in these words:

"I didn't want my son to arrive home to find that such a terrible thing had happened and he walked round the back of the house here and I put the television on and as he walked in, I said "this terrible thing has happened" and I just saw the first tower fall as he came in the door...I was stood here and I thought, I could feel my whole inside emptying off to the floor, it was really strange like this big puddle of me down there..."

This testimony expresses some of the aspects described in the chapter on genetic phenomenological analysis, i.e. there is a situation that provokes a disruption between the sedimented dimensions of the experiential self and the factual experiences of life. Although we do not yet have information about the passive syntheses sedimented in the experiential self that could have contributed to a spontaneous reawakening of existential anguish, we do know that the situation was unleashed at the moment the twin towers fell. But Marie also describes a situation that is crucial: there is a continuous two-way flux between the 'inner' world of the self and the 'outer' world of the surrounding environment. A dramatic change in one of the systems influences the other. This existential tension is here called *paradoxical reversibility* (see Chap. 2).

Rudolf Bernet, in connection with the work of Merleau-Ponty, mentions how the gaze of the subject is invisible to himself and in himself; but when one is before a painting, through the transformation or impact of it, the gaze recovers through a reversible process. "The gaze of the picture, (like the gaze of the thing) reverses the subject like a glove pulled inside out, exposing the inside while at the same time internalizing the exterior of the picture (or of the thing)" (Bernet 2003, p. 95). The painting in question could be another person, a factual experience, a world, and the process may result in conflict in the presence of a traumatic situation. Faced with a factual experience, the person's "gaze" becomes reversible; the experiential self sees its 'inner' side (intentional experiences sedimented in the zero-consciousness) exposed in the world, while simultaneously the 'outer' experiences occurring in the surrounding world are interiorized. The process operates at a pre-reflective level, and is paradoxical, because it abruptly exposes dissociated processes of the experiential self (hidden motivations). It is the disruptive result of intentional motivations sedimented in associative networks that have become dissociated from the self. The existential conflict arises from intersubjective interactions; the self-world interrelationship is expressed in this case in an experience of one's "inside emptying off" when Marie was confronted with a traumatic experience in the interrelational world. This notion is related to Heidegger's concept of *fallen*. The *Dasein* may fall unauthentically in the daily world. The term *'fallen'* means 'falling *at* the world' or 'collapsing *against* it' (Heidegger 1962, p. 220), which translates and expresses the existential tension that occurs in paradoxical reversibility. When the *Dasein* falls into unauthenticity, it collapses into the world, which involves a collapse in relation to oneself. Moreover, the profound impact upon the structure of self is manifested in the self-body unity. The psychological experience is given through an embodied subjectivity, and an experiential trauma is manifested with the involvement of corporality. Indeed, it is this that connects it to the experiential world. As Sartre has shown, the consciousness may spontaneously become anguished without *any apparent reason or motive* (Sartre 1994). Heidegger also stated that anguish can arise in the most innocuous situations (Heidegger 1962). Anguish makes itself felt and in part is manifested by the loss of meaning following a traumatic episode:

"I was driving along, walking, thinking, looking at everyone just buffing about and thinking "Why are they behaving so normally? Why do they look happy? Why are they smiling? Why do they look normal?" because I didn't feel normal at all…"

As Stolorow reflected, trauma is in essence an "experience of unbearable affect" (Stolorow 2007, p. 14), and one of the aspects that results from that experience is that the person feels strange, and begins to experience the world in a way that is incommensurable with the experiences of other people. That is to say, there is a loss of connection with the surrounding world. The incommensurability of worlds also occurs when "the absolutized horizons of normal everydayness" (Stolorow 2007, p. 16) (i.e. everything in our daily lives that contributes to a sensation of stability, control and predictability) are drastically undermined. Once more the inalienable bond between self and world is highlighted. Heidegger broaches the issue of existential anguish as a feeling of the *uncanny* (Heidegger 1962). In that experience, the person feels "strange in the world"; he is no longer 'at home' or belongs in the world. In the case of Marie, she actually worked closely with death and was constantly exposed to emotionally powerful situations, where she was able to maintain a strong professional posture, as she explains in a dialogue with her psychotherapist: "I work with lots of care professions…caring professions are very difficult because they take on a lot of emotional baggage from other people…I work with dying people a lot and she said, you know, "You can't get in a more emotional situation than that and…because you're giving all the time, you have to be there and strong and cope and give the vial of morphine and say "yes, this is what they need, they need this amount, they need that…" and the decisions that you're making or…you have to be so professional…but yet you come out of there and you often feel a quivering wreck that…you're not allowed ever to show that "

Although she had always been a strong person, able to deal capably with death and the emotions of others, she now felt herself to be a "quivering wreck." She was just like the buildings in New York, symbols of imposing power, which could come tumbling down with an impact from outside. Her son came into the house just as the first tower collapsed, as if reflecting the precarious nature of the absolutisms of existence, affecting the structure of Marie's worldview, which till then had been unshakably firm even in the presence of intense emotions. As usual, her first reaction was "life is fine"; but the absolutism of existence had been radically shaken, making her feel "empty", and placing her before the hollowness of the void. From then on, her anguish began to impinge upon her life. She started to feel strange in the world. The whole familiar dimension of personal experience that usually made her feel secure and calm had begun to rupture and as stated by Heidegger "everyday familiarity collapses" (Heidegger 1962, p. 231). At these moments, the incommensurability between the world of the person that has experienced the psychological trauma and the world of the others is manifested by an inability to communicate with or be in harmony with significant people. Marie's husband tried to play down the events and empathize with her experience, but she could not *feel* any contact with him. But what was there in Marie's history (that is to say, in the passive geneses constituting temporal awareness) that could have contributed to this daily life experience suddenly becoming a psychological trauma?

Another detail about Marie's situation was that her anguish became even more acute when one doctor told her: "I want you to go home now because if you don't you're going to be ill for a very long time." The same doctor offered an immediate explanation: there was something serious *in herself* that had unleashed the situation in which she found herself. Thus expressed, the doctor's concern had negative repercussions. Marie went home and closed herself away in fear, sad and unable to communicate with others, convinced that there was something very serious hidden away in her past that was causing her state. Existential anguish does not 'see' or 'situate' the thing that has become a threat to one's being. Anguish is revealed precisely by being present without being identified; thus, anguish 'does not know' what it is anguished about. But that anguish which is 'nowhere', in the sense that there is no identifiable cause, is simultaneously so present that it can be overwhelmingly oppressive. The being-in-the-world manifests its anguish to itself (Heidegger 1962). Generalized anguish is manifested in anxiety, also present in the first encounter with the psychotherapist: "…what also at the time of that was significant for me was that she…you know when I began to unravel, I was saying to her in the beginning, I guess people come to you, there's usually something deeply seated in the past, isn't there? Because that's why they would see a counselor and she said "Oh, not always" and "I think because I truly, truly can't think of anything in my past that would lead me to be like this" and so she said "Well, tell me just about your life as it is" and "just think, just think what has happened."

Marie was profoundly anxious and the 'explanation' that had been given for the way she felt aggravated her perception of herself and the world, as she could not see anything in her past that might explain the situation. This excerpt reveals dimensions essential to existential psychotherapy which are corroborated by the data from this research. The therapist's first goal is to describe the being-in-the-world and make explicit the inter-relational space. Rather than offering any interpretation or attempting to provoke change in the other, the process involves the phenomenological description of the relational processes. In this case, the psychotherapist placed herself in a posture of *un-knowing* (Spinelli 2007). When Marie first sought out the therapist, saying that people would be looking for her thinking that something really bad had happened in her life, the therapist replied: "Oh, not always! Tell me just about your life as it is, just think, just think what has happened." This was one of the most significant moments of psychotherapy for Marie. The existential approach has as its fundamental principle the promotion of a relational space of trust, which is also confirmed by research in psychotherapy. The therapist was understanding about Marie's fears and anxieties, especially as regards the idea that there might be something malignant in herself. Marie felt a strong empathy, as if the therapist was in tune with her concerns, especially when she played down the situation and asked her to speak only about herself and her life. There was a very strong connection at that moment. As Marie said, the therapeutic space "wasn't alien territory" and despite being very nervous at first, she soon grew comfortable and noticed the first seeds of what is designated by *relational epoché* (Sousa 2015). As we shall see, this crucial step in therapy enabled Marie to have the trust to uncover sedimented associative processes that had been suppressed in dissociations. When the therapist said "tell me about your life," Marie found herself talking about the death of her father that had taken place 2 years before. Then, she spoke of her mother, who had died a long time ago, and in bringing up the subject of her father's death, she realized how it had had an enormous impact on her, although she had avoided facing it in that way.

"Yes, she said "tell me what you do. What…what's happened in your life"…my father had died, in fact, in 1990 and… and that really, I hadn't realized probably it had impacted me so much. My mother had died a long time ago and I think, he… his loss, and I was really close to him, and I think his loss was great to me and of course he was the end of the generation, the oldest generation in my family, so it was suddenly, my husband and I, my sister and I we were both, you know, my sister and all the people in the family now". But the disclosure of these memories was surprising to her. On the one hand, she started to realize that she was describing important life situations that had not been properly reflected on, and which unleashed important affective processes (such as a sense of loss, end of a generation, etc.). On the other hand, she continued to see no reason why it had all come to the surface at that particular moment of her life, beyond the fact that she had felt bad when she watched the collapse of the twin towers. However, she had already embarked on a particularly important process: the phenomenological investigation of memory. This quest involved probing contexts of simultaneity and succession of meanings that were interrelated in the temporal flow of consciousness. So retentions and memories that were submerged in imperceptible processes were reawakened. The disclosure, even though it involved only a tiny portion of a memory, was in turn able to shed light upon other memories, make connections between memories that were not initially connected, and make explicit their experiential meanings. "That was quite... ...strange thing...and I didn't expect to even think about that and it occurred to me. ...No, I think it occurred to me during, during...you know, as I talked to her and I thought maybe that has, you know...I said to her, I remember saying to her "I can' t remember anything really significant that happened that lead to this point apart from the twin towers falling."

But from that point, because Marie had found a safe trusting space—a real relationship with the therapist—, phenomenological description enabled her to reactivate in the reflective consciousness a whole associative process of passive geneses sedimented in the retentional chain of temporal consciousness. The important things here was that reduction is simultaneously an unveiling of associative processes of retentions and memories that are in the zero consciousness, and therefore outside the sphere of the active consciousness. But, in addition to that, this was also co-reduction, as it applied in the intersubjective space, in the presence of two co-subjectivities with an experiential connection, as described in the section about double reduction and intersubjectivity. But firstly let us look at how the clouding-over process (which had led to significant intentional experiences losing their force until they became sedimented in the "affective zero-consciousness") began to be revealed. Through a nodal point (the death of her father), Marie was able to broach the death of her mother, and then the death of her grandfather, which had occurred when Marie was 6 years old. Her grandfather lived in the same house as herself, her parents and sister. However, when he was rushed into hospital one night, her mother failed to tell the children how serious his condition was. Hence, when it was confirmed that he had died, Marie realized that she had not had the chance to say goodbye. "...and going back, again my granddad died when I was six or seven and, and hadn't, my family...he died fairly suddenly but...he lived with us or we lived with him... and my father had gone to off...we stayed... so that was my mother, my granddad, my sister and myself in the house and then one night he got taken to hospital and I never saw him again, he died, and my mother came and told us that he'd died and...I was never able to say goodbye to him and... and I think that, you know, again my therapist allowed me to...see, that is the significant thing she said to me "Well that's an awful thing for a small child to cope with"...well nobody had, nobody had ever said that to me before, you know... ...that...she... she just enabled me to see it as a significant event." At that moment, the therapist validated Marie's experience by reaffirming that it was a difficult situation for a 6-year-old child to have to deal with: "she (the therapist) said "well that's an awful thing for a small child to cope with"... well nobody had, nobody had ever said that to me before, you know...". But as well as recognizing and validating Marie's subjective experience, the therapist also promoted what we have defined as one of the aims of genetic analysis, namely the process of *reflective reactivation* and other therapeutic interventions that enhance a kind of internal alterity, which in turn, can promote an investigation into the constitution of meanings in the passive geneses through a privileged interrelational space. The process of reactivation flows from memory to memory in connection with the present lived experience. From the fall of the Twin Towers and the death of her father, these more recent events led to the death of her grandfather, which was experienced as an emotional trauma. From this point, Marie continued to make associations, discovering a repetition of that trauma in the death of her mother: "I think, that's where I'm coming from...and also when my mother had died...she died when I was 22 or 23 and I was working down here so I couldn't...I kept going home and my father two or three times called me saying she was very, very ill and I went and she didn't die...and I wasn't there when she did die, my sister was at home, she'd just got there and I didn't...and when I, by the time I got home my father had my mother taken from the house because he thought it would distress me to see her and I didn't then like say to him that actually I would actually like to see her because I didn't want to upset him, so... and then she was buried and...or cremated...

and, so I never saw her again and I think talking to the therapist enabled me to see that, you know, because in a way as she said it was like when my granddad died and had gone and didn't come back, the same thing happened with her because I wasn't there and I couldn't see the reality of it although I knew it...so it was, it was a, it was a significant thing." In fact, Marie had experienced the deaths of two very significant people, but had not integrated them or managed to 'see the reality of it'. And just as in her professional and personal life, where she did not feel that she was authorized to display affects and emotion before pain and death, in these situations too, with the death first of her grandfather and then of her mother, she had cultivated the belief that she was not supposed to share her affectivity. The death situations were traumatic but as the function of the self is self-preservation, it develops strategies for dealing with disruptive interrelational experiences. The emotions, the experience of the death of significant people, were dissociated from her active self, although *the original meanings of the experience had been sedimented in the zero consciousness.* This is the crucial reason why Husserl's concepts of association and reactivation have a double meaning in the therapeutic context, as we have mentioned. On the one hand, association and reawakening are psychological processes that operate at the pre-reflective level and help explain the psychological origin of existential tensions. On the other, it is argued in this work that they express forms of therapeutic intervention in the sphere of genetic phenomenological analysis.

Let us look at the first point. Associative processes of intentional motivations largely occur without any awakening of self-awareness. They not only link experiences that have a direct relationship with each other, but also forge connections to constellations of meanings that have not previously been related. In part, these networks of associations of meaning contribute to the passivity of facticity, the subsoil of the background of lived-experiences, which form the experiential atmosphere of subjectivity. But as we have seen, an affective allure may occur when, for some reason (cognitive or emotional), through some prominence or contrast, a particular experience is reawakened and erupts into the self. The concept of reawakening means that an experience that has been dissociated from the experiential self produces a psychological trauma through a paradoxical reversibility. Both processes are an integral part of usual psychological life, but may also be expressed and make sense in situations of conflict. Secondly, we should emphasize how both concepts involve a dimension of *intervention* in the sphere of existential psychotherapy. As passive geneses are formed through associative processes, a phenomenology of association is encouraged through phenomenological reduction, in order to promote the description of the geneses constituted in the retentional chain and of the memories of lived experience. We have seen how Marie managed to articulate important aspects of her person and surrounding world starting from nodal points of memory, as a result of the phenomenology of association initiated by the psychotherapist. Reawakening is a psychological process that can occur pre-reflectively, but in psychotherapy *reflective reactivation,* is induced by a process in which genetic analysis plunges into the constitution of the meanings sedimented in the passive geneses. The aim of the reawakening in psychotherapy is to shed light on life experiences that have remained in the antechamber of the self and which, for different reasons, may be suppressed, denied or evaded. This is not just a matter of archaeological rummaging into the past; rather, it involves scrutinizing lived experiences of the past, present or future in the temporal consciousness. The applicability of reflective reactivation implies that it is based on a therapeutic relationship of trust, involving great relational harmony. Psychotherapy is often divided up in the literature into the therapeutic relationship versus specific interventions. Here, it is argued, *both* are integral parts of the therapeutic process. Reflective reactivation is something that can only happen in a privileged relational space of trust, and is aroused by certain interventions identified by the static method: phenomenological description, questioning, active listening, reformulations and clarifications, challenging assumptions and beliefs. Reflective reactivation is a process that promotes a differentiation in the self, enabling it to achieve a distancing in relation to the meaning of experiences. In this sense, it has similarities with what is called *productive thinking* (Bohart 2002). Though not a phenomenologist, Bohart emphasizes how productive thinking, which can only be developed with a good therapeutic alliance, is a crucial dimension of psychotherapy, characterized amongst other aspects by an inwardly focused attention. This is the adoption of a phenomenological posture, in which the person manages to create a distance in relation to his/her experiences and beliefs, undertake an uncritical examination of him/herself, and thereby gain access to the affective dimensions of experience. What is not open to dialogue cannot be challenged or invalidated (Stolorow 2007). "Yes, yeah, and it wasn't until talking to therapist that I...was able to, even....that I even thought about such things. No, no. I think I, probably by nature tend to think about things and go "Oh, no, don't think about that". So,

I think I tucked a lot of things away." Although the death of Marie's father had in some way helped bring about an emotional readjustment (given that she was able to see her father before and after he died, including in the company of her daughter), it was only during psychotherapy that she managed to *re-flect* and integrate the emotional processes and articulate the things that had been hidden and dissociated. Despite the strangeness, she now understood how a present experience, with apparently no direct connection (i.e. the fall of the two towers) could in fact have had an impact upon her experiential process. "She (therapist) encouraged me to talk about what I considered to be normal things... that suddenly became significant... that, you know, to me life, this aspect of life I would expect, you know, you would your grandparents die, your parents die, you expect everybody to die...and again I think it was like when nine eleven happened and I couldn't work out why it was so, so... had such a profound effect upon me. And I still find it strange now but it was the therapist that allowed me to think what actually...that it's not unreasonable for that to have happened." As shown by Marie's, the therapeutic process allowed the *release of emotional and cognitive experiences* through *validation of experience*. This is in keeping with an aspect mentioned in relation to genetic analysis: reflective reactivation presupposes an affective reflectivity. It takes place in the context of a real human encounter, and when fully achieved, implies the cognitive and emotional integration of life experiences. There is an enormous difference between speaking about emotions and traumatic experiences, and *re-living* them in a human relationship (Greenberg and Paivio 1997). In Marie's case, she acquired a new awareness that now enables her to face her life beyond purely rational processes and to connect the events of 9/11 to her experience of anguish. As this testimony shows, now that she has managed to release the cognitive and emotional experiences that had been dissociated, she has become conscious of what we call the paradoxical reversibility, i.e. the mutual two-way influence between the self and the world (or the presence of the being-in-the-world) and how this may manifest itself as psychological disturbance when some life experiences are not properly thematized and integrated: "I linked it only after talking to her, during that time, and probably since then as well, you know, the more I thought about it the more I think "Hey, you know, she, she was right really" but these things they are sort of crude aren't they? They accumulate...and if you don't...if you can't offload it or release it or make sense of it in some way, well deal with it at the time I guess, then it will stay there and....come out at some peculiar time in your life and if some other thing came out of it, that was." Even psychotherapeutic literature that is not specific to the existential approach mentions that when people deal with experiences of dread that are particularly painful for the self and manage to assume a phenomenological posture in relation to themselves, they develop capacities and resources that enable them to integrate and re-live experiences that were previously intolerable (Greenberg and Pinsof 1997). The therapist's posture was not to "provoke change in the client". Rather, it was to focus on the main principle of the existential approach, the quality of the encounter, which includes a trusting relationship in a safe environment (Spinelli 1997). The central question of psychotherapy is not to provoke change in behavior. The main factor is the re-establishment of *meaning* of the lived experience. Also on this point, the literature indicates factors that corroborate the principles of the existential approach. The capacity to deal with traumatic psychological experiences involves the possibility of rethinking internal experiences and not only conditioning external experiences or behavior. There occurs a change in meaning, not only in behavior; and the change occurs from the reformulation of the person's rational and emotive capacities (Greenberg and Pinsof 1997). This process is related to what has been said about the application of phenomenological reduction in a face-to-face encounter in the intersubjective space, which Hussserl called "mirroring"—an original and reciprocal experience of co-existence. The therapeutic space *is a reduction* of objective time and the space of the natural attitude. These are the indices that make possible a profound emotional human experience. Co-reduction of the intersubjective psychotherapeutic space promotes an *original experience of co-existence*, but that happens because the reduction is performed in objective time and within the space of the natural attitude. While Marie's "cure" did not occur exclusively within the therapeutic space, as she herself pointed out, the sessions were its time and its space: "it was my time, and that's how I felt, the relief that somehow I'd found this little oasis, that was for me, for my...me and my time." The application of genetic phenomenological analysis also demonstrates how inner time-consciousness underpins pre-reflective consciousness and the experiential self. The temporality of consciousness is the royal route to analysis of the experiential world of subjectivity. The flow of retentions and protentions are a chain of *experiences*, largely sedimented in the zero consciousness without having been thematized, while others subsequently intertwine in associative networks of pre-reflective intentional motivations. As Husserl argued, far from having a formal abstract explanation, inner time consciousness theory, when applied to the facticity of the person, is the cornerstone of our understanding of personal identity. As has been seen, psychological trauma seriously compromises the unity of temporal consciousness, and the consequence of dissociation is a disorganization of personal meaning maintained by temporality. The re-establishment of this meaning is elaborated both through relational processes intrinsic to the therapeutic process and by connections of meaning re-elaborated by the person. So it is clarified that existential psychotherapy always maintains a connection between the concept of the experiential self, with its processes of passive geneses, and the notion of the person, which is another dimension of the development of identity.

CONCLUSION

The aim of this text is to present and define a model for existential psychotherapy, based on the static and genetic phenomenology of Edmund Husserl. In addition, I have sought to propose a theoretical model that integrates the main therapeutic factors regarded as effective by scientific research, in existential clinical practice. Another of my central aims was to provide an explanation of intervention stances and techniques of an existential nature. It is still not uncommon to hear it asked how an existential psychotherapy 'works'. This book makes a small contribution to answering this question. I believe I am aware of the various limitations of this text. I am also quite sure that other observations will be presented which will help me reflect on the task I have sought to undertake. Indeed, it is beyond the possibilities of a book such as this to consider all the factors involved in the complexity of psychotherapeutic processes. I believe I am also aware that many of the positions I defend in this book are not consensual in the existential psychotherapy community. However, our diversity is part of what makes this field so fertile. Following the example of one of the most elegant authors of existential phenomenology, Paul Ricoeur, I also believe that the explanation will help us to a better understanding, and that understanding is fundamental for us to be able to explain the phenomena of existence. So I have proposed a theoretical model of existential psychotherapy that follows this premise. I leave it to the reader's critical judgment to decide on its usefulness. Any observation, comment or question is welcome: daniel.sousa@ispa.pt

REFERENCES

Bernet, R. (2003). Gaze, drive and body in Lacan and Merleau-Ponty. In J. Corveleyn & P. Moyaert (Eds.), *Psychosis: Phenomenological and psychoanalytical approaches.* Leuven: Leuven University Press.

Bohart, A. C. (2002). How does the relationship facilitate productive client thinking? *Journal of Contemporary Psychotherapy, 32*(1), 61–69.

Greenberg, L. S., & Paivio, S. C. (1997). *Working with emotions in psychotherapy.* New York: Guilford Press.

Heidegger, M. (1962). *Being and time.* Oxford: Basil Blackwell.

Safran, J. D., & Muran, J. C. (2000). *Negotiating the therapeutic alliance.* New York: Guildford Press.

Sartre, J. P. (1994). *A Transcedência do Ego.* Lisboa: Edições Colibri.

Sousa, D. (2015). Existential psychotherapy. The genetic-phenomenological approach: Beyond a dichotomy between relating and skills. *Journal of Contemporary Psychotherapy, 45,* 69–77.

Spinelli, E. (1997). *Tales of un-knowing: Eight stories of existential therapy.* New York: New York University Press.

Spinelli, E. (2007). *Practising existential psychotherapy. The relational world.* London: Sage.

Stolorow, R. (2007). *Trauma and human existence.* New York: The Analytic Press.

APPENDIX

Conclusion

The aim of this text is to present and define a model for existential psychotherapy, based on the static and genetic phenomenology of Edmund Husserl (Table A.1). In addition, I have sought to propose a theoretical model that integrates the main therapeutic factors regarded as effective by scientific research, in existential clinical practice. Another of my central aims was to provide an explanation of intervention stances and techniques of an existential nature. It is still not uncommon to hear it asked how an existential psychotherapy 'works'. This book makes a small contribution to answering this question. I believe I am aware of the various limitations of this text. I am also quite sure that other observations will be presented which will help me reflect on the task I have sought to undertake. Indeed, it is beyond the possibilities of a book such as this to consider all the factors involved in the complexity of psychotherapeutic

© The Editor(s) (if applicable) and The Author(s) 2017   217
D. Sousa, *Existential Psychotherapy*,
DOI 10.1057/978-1-349-95217-5

Table A.1   Existential psychotherapy

Psychotherapeutic Process Form
Version 2.0

Name _____ Age:____

Session # ____ Date: _____

Request:_____

_____

_____

_____

_____

_____

Expectations_____

_____

_____

_____

_____

_____

_____

Narrative of the Existential Project:_____

_____

_____

_____

_____

_____

_____

_____

_____

_____

_____
_____
_____
_____
_____
_____
_____
_____
_____
_____
_____
_____
_____
_____
_____
_____

Existential Conflicts: _____

_____
_____
_____
_____
_____
_____
_____
_____
_____
_____

Therapeutic Goals:_____

_____
_____
_____
_____
_____
_____
_____
_____
_____

Therapeutic Contract:_____

_____
_____
_____
_____
_____
_____
_____
_____

_____

_____

Sedimentations:

• Self

• Other

• World

Leading Clues: _____

_____
_____
_____
_____
_____

_____
_____

Relational Stance (Client):_____
_____
_____
_____
_____
_____
_____

Level of Collaboration / Tasks_____
_____
_____
_____
_____
_____
_____
_____

Feedback and Monitoring:_____
_____
_____
_____
_____
_____
_____
_____
_____
_____
_____
_____
_____
_____
_____
_____
_____
_____

NOTES

processes. I believe I am also aware that many of the positions I defend in this book are not consensual in the existential psychotherapy community. However, our diversity is part of what makes this field so fertile. Following the example of one of the most elegant authors of existential phenomenology, Paul Ricoeur, I also believe that the explanation will help us to a better understanding, and that understanding is fundamental for us to be able to explain the phenomena of existence. So I have proposed a theoretical model of existential psychotherapy that follows this premise. I leave it to the reader's critical judgment to decide on its usefulness. Any observation, comment or question is welcome: daniel. sousa@ispa.pt

REFERENCES

Ahn, H., & Wampold, B. E. (2001). Where oh where are the specific ingredients? A meta-analysis of component studies in counseling and psychotherapy. *Journal of Counseling Psychology, 48*(3), 251–257.

Anderson, T., McClintock, A. S., Patterson, C. L., Himawan, L., & Song, X. (2016). A prospective study of therapist facilitative interpersonal skills as a predictor of treatment outcome. *Journal of Consulting and Clinical Psychology, 84*(1), 57–66.

APA Presidential Task Force on Evidence-Based Practice. (2006). Evidence-based practice in psychology. *American Psychologist, 61*, 271–285.

Baardseth, T. P., Goldberg, S. B., Pace, B. T. Wislocki, A. P., Frost, N.D., Siddiqui, J.R., … Wampold, B. E. (2013). Cognitive-behavioral therapy versus other therapies: Redux. *Clinical Psychology Review, 33*, 395–405.

Benish, S. G., Imel, Z. E., & Wampold, B. E. (2008). The relative efficacy of bona fide psychotherapies for treating post-traumatic stress disorder: A meta-analysis of direct comparisons. *Clinical Psychology Review, 28*, 746–758.

Beutler, L. E., Forrester, B., Gallagher-Thompson, D., Thompson, L., & Tomlins, J. B. (2012). Common, specific, and treatment fit variables in psychotherapy outcome. *Journal of Psychotherapy Integration, 22*(3), 255–281.

Bordin, E. S. (1994). Theory and research on the therapeutic working alliance: New directions. In A. O. Horvath & L. S. Greenberg (Eds.), *The working alliance: Theory, research, and practice* (pp. 13–37). New York: Wiley.

Caldas de Almeida, J. M. (2013). *Estudo epidemiológico nacional de saúde mental*. Lisboa: Faculdade de Ciências Médicas.

Castonguay, L. G., & Beutler, L. E. (2006). *Principles of therapeutic change that work*. New York: Oxford University Press.

© The Editor(s) (if applicable) and The Author(s) 2017
D. Sousa, *Existential Psychotherapy*,
DOI 10.1057/978-1-349-95217-5

Cooper, M. (2008). *Essential research findings in counselling and psychotherapy: The facts are friendly.* London: Sage.

Cooper, M. (2003). *Existential therapies.* London: Sage.

Crits-Christoph, P., Connolly Gibbons, M. B., Crits-Christoph, K., Narducci, J., Schamberger, M., & Gallop, R. (2006). Can therapists be trained to improve their alliances? A preliminary study of alliance-fostering psychotherapy. *Psychotherapy Research, 16*(3), 268–281.

Cuijeprs, P., Driessen, E., Hollon, S. D., Van Oppen, P., Barth, J., & Andresson, G. (2012). The efficacy of non-directive supportive therapy for adult depression: A meta-analysis. *Clinical Psychology Review, 32,* 280–291.

Direção-Geral de Saúde [DGS]. (2015). *A saúde dos portugueses. Perspectiva 2015.* Lisboa: Direção-Geral de Saúde.

Furtado, C. (2013). *Psicofármacos: Evolução do consumo em Portugal Continental (2000–2012).* Lisboa: Infarmed.

Geller, J. D. (2005). Style and its contribution to a patient-specific model of therapeutic technique. *Psychotherapy: Theory, Research, Practice. Training, 42,* 469–482.

Goldfried, M. R., Patrick, J., Raue, P. J., & Castonguay, L. G. (1998). The therapeutic focus in significant sessions of master therapists: A comparison of cognitive-behavioral and psychodynamic-interpersonal interventions. *Journal of Consulting and Clinical Psychology, 66*(5), 803–810.

Goldfried, M. R., & Davila, J. (2005). The role of the relationship and technique in therapeutic change. *Psychotherapy: Theory, Research, Practice, Training, 42,* 421–430.

Greenberg, L. S., & Pinsof, W. M. (1986). Process research: Current trends and future perspectives.In L. S. Greenberg & W. M. Pinsof (Eds.), *The psychotherapeutic process: A research handbook* (pp. 3–20). New York: The Guilford Press.

Jacobson, N. S., Dobson, K. S., Truax, P., Addis, M. E., Koerner, K., Gollan, J. K., … Prince, S. E. (1996). Component analysis of cognitive-behavioral treatment for depression. *Journal of Consulting and Clinical Psychology, 64*(2), 295–304.

Lambert, M. J. (2005). Early response in psychotherapy: Further evidence for the importance of common factors rather "placebo effects". *Journal of Clinical Psychology, 61*(7), 855–869.

Lambert, M. J. (2010). Yes, it is time for clinicians to routinely monitor treatment outcome. In B. L. Duncan, S. D. Miller, B. E. Wampold, & M. A. Hubble (Eds.). *The heart and soul of change: Delivering what works in therapy* (2nd ed., pp. 239–266). Washington, DC: American Psychological Association.

Lambert, M. J. (2015). Opening address. Advances in measuring, monitoring & feedback. Presented at the Ninth Annual Counseling Conference of the University of South Carolina. Columbia, South Carolina.

Levitt, H., Butler, M., & Hill, T. (2006). What clients find helpful in Psychotherapy: Developing principles for facilitating moment-to-moment change. *Journal of Counselling Psychotherapy, 53*(3), 314–324.

Little, J. H. (2010). In B. L. Duncan, S. D. Miller, B. E. Wampold, & M. A. Hubble (Eds.), *The heart and soul of change: Delivering what works in therapy* (2nd ed., pp. 167–198). Washington, DC: American Psychological Association.

Luborsky, L., Singer, B., & Luborsky, L. (1975). Comparative studies of psychotherapies: Is it true that "everyone has won and all must have prizes"? *Archives of General Psychiatry, 32*, 995–1008.

Marcus, D. K., Kashy, D. A., Wintersteen, M. B., & Diamond, G. S. (2011). The therapeutic alliance in adolescent substance abuse treatment: A one-with-many analysis. *Journal of Counseling Psychology, 58*(3), 449–455.

Marcus, D. K., O'Connel, D., Norris, A. L., & Sawaqdeh, A. (2014). Is the Dodo bird endangered in the 21st century? A meta-analysis of treatment comparison studies. *Clinical Psychology Review, 34*, 519–530.

May, R. (2000). *A psicologia e o dilema humano.* Petropolis: Editora Vozes.

Ministério da Saúde, Alto Comissariado da Saúde, Coordenação Nacional para a Saúde Mental. (2008). *Plano Nacional de Saúde Mental 2007–2016—Resumo Executivo.* Lisboa: Coordenação Nacional para a Saúde Mental.

Norcross, J. (Ed.). *Psychotherapy relationships that work* (2nd ed., pp. 25–69). New York: Oxford University Press.

Nyman, S. J., Nafziger, M. A., & Smith, T. B. (2010). Client outcomes across counselor training level within a multitiered supervision model. *Journal of Counseling & Development, 88*, 204–209.

Okiishi, J. C., Lambert, M. J., Nielsen, S. L., & Ogles, B. M. (2003). Waiting for supershrink: An empirical analysis of therapist effects. *Clinical Psychology & Psychotherapy, 10*(6), 361–373.

Orange, D., Atwood, G. E., & Stolorow, R. D. (1997). *Working intersubjectively contextualism in psychoanalytic practice.* New York: Psychology Press.

Rosenzweig, S. (1936). Some implicit common factors in diverse methods of psychotherapy. *American Journal of Orthopsychiatry, 6*, 412–415.

Sousa, D., & Vaz, A. (in press). A descriptive phenomenological exploration of significant events in existential therapy. *Journal of Humanistic Psychology.*

Sousa, D. Tavares, A., & Pestana, A. (in press). Eventos significativos em psicoterapia existencial. In A. M. Feijoo & M. B. Lessa (Eds.), *Fenomenologia e práticas clínicas II.* Rio Janeiro: IFEN.

Sousa, D. (2014). Phenomenological psychology: Husserl's static and genetic methods. *Journal Phenomenological Psychology, 45*, 27–60.

Swift, J. K., Greenberg, R. P., Whipple, J. L., & Kominiak, N. (2012). Practice recommendations for reducing premature termination in therapy. *Professional Psychology: Research and Practice, 43*(4), 379–387.

Tasca, G. A., & Lampard, A. M. (2013). Reciprocal influence of alliance to the group and outcome in day treatment for eating disorders. *Journal of Counseling Psychology, 59*(4), 507–517.

Thoma, N. C., & Cecero, J. J. (2009). Is integrative use of techniques in psychotherapy the exception or the rule? Results of a national survey of doctoral-level practitioners. *Psychotherapy Theory, Research, Practice, 46*(4), 405–417.

van Kaam, A. (1958). *Existential foundations of psychology.* Pennsylvania: Dimension Books.

Wampold, B. E. (2010). *The research evidence for the common factors models: A historically situated perspective.* In S. D. Miller, B. L. Duncan, M. A. Hubble, & B. E. Wampold (Eds.), The heart and soul of change (2nd ed., pp. 49–81). Washington DC: American Psychological Association.

Wampold, B. E. (2015). Routine outcome monitoring: Coming of age—with the usual developmental challenges. *Psychotherapy, 52*(4), 458–462.

Wampold, B. E., Mondin, G. W., Moody, M., Stich, F., Benson, K., & Ahn, H. (1997). A meta-analysis of outcomes studies comparing bona fide psychotherapies: Empirically: "All must have prizes". *Psychological Bulletin, 122,* 203–215.

INDEX

Printed by Printforce, the Netherlands